D0878548

Twins Found in a Box

Adapting to Adoption

By

Jeannine Joy Vance

© 2003 by Jeannine Vance. All rights reserved.

No part of this book may be reproduced, stored in a retrieval system, or transmitted by any means, electronic, mechanical, photocopying, recording, or otherwise, without written permission from the author.

ISBN: 1-4033-9137-8 (e-book)
ISBN: 1-4033-9138-6 (Paperback)
ISBN: 1-4033-9139-4 (Dust jacket)

Library of Congress Control Number: 2002096429

This book is printed on acid free paper.

Printed in the United States of America
Bloomington, IN

1stBooks - rev. 01/07/03

ACKNOWLEDGMENTS

Thanks to all my family and friends who gave support. The only reason this book could get written, revised (too many times to count), and edited is because ever since I have known him, which now has been half my life, my husband has worked like a maniac to support our family so I could stay home and write. Thanks Xuan! Jeanette and Dad continuously read the manuscript and gave me thumbs up signs for every dreadful revision. Vanessa patted my back and said I was doing a great job while I slouched in front of the computer depressed with the thought, "What did I get myself into?" and "Why the hell am I doing this?" Allison said that my book was "great and wonderful" before she could read. Jenny Johnson served as my own personal cheerleader with frequent calls of support and up-to-date gossip about what the rest of the world was doing. I want to thank my spiritual reading group friends for teaching me what unconditional love really is: Carol & John Raby, Michelle Barker, Marie Miller, Freda Horn, Julia Harris. I will take what I've learned from you with me wherever I go! Thanks to my writing group friends for motivating me to keep writing even though I constantly complained about it: especially Elfi Hornby, she is my inspiration because she believed in my writing ability when I didn't; Sharon Leitheiser and Kelly Creso also supported me throughout the process. And finally, thanks to Radhika Kumar for editing my mess and turning my brain into mush with her questions and comments. My book would not be what it is today if it wasn't for all of you!

Dedicated to:

Vanessa, Alli, Dustin, Perris, Kyle, Nina,
Jessica, Steven, Peter, Phong, Kevin, Eric,
and to future children

TABLE OF CONTENTS

PREFACE

I don't know much about my birth and what I do know lacks details. Jeanette and I were found in a cardboard box on a street corner in Seoul, Korea. An unidentified passerby discovered the box and then took us straight away to the nearest police station. From there we were immediately sent to a Christian orphanage located within the city. We found out later that our American parents had planned to adopt only one baby girl. Plans changed when the adoption agency announced that there were two babies available: twins. Would they consider adopting both?

"Yes!" was their reply. Action was taken immediately to get us into their home in Washington State. They had only to go to the nearest United States airport to retrieve us. I arrived, like a gift, just before Christmas. Jeanette was ill and arrived few months later. Mom named us Jeannine and Jeanette because both names mean "Gifts of God." As babies, we drove Mom and Dad crazy with our incessant crying. They told us repeatedly that had they adopted us first, they would not have had any more children. At first, they blamed our colic on the foreign environment and the switch in time zones. The unfamiliar Western sights, sounds and smells and the change in routine made us hyperactive. During the nights, we were ready to play and interact; during the days, we were tired and cranky and wanted to nap.

In contrast, my parent's older children, Michael and David, slept through parties and social gatherings when they were babies. When they woke, they were content and caused no trouble. Mom and Dad could even take their sons to the movies without disturbing a soul. Not so with Jeanette and me—we were constantly crying. When Mom finally got me to sleep, Jeanette would wake and Mom would have to feed, change, and rock her until she finally calmed down. One of us was always awake and crying for attention.

On several occasions, Mom and Dad told us what motivated them to adopt a girl. Jeanette and I were to serve as replacements. A short time before they adopted us, they had lost their own daughter, Michelle, at birth. Mom's pregnancy had been normal and uneventful.

ix

Even up to the day before her scheduled C-section the doctor had announced that everything looked good. Dad wouldn't even need to be at the hospital, the doctor had said. He could take the boys home and wait for the call with the news. The news of the stillborn birth came as a complete shock. Dad didn't ever see his daughter as the hospital took care of the baby's body. Dad told us that it was as if the baby didn't even exist.

Mom, on the other hand, didn't talk about her loss and probably suffered silent emotional distress. All her emotions were boxed-up and buried inside. Two babies found in a box could not replace the love of a real child. Did she truly see us as "Gifts from God?" I often wondered if Mom regretted her decision to adopt us.

The impulse to adopt came to Dad from what he calls the "Spirit of the Moment." He felt divinely inspired. He hoped it would help Mom cope with her loss. He suggested the idea to Mom, not realizing the long-term ramifications. Dad thought adoption was just the "right thing to do." Mom was not as enthusiastic, but she accepted the idea. The two of them did not weigh the pros and cons by discussing adoption extensively and they did not talk with other adoptive parents before calling an adoption agency. In the 1970's it took only as long as two months to obtain a baby. Dad's noble intentions caused them to feel good.

"Did we fill your life with joy?" I asked Dad once.

"No." Dad laughed and then joked. "With misery. And the misery has not yet ended."

My mother was a beautiful little girl. Her Shirley Temple curls and sparkling eyes jump off the black and white photos in the family album and tug at my heart. When I study her photos as a baby, girl, teen, and young adult, I am amazed at her striking beauty and joy for life. I had always heard about her beauty and her popularity at school and within her family, but I need to see the proof in the photographs. In each photo as an infant, in school plays, graduation, wedding, and as a young bride with Dad, her smile is contagious. She and Dad were very happy before his injury. They had hopes and dreams for a perfect future filled with love and wedded bliss. As a young couple, they hugged and smiled for the camera. Their lives were completely secure—free of pain, sorrow, and knowledge that one day, their dreams of a happy future could be destroyed by one incident—a catastrophic hang-gliding accident. After Dad's injury, Mom couldn't smile for the camera any longer. All hopes and possibilities disintegrated into thin air at the top of Dog Mountain where Dad's injury occurred. No more smiles.

Dad's accident revealed some of the hidden dynamics in our family and really tested our adaptive skills. Before the accident, Jeanette and I were merely adapting to junior high. After the accident, we were unexpectedly trying to prove our worth but feeling more and more like outsiders. This book is an account of that period in my life.

Chapter 1

Dazed and Confused

Jeanette and I spent the whole summer of 1984, the summer before Dad's accident, anticipating the new school year in a new school. We loved the thought of getting out of the house and experiencing freedom. I loved the unknown: the possibility of being able to live and create whatever future I wanted, and junior high, I thought, would be the stepping stone. I still couldn't decide what I wanted to be when I grew up; I loved anything that had to do with art, interior design, cultural awareness and creativity. The future was bright and happy and I was ready to experience the world.

Fall had always been my favorite time of the year because it was an opportunity to make a fresh start. I was also enchanted by the way the maple leaves fell in September. They floated, turned and gently covered the raw earth, like a vibrantly colored quilt. Jeanette and I gathered bundles of leaves and pretended they were pom poms. Then we would make up cheers and routines for our new school Lakota Junior High.

"Two, four, six, eight, whom do we appreciate? Lakota Falcons! Yeah! Go, Falcons!" My dream of cheerleading started in first grade and refused to go away as I grew older. Jeanette and I attended a private Lutheran school until third grade. Then our parents transferred us to the local public school. At the private Lutheran school, we were popular and well-liked. Because we were twins, we even came close to being chosen as miniature assistants to the ninth grade cheerleaders. That was every first grade girl's dream. However, at the last minute a cute little girl with dark brown curls was chosen. We were so close! I hoped that, even though I wasn't very coordinated, I could try out for cheer squad during the coming year.

The public elementary school had been fun at times, but was hard to adjust to and was a little difficult. Twins were immediately

1

assigned to separate classrooms, which was a rude shock. I had never been separated from Jeanette for more than an hour. The thought of spending six hours each day without her was daunting. In fourth grade, the teachers picked me to play Toto for the production of *The Wizard of Oz*. They told the class, "We have the perfect person picked out to play Toto! This choice was a no-brainer." Then their eyes met mine. "This part goes to Jeannine!" Satisfied smiles ignored my frown. I tried not to look at my classmates or the teachers. I tried my best to disappear and when that didn't work, I just ignored the smirks around me, feeling my heart drop to the floor with humiliation.

I was told to crawl behind Emily, the teacher's daughter, who happened to be picked to play Dorothy, while she skipped around the audience, humming the tune: *We're Off To See The Wizard, The Wonderful Wizard Of Oz*. I complained during our practices that she skipped too fast, my legs were cramping up and my palms were getting gray and scummy. "Do I have to follow her around on my hands and knees?"

"Jeannine," Emily's mother said. "It wouldn't make sense if you just skipped along beside her—now would it? You're playing the part of a dog. A cute little dog. Crawling on your hands and knees makes sense." Then she patted me on the head and exclaimed, "You're so cute! You're perfect for the part!"

Georgette, a tall, lean friend of mine, was chosen to play the witch from the west because of her large and bowed nose. I was supposed to jump on the stationary bike with her and bark at the audience; she was then supposed to let out a huge, gruesome laugh. We endured several distraught thoughts over playing these parts.

Leslie was chosen to play, Glinda, the good witch from the north, either because she was a cute blond or because her mother was involved in PTA—I was never sure which. She wore a thick white dress and tapped us with her glittery wand just for the fun of it. She smiled and glowed. Young boys, who had never experienced "falling in love," suddenly fell off their chairs when they saw her.

Emily was so happy to be Dorothy that during the final recitals she nearly ricocheted off the gym walls, grinning at all the grownups like the Grinch who stole Christmas, while I lagged behind, panting and choking on the dust and debris. The audience thought we were magnificent. The teachers said we had earned the right to keep the names of the characters we portrayed, so for the rest of the fourth grade school year I was called Toto.

In sixth grade, Jeanette and I came close to getting picked for the theatrical production of the *King and I*. Compared to the *Wizard of Oz* production at school, this was considered big time. Tryouts were at the Paramount Theatre in Seattle. The directors and producers were in the process of searching the entire United States for Asian twins. There were only six sets of twins who made the Seattle finalists and Jeanette and I were in the mix. All we needed to do was bow in a kneeling position in front of a large group of important people. Unfortunately, we were unable to bow without experiencing pain in our bony knees. To add to my bad acting skills, my arms were not straight enough when I reached to the heavens and then to the floor and I was too stiff to touch the floor completely with my forehead. I winced every time we were told to change positions and I wasn't quick to obey the commands. I silently wished the directors would pass out cushions. And I wondered why we had to kiss the ground for the bald man. What was so great about him? I was full of questions. I didn't like following the rules. I did not understand the concept of "acting".

After what seemed hours of bowing and kissing the ground, my parents were told that even though we were the most identical of all the sets of twins and the oldest in the group, we were an inch too short for the part.

Mom stared at the two girls who were chosen. "They're not even twins!" she whispered discreet, but bewildered at the decision. "You girls should have been chosen."

"You girls were so close!" Dad said. By the time we returned home, they had accepted the decision.

"Well girls," Mom told us, trying to look on the bright side, "If you were chosen, you would have had to take your braces off because they're considered a modern appliance."

We nodded and agreed. I wanted to keep the braces in so I could have straight teeth, especially since we were entering junior high. I wanted to make a good first impression.

Yes, God definitely has a happier plan mapped out for me in junior high! My faith in God was stronger than ever. He would have a grand life ready for me to wear. Jeanette and I did what we could to prepare for our first day. Our new school supplies were packed in identical purple duffel bags next to the entrance of our bedroom, ready to go. Mom had bought us new pencils, packs of college-ruled paper, and brand new notebooks. We had gone shopping with her a few weeks before for our new school clothes. The most impressive outfit in my closet was what we called our "Michael Jackson" jackets and Sara Jeans bought at one of the shops in the local mall. Mom actually let us choose them and I couldn't wait to flaunt it in front of my classmates. My coat was turquoise and Jeanette's was lavender. The stylish Sara Jeans had sparkling threads sewn throughout the denim material. They were still a little too big, but all we needed to do was roll up the bottom to keep them from dragging. When I looked in the mirror before I left for school, I was happy—in fact, I thought I looked cool. Maybe not perfect, but still cool. Mom never did get around to taking in the seams or shortening the jeans, like she had promised. But at least we had picked them out ourselves. Not like in elementary school, where we received our new school clothes sitting upon our parents' bed, like panting basset hounds. Mom would pull out outfit after outfit, happy with her choices, but ignorant of our tastes. Now we were entering junior high, wearing our Michael Jackson jackets and Sara Jeans, which were so awesome! We couldn't wait to start school!

As I walked into the big brick building, I noticed that I didn't make a remarkable first impression. Compared to the other students, I was scrawny, crooked, dressed in children's clothing and still needed to grow into my large hands, feet and teeth. I looked like an underdeveloped mole. Double that image and you had Jeanette and me.

"Chinks!" taunted a rowdy busload of elementary aged school children. "You two are Chinks!" They stuck out their tongues and pulled back their eyes, a few boys raised their middle finger at us and shouted, "Go back to where you come from! You don't belong here!" The bus rushed off with a roar, leaving me to mop up the words like a dry sponge.

4

"Jeanette, did you hear those kids making fun of us?"

"What?"

"Those little kids were making fun of us, calling us names, pulling back their eyes and stuff." The world was full of surprises. *Why do they want us to go back to where we came from?*

"I must have missed it," she said.

I was confused. In my head I knew I wasn't a Chink, I wasn't even Chinese. I was clearly an American, like my family. I came from Korea, but it didn't necessarily mean that I was Korean. I was as American as those kids. My parents did not prepare me for the mocking hand gestures and name-calling. The disapproving stares and prejudice immediately told me that my twin sister and I were less. Couldn't those kids see that we loved everything American, like McDonald's hamburgers, Michael Jackson, and rollerskating? Why couldn't they see that we found the Rubik's Cube, Pac Man and Star Wars amusing, like everyone else? Did they not know that we belonged to a white family, just like they did? For the first time, we realized the color of our skin was not accepted or even tolerated. Worse than not belonging was the feeling of being unattractive and unlikable. I felt the rejection, like cold water thrown in my face.

Once we found our lockers, I stuffed my purple duffel bag into the skinny space and listened to the cheerleaders make friendly talk amongst themselves. *Wow, they're so pretty! I wish I was one of them. Who knows, maybe we can be friends.*

A girl dressed in a red, black and white cheerleading uniform asked her locker partner, "What's your middle name?"

"My middle name is Lisa," her locker partner bounced back with flair and style.

The Brooke Shields look-alike flipped long brown hair back and then pulled it up into a high ponytail. "That's a pretty name." With a thin toothed comb, she backcombed the top into a palm branch and sprayed the entire area with extra-stiff hairspray. I tried not to look.

"What's your middle name?" I overheard her ask the cheerleader next to her.

"Rose."

"Cool. Hey that's my grandmother's name!" Brooke look-alike exclaimed with pure love. She placed a piece of watermelon bubblicious gum into the girl's hand. Rose-middle-name was now officially a member of the cool group. Without a thought, the girl unwrapped the fat piece and popped it in her mouth. Meanwhile, I rolled my eyes at their brainless banter, wishing at the same time that they would include me.

"What's your middle name?" The Brooke look-alike asked another proud-to-be-alive cheerleader.

"Marie!" The girl held her books closely to her heart, then shifted her weight from one smoothed waxed leg to the other. Must be a cheerleader move, I assumed.

"Wow, like that *has* to be the most beautiful middle name of all time." Brooke look-alike tossed the girl a piece of gum.

"What's your middle name?" The Brooke look-alike asked into the air. The question bounced off one of the ping pong tables, and landed close to me.

I looked around. *Was she talking to me?* No one answered, so I did. "Joy."

The four cheerleaders, with Brooke look-alike the tallest of the bunch, turned and stared me up and down with their eyes. I wondered what the problem was. Yes, my pants were baggy, and my hair was long and stringy. No, I was not wearing cover up, liner and lipstick or "shoulder duster" earrings or giant florescent hair bows. Yes, I was aware that I was completely out of style. Cute giggles turned into wild outbursts and then coughing and choking into Kleenex for extra sensitive skin.

"Joy?" the Brooke look-alike said with a shudder. "Your middle name is freakin' Joy? What kind of middle name is that?"

I laughed with them. "Yeah, you *are* right. It *is* pretty stupid," I agreed, but wondered why they were making such a big deal. I thought they would readily accept me because of my American name. Perhaps, if I had been a little older and wiser, I might have thought, 'What's with this middle name crap? How annoying!' But on my first day in junior high, I was eager to be accepted at whatever cost. Fortunately, some religious sense came knocking: I was a servant for Jesus and should be willing to take ridicule for a chance eternal relationship with him.

"Oh, my God, what *are* you?" Brooke look-alike asked. A bright pink bubble waited for my response.

At first I thought she meant my nationality, but the loud popping and smacking noises she made with her gum told me she didn't care if I came from Korea or China, the two totally separate countries meant nothing to her. According to her, whoever had tan skin should be packed up and shipped off together.

She pulled back her eyes. "Chinese, Chinese!"

The excitement of junior high disappeared then. At home, we were taught that our thoughts should be kept private; at school, the kids shared their opinions openly. *Why do they assume I'm Chinese? Duh, I'm American!* But the words refused to come out. *What's wrong with me? Why can't I speak my mind?* I couldn't at home, at church and now, I discovered, even at school.

So... it's not cool or acceptable to be Asian. In fact, they despised us. It didn't take a mad scientist to figure that out. And American names don't help the situation—I was still an outsider, intruder, alien or whatever she wanted to call me. Talk about a defining moment! Suddenly, standing there in my baggy clothes, I didn't feel adequate—I felt smaller than my almost five-foot stature. *I look halfway decent*, I told myself over and over again, having no faith in my chant and nothing in my world to confirm the semi-positive affirmation I tried to force myself to believe.

"You're so tiny! You shouldn't be in junior high; aren't you supposed to be in grade school?"

What was all the fuss about? After all, I *had* to be at least a quarter inch taller than the cheerleader standing next to her. Discreetly, I measured myself against the shortest cheerleader with my eyes—just to make sure. Maybe I was wrong; maybe she *was* taller than I was.

In her matching outfit, Jeanette sauntered up to the lockers, crammed her identical purple duffel bag inside and exclaimed, "Man Jeannine! I got totally lost. This place is huge."

"Like, oh, my God. One ugly girl is bad—" Brooke look-alike whispered. "But two is just plain scary. Look, they both play the violin. Weird."

7

I wished I was European. If I had been then the kids would have found me intriguing, maybe even cheerleading material. What was I supposed to do when faced with racism? Run away and hide? Spit in their faces? I couldn't do either of those, so I just stuffed the violin quickly into the locker. When I slammed my locker door shut, loose papers floated around me. My hands grasped at empty air while trying to snatch them up quickly. I probably looked like a pantomime.

Jeanette looked up at the girls in admiration. Pointing to the Brook look-alike, she whispered, "Wow Jeannine, I like her hair." Then she immediately left the scene to find her class.

Brooke look-alike slapped her knee. "Like, I think you have the wrong school. Go back to China!"

I hated myself for being too scared to speak out in my own defense. I hated myself for not wearing my American pride.

"You're a *geek* of nature. You know that, don't you?" She continued playing Master of the Universe.

I pretended to ignore her. *Who do you think you are? God? So this was what the junior high world was all about. So this was as good as it got in the material world.* I thought about what I had been taught in church about suffering. I should have been prepared for the ways of the junior high world. In Colossians 1:24, Paul foretold that living as a Christian in an unChristian world involved suffering. As a Christian who served Christ and shared him with others, like Paul I should expect some sacrifice and pain. Painless Christianity was a contradiction. There were only two choices in life, to follow the material world or to follow the ways of Christ. The teachings of church were definitely worth striving for.

"Jeannine Joy, Jeannine Joy," she taunted. "What kind of middle name is that?"

The cheerleaders left with their arms linked, chanting Jeannine Joy, Jeannine Joy. They embodied school spirit, or, better yet, Lakota's pride. I half expected to see bumper stickers on their rears when they turned around to leave, announcing that "Lakota will Win," and "God bless Lakota's cheersquad!" *Why can't God bless the meek, as well? Are we not as valuable? Do we not deserve blessings?* The cheerleaders were definitely flaunting their Lakota pride. Pride was something I didn't deserve and had not achieved yet. Lucky?

Yes. Proud? No. I could not pretend that I was the best of a class, group or a society, and I couldn't even try to give the impression that I was better than someone else because of who I associated with or because of an outfit that made a statement. No wonder so many students rebelled against cheerleaders and school spirit, even though they desperately wanted to fit in and be accepted.

While I tried to find my classes in the sprawling junior high building, kids smirked and looked away. Boys and girls formed groups like clusters of cheerful forget-me-nots and laughed their way into classrooms. Everyone was so happy! The students seemed so proud of who they were or who they were blossoming into. They came from good, supportive all-American families. No one was scared out of his or her mind, like I was. My eyes bulged at the sight of so many students and the realization that junior high kids were so aware of what was "in". After all, Mom had said the shops in the mall were for high school kids and that we were still much too young to shop there. Except for the Michael Jackson jackets and Sara Jeans, which we'd chose, Mom found age-appropriate outfits from the children's section in Sears and J C Penny catalogs. I lost faith in what Mom told us when I saw the girls flaunt their new stylish clothes. *Why do the girls look like teenagers, even adults, even though they're so young? Why won't my body catch up with my mind?* I questioned Mom's authority for the first time in my life.

The gods were now Michael Jackson, Cindy Lauper, and Madonna, according to the kids at school—and not following the gods was worse than death. Outfits included a single shiny white glove, parachute pants, jackets adorned with zippers for the guys, and ratted, multi-colored hair, rubber bracelets, and lace tights for the girls. Somehow, the girls were able to fit into the mall clothes perfectly. Shouldn't layers of oversized shirts worn with thick belts, tight miniskirts, form-fitting jeans, neon sweatshirts with matching glow-in-the dark barrettes, and ankle socks be reserved for grown-ups? I was wrong and discovered a new feeling inside—envy. I had never felt such intense emotion before. My feelings of insecurity doubled. Somehow I needed to convince Mom to let us go shopping again for new and popular school clothes, but this idea remained a sinful fantasy. Clothes fashioned after the "media gods" were wrong in Mom's eyes and in the eyes of the church.

Jeanette didn't have a problem being labeled a nerd and she didn't notice that she was completely out of style either; I, on the other hand felt the world around me shifting and I wanted desperately to belong. During first period, I scanned the class for kids who looked easy to approach. An Asian girl about my size, wearing tight pants decorated with paisleys and a wool oversized sweater, sat only a few desks away.

"I like your pants; they're cool." I humbly told her. My Sara Jeans were long in the crotch and rolled up a couple times. No one wore pants that were loose and baggy. I envied her short permed hair also, but was too afraid to say anymore.

"Thanks. Hey, do you want to sit by me?" She patted the desk next to her. I was thrilled, but didn't show any emotion. I just said, "Sure," and took the seat, thanking God at the same time.

After class, I found out her name was Ly when she complained, "My name is pronounced Lee. I hate it when the teacher calls me Lie."

"Hey, I hate it when the teachers call me Jeannie, instead of Jeannine. And I also hate it when people call me cute."

"Me too!" Ly confided.

Good, I made a friend!

I tried to make another friend in my PE class. After a game of touch football, I told a skinny brunette girl who looked easy to approach, "Hey, you did a good job!"

Unfortunately she thought I said, "Hey, you look like a dog!" That didn't go over well with the girls in the locker room. From that day forward, I was on her "shit list", including the "shit list" of all her friends. Of course, I was too shy and too stupid to clear up the misunderstanding.

Jeanette and I found each other in the cafeteria for lunch and then our friend Jenny showed up. *Good!* Jenny had been our friend since kindergarten. Boy, was she stylish! She had already blossomed into a tall longhaired blond, wearing an oversized United Colors of Benetton sweatshirt and snug fitting Guess jeans. She was so lucky! Her mom let her wear that stuff.

Jenny looked at Jeanette. "Hi Jeanette."

She looked at me. "Hi Jeannine."

Jenny was the only one at school who could tell us apart. "Want to eat lunch?" she asked.

"Sure!" we chimed. Jenny actually *wanted* to eat lunch with us! My religious reservations about her were put on hold. Ly walked up and laughed at the sight of Jeanette and me. We looked to each other and shrugged. "What?" Our identical voices echoed, in stereo, bouncing against the kids' chatter in the hall.

"There's two of you!"

"So."

"No wonder," she said to me and giggled again. "I thought that you got snobbish on me." She pointed to Jeanette, "When I told her to sit by me in history class, she just looked at me weird."

The group of cheerleaders gathered around. They stared down at us in disgust and then patted Jenny and Ly's shoulders. "Hey you guys. Eat lunch with us."

I gazed at my inadequate purple tennis shoes bought from Kmart and waited for Jenny and Ly to agree and walk away. The cheerleaders didn't even ask them, they just stood there like ice princesses and demanded. *What spoiled brats!*

"No thanks," Ly replied. Jenny sneered back at the girls and faced Jeanette and me. Their response to the cheerleaders caused me to look up in surprise. At the same time, my mouth dropped open. They just passed up eating with the cool group. They didn't go along obediently, like I would have done.

The cheerleaders flipped their hair and sauntered off, "Suit yourself." Lakota's pride followed them like a cheerful shadow.

Ly, Jenny, Jeanette, and I walked around the cafeteria, like lost souls, searching for an empty table. There wasn't much room and I learned by watching that we couldn't sit just anywhere. The cheerleaders—proud and loud—found a table and slowly unpacked their lunch while pointing to and giggling at whoever accidentally sat at the table next to them.

The four of us found an empty bench in the hall and sat down. "I like your clothes you guys," I commented. "I wish my mom would let me wear stuff like that."

"Thanks," Ly said, "The material is from Malaysia, and the earrings are from Cambodia. Do you want to come over to my house some time?"

"Sure!" My heart raced at the prospect.

Like Princess Diane, Jenny sported *two* watches. Both were made by Swatch; one was in primary colors and the other had a gray face and red straps. "I like your watches," Jeanette said.

"Thanks," she pointed to the gray and red one. "Keith Harring designed this one."

"Oh."

"He's a graffiti artist."

I had never heard of the artist. Later I learned that he was gay, which caused me to wonder if Jenny was really a Christian.

"You guys!" Jenny exclaimed. "I've just heard a rumor that Duran Duran is coming to Seattle."

"Oh."

"You *do* know who Duran Duran is, don't you?"

"No."

"Have you heard of the group Scritti Politti?"

I scrunched up my nose. "Scritti Po—what?"

"You *do* listen to Culture Club, don't you?—Have you heard of Depoche Mode?—I'm sure you've at least heard a song or two from The Cure?"

"Culture what? Depoche what? The Cure who?"

"Next time I go to Time Travelers I'll take you with me."

"Time Travelers?"

"Yeah, you know, the music store on Second Avenue."

"Oh." Of course we couldn't tell her that Mom *still* picked out our clothes—buying albums and going to concerts would be completely out of the question. *What if she found out how strange Mom is? Would she understand our strange family and still like us? Should I befriend someone who is so awake and confident?* Sure, I had learned from our elementary school days that Jenny considered herself a Christian, and she possessed most of the necessary elements needed to make a good Christian. She was honest and humble, she kept her promises, and she did her best to help friends in need. But she was wearing a watch designed by a gay artist and homosexuality is against

12

God. Jenny was also known for analyzing behavior and questioning adults, and she didn't immediately comply with the scriptures or what the church commanded. Was she "born again"? Did she attend church every Sunday, like we did? Was she willing to share the Gospel with anyone and everyone, like Paul instructed? As a sincere Christian, these were crucial questions I had to ask myself before considering any friendship.

Jeanette nibbled on her soft brown banana and compared her class schedule with her copy of the school map given to all the seventh graders. "Geez, is this thing right? Where are we?"

"You're holding the map upside down," Jenny said. "Try looking at it this way."

"Oh," she turned the map around and studied some more. "...Are you sure?"

Geez, Jeanette could be so oblivious at times, I just shook my head. I couldn't believe that people actually thought I was anything like her when we were clearly different! Couldn't they see beyond our identical outfits, hair, and facial features, like Jenny could?

Chapter 2

Born Losers

Jeanette and I adapted awkwardly to junior high. David, our older brother, was a senior at Charles Wright Academy. As far as my parents were concerned, their lives and the lives they wanted for us were all going according to plan—except, of course for Mike. My oldest brother Mike refused to conform to their concept of a good Christian son, causing them years of disappointments and heartaches. Mike had not done well in school. Since he was two years older than David, his goal was to at least earn a General Equivalency Degree (GED) before David graduated. Mom agreed to take Mike to school so he could actually follow through with his plan. When she pulled to the curb at Federal Way High School, and Mike got out of the car, I noticed a lump in his sock.

Without thinking, I blurted out, "Mom, why is Michael's ankle shaped so funny?"

"What are you talking about, Jeannine?"

"Look at his ankle; there's something in it."

Mom startled me with a sudden spurt of frantic movements. She pulled off her seat belt, opened the door to the gold, '67 Cadillac sedan with a hurricane's force, threw her hands in the air and yelled Mike's name. "Michael, Michael! Get back here!" Students from the parking lot stopped talking and looked in our direction.

Mike turned around and ambled back to the car. "Yeah?"

"What's that in your sock?"

"I don't know what you're talking about." He glanced down at his feet and shrugged. "Nothing."

"Don't play games with me. I'm too smart for that. It's cigarettes, isn't it? I knew it. I knew you were smoking. I could smell it on your clothes. Give me that pack, before I rip them out myself!"

Mike grudgingly obeyed before Mom shouted any louder and caused a bigger scene. I immediately realized that I should have kept my mouth shut about the lump.

"Michael, when are you going to turn your life around?" She stated through gritted teeth. "Why are you doing this to the family? If you don't stop rebelling you're going to ruin your life."

"Yeah? Well, so what?" Mike circled around, only this time he slouched while heading back toward the building. "I don't give a crap anymore."

I sat in the back seat feeling guilty and horrible for him. God, how could I be so stupid? It was my fault. I shouldn't have pointed out the lump; I should have known better.

While Mike was at school, Mom searched his room for more signs of evil. Eventually she found 'forbidden fruits,' like candy bar wrappers, cigarettes, and *MAD* magazines. Each item added to her suspicions that she had a troublemaker on her hands.

After school, Mom tried sweet talk. "Michael, why are you doing this? Why are you smoking, listening to this garbage music, rebelling? We just want you to grow up to be a good, decent citizen. Is that too much to ask?"

"In this world? Yes it is," he retorted. "This place sucks."

"It's his long hair," Dad announced, after arriving home from Boeing. "And those stupid rock star idols of his. What's this world coming to?"

"I don't know why he's acting out. We're giving him a good Christian home. He used to be such a docile baby," Mom wondered aloud.

"Yes, you're right. At least we're raising him in a Christ-centered family. The only thing we can do at the moment is pray for him to come to the Lord and leave the rest to God," Dad said.

"Sooner or later he'll come to Jesus," Mom agreed.

As a substitute for counseling, Mike was assigned to listen to the discipline tapes of Dr. Dobson, a celebrated child psychologist and Christian. Mom and Dad were great enthusiasts of Dr. Dobson. He pointed out in his book "Parenting Isn't for Cowards" that *some kids seem born to make it and others are determined to fail and that too often parents are too quick to blame themselves for how their children*

15

turn out. He advised millions of parents through his books and even spoke at the White House while President Reagan was in office. Mike obeyed my parents and listened to the tapes, but I interpreted the shaking of his head as *no way*, and the rolling of his eyes as implying that he couldn't believe Mom and Dad actually believed that crap. Jeanette and I were next in line to have private sessions with Dr. Dobson on tape. David was already a cooperative child, so when it came to him, the lessons weren't so imperative.

Despite Dr. Dobson's wisdom, Mike continued on what our parents thought was a destructive path, growing more isolated and insignificant in the process. "I'm the milkman's son—you know that don't you?" he stated to Jeanette and me. "I'm nothing like Dad or David or Mom. I don't know where I came from."

Jeanette and I chuckled at the thought. Although Mom and Dad were still angry with him, he joked regularly, even at dinner time.

On the evening after Mom discovered Mike's cigarettes, she said, "Michael, it's your turn to say grace." Usually she supervised grace before she left for the living room with her meal.

"GRACE!"

Mom sighed and we knew that her sigh meant: "Be serious".

"Rub a dub, dub, thank God for the grub."

Mom sighed again.

Michael looked down at his plate, which held sweet and sour chicken over Uncle Ben's Rice—our favorite and Mom's specialty. We had lots to be thankful for. This time, he prayed seriously. "Dear Jesus, thank you for the food and the nice day. Amen." That was as long and enduring as his prayers ever got.

Rarely did the family eat dinner together. Dad ate his serving in the unfinished master bedroom; Mom ate alone in the living room amidst her things; both watched a television programs to their liking. Mike, David, Jeanette and I ate together, but independently stared into the soft September drizzle. Outside the large plate glass window, Mom's rhododendron and azalea bushes, pruned ferns and delicate pansies drooped. Off in the distance, we could see the row of Dad's Cadillacs and Limousines as if they were a school of humpback whales beached under maple trees.

David left the table for the doors of the refrigerator.

16

"What do you need, Honey?" Mom asked from the living room.

"Something to drink."

She beat him to the refrigerator. "Here, Sweetheart, take one of these Snapple juices. Which flavor do you like? There's mango, orange..."

Jeanette, Mike, and I ate in silence. The thought of getting something out of the refrigerator remained a fantasy; reality told us it was a crime. *Snapple. I wonder what that tastes like!* David ate and drank what he wanted. Mom called him sweetheart, but there was a valid reason.

Consistent with Dr. Dobson's theory, Jeanette, Mike and I were considered *Strong-Willed Children (SWC)*. After interviewing 35,000 parent participants in a study Dobson came to several conclusions: the first being that *in the human family there are nearly three times as many SWC as Cooperative Children (CC). And that these characteristics are basically inherited.* According to Mom, Dr. Dobson's theory was right on the mark. Jeanette and I were following the rebellious route Mike had taken. We couldn't seem to get the hang of little things, like tying our shoes or riding a bike, and our coordination seemed to lag. Curiosity often got the best of us. We wanted answers that made sense so we could make sound decisions based on all the information we were given. Weren't we capable of making decisions? And if not, why not if God had given us freewill? Mom didn't understand our questions. In her opinion, we were *strong-willed children.*

David was a *cooperative child.* When he was seen with his hand in the bread drawer, Mom joined him and suggested treats that might go perfectly with it. But most of the time he didn't have an appetite and Mom wondered why the rest of her children were greedy and always hungry. When the rest of us were found with our hands in the bread drawer, we were called thieves and the *Little Spanker* appeared. Yet she didn't abuse us, not unless one considers conventional spankings from a skinny tree branch abuse because a piece of bread or some cereal was missing. Spankings were the most effective training tool parents had access to. The thought that a non-Christian parent could raise healthy happy kids with respect and kindness never crossed my mind or the mind of my elders. Instead, we conformed to

Dr. Dobson's rules. Michael, Jeanette and I deserved to get hit with a stick for noncompliance, although we could never figure out why David was never spanked for his curiosity. In our house, a spanking was called good old-fashioned discipline, straight from the Word of God. The Bible says if parents spare the rod, they'll spoil the child. "Spanking caused no emotional damage if done properly," Dr. Dobson declared confident and sure; after all, he had God to back him up. And two minutes of crying after corporal punishment was sufficient amount of time for a child to recover. In fact, he recommended using a neutral object of some type for the punishment as the hand should be seen as an object of love. He warned that if a parent used a hand, the child might develop a pattern of flinching when a parent made an unexpected move. Flinching would *not* be a problem if a parent took time to search for a neutral object. In our case, even though Mom took time to find a neutral object, I still caught myself flinching when she reached up to retrieve a dish from a cupboard or an item from the refrigerator. Dr. Dobson was incorrect in that department.

Why is it okay for David to get food whenever he wants, but not okay for Mike, Jeanette, and me helped ourselves to more? Why is she totally trusting with David, yet refuses to have confidence in the rest of us? Our instincts told us that Mom didn't love us the same way she did David. We reasoned that our feelings were jealousy and envy and should be discounted, like the doctor pointed out. Complaining or even suggesting that Mom favored David was blunt disrespect. Who were we to complain?

Mike chewed on the chicken and stared at the floor until there was nothing left to think about. I felt sorry for him. Mom and Dad ignored his humor and his potential; instead they focused on what they believed to be his flaws. Their oldest son didn't try very hard at maintaining his grades and he was interested in rock-and-roll from the seventies. Mike swore that he could turn Jeanette and me into "rockers" too, by teaching us how to play the electric guitar. "Once you get the hang of 'Mary had a Little Lamb,'" he said, "then 'Stairway to Heaven' by *Led Zeppelin* is a cinch!" He also used natural talent to carve guitars from scraps of wood found at the beach, or to draw comic strips and sketches of army tanks and planes.

Our parents didn't know that even though Mike grew his hair out long and smoked behind their back, he cared for the well-being of his little twin sisters. "If you guys ever start smoking, I don't know what I would do," he scolded. "No, I *do* know—I'd beat you up! Believe me, it's a bad habit. I wish I had never started." His concern prevented me from ever picking up the habit.

Bedtime was eight o' clock, and bedtime always arrived too fast for Jeanette and me. I rested in bed, listening to the summer birds and thinking. Mom called me disobedient and manipulative because of my wandering and exploring mind. I interpreted her orders and strict belief system as obsessive parental control and power. Jeanette and I were, after all, twelve, and soon to be teenagers. Our rebellion had nothing to do with wanting to cause trouble within the family and everything to do with the desire to grow up and become independent.

Finally, I just couldn't lie in bed any longer—I had to do something. My restless mind was driving me crazy! I gathered some old notes from school pals and crept to where the living room and my sleeping area connected. I sat behind a few of Mom's boxes and spread out my notes. The rooms were dark though, and I couldn't make out the words on the papers. *Maybe if I scoot out into the living room a little more, I'll be able to read the notes with some light.—Ah, that's better.*

Suddenly the papers were snatched out from my hands. I looked up. A large, dark silhouette stood over me with the flashlight in my face. It was Mom. "What are you doing?" she demanded.

"—Reading?"

You're supposed to be in bed!"

"Why?"

"You didn't ask permission to get out of bed!" She pulled me up by the arm. This time, I resisted her gripping fingers and reached for my notes, but she lifted them to the ceiling. When she grabbed at my hair, I decided that, this time, I would pull her hair too. I yanked; she screamed. A jumbled fight followed. In the end, I found her sitting on top of me, with my hands held down by her legs. It was as if I had lost a wrestling match—only my opponent weighed at least fifty pounds more than I did.

"Allen! Allen! Help me!" Mom screamed and panted. "I don't know how much longer I can hold her down!"

I wiggled, but to no avail. I was trapped and losing air by the second.

"Allen! Allen! Come here and help me!" she panted.

Thundering footsteps caused the floor to quiver from under me. When Dad appeared, he took one look at us and laughed.

Mom's worst fear about Jeanette and me had been realized. "It's not funny, Allen. These girls are turning into troublemakers." Our stubborn nature had already manifested itself in rebellion. Why were we so curious? Why wouldn't we take no for an answer? Why were we so restless, especially during important times, like bedtime and church services? Why couldn't we just "get" it? Why couldn't we learn the ways of the world with ease? The answer, according to Dr. Dobson, was that we were *strong-willed children.*

Nothing was said about teaching children to think for themselves—that the parent's job was to teach self-sufficiency by trusting children to make their own decisions. No, children were not capable of discerning right and wrong and then acting accordingly. Children were not capable of making sound decisions at all.

Mike, Jeanette and I didn't talk about our feelings, but we couldn't ignore them either. Dr. Dobson said that emotions were dangerous. *They were weapons Satan used and humans were vulnerable creatures who could not withstand these satanic pressures without Divine assistance. Emotions must always be accountable to the faculties of reason and will. That accountability is doubly important for those of us who purport to be Christians.* In no way did we think the doctor's teachings were significant to our development. Once, I whimpered to Mom, like a squeaking mouse, that she liked David the best. She denied my accusation immediately. I left the kitchen, wondering what my problem was.

"Jeannine, there is a big difference between *liking* and *loving.* Sometimes I don't like you, but I will always love you." Of course, she meant to be kind, but I spent many moments trying to figure out that comment. *Why doesn't she like me?* Who knew that later in life those feelings of insecurity would choke our throats and block our growing into well-adjusted adults? Who knew that the negativity would be nearly impossible to overcome? Who knew that forgetting who we really are could cause us to walk with drooping shoulders? Who knew that thoughts and intentions were so powerful? Who knew that a child needed to be *liked* in order to feel whole? Mom's inability to *like* Jeanette and me was the reason we felt closer to Dad; with him we felt important and confident. Unfortunately, Dad refused to see Mike's inner capabilities. He sided with Mom when it came to Mike's rebellion.

The morning after I had been caught out of bed, David and I peeled hard-boiled eggs over the garbage can. Suddenly, a premonition overwhelmed me. "David, you're going to have a horrible life. I just know it," I said.

"What? What are you talking about?"

"Because you are such a great Christian! In the Bible, all the great prophets had horrible lives. Lives that were tested with adversity."

"No, I'm not." He rejected my words, and didn't respond the way I had expected. I thought, for sure he would be amazed at my prediction, but instead he said, "And I don't appreciate what you are saying."

"No, really," I added, believing that I was bestowing a great compliment. "I'm learning about this in Sunday School. You're like Job. He lost just about everything, but he still had faith. God found favor with him—" And Mom found favor with David, as well. She appreciated his talent and his compliance. He had inherited Dad's natural ability to reason and analyze. Dad and David were Rubik's Cube/Atari/Star Trek nerds, who were destined to turn into computer geeks. David was following Dad's footsteps: He actually wanted to excel in school—not like Michael, who thought the educational system and all the trappings that came with it, such as stuck-up kids and know-it-all teachers, "sucked big time".

David stomped his foot.

I tried to explain, "And I'm learning stuff about Joseph too, how his brothers sold him into slavery—"

He pulled off the shell to his egg with more vigor than I'd ever seen him. "Yes, I know about Job and Joseph." He stopped to stare at me. "Are you crazy? Don't tell someone they are going to have a horrible life. That's so rude!"

21

"But he could interpret dreams and then he ended up being the king of the land!" I stopped talking even though I knew many more Bible stories about great Christians. Why was he so angry at my statement? I even pushed him to ask Mom and Dad—they wouldn't dismiss my profound insight. It sounded stupid, but it wasn't unusual to compare David with Bible heroes. Take for instance, the Bible story of David and Goliath. With only one smooth stone, David killed Goliath, resulting in God's favor and the people insisting that he be crowned king. I thought that that was the reason Mom gave David the name in the first place. Didn't she name him after the David in the Bible who beat the system by killing Goliath?

Mom and Dad not only liked and loved David, they also believed in him. They made it known that they would always be available to protect and defend; they wanted him to be *liked* at school and in the world, and they just knew, somehow, that David would one day become a success story. I wouldn't admit it then, but of course we were resentful. *Oh no, another negative emotion brought to us on a dirty dish from Satan.* Our parents' faith and hope in David made us all believe in him. He was such a great Christian that I fully expected him to have a horrible life, like the Bible heroes Job, Joseph, Jeremiah and of course, the greatest of all and the Son of God, Jesus. Don't all great prophets have horrible lives?

I believed in my insight with the confidence of a stubborn twelve-year-old. Mom would definitely agree that David's faith was comparable to the conquerors in the Bible. If anyone was to be king in our family, it would be David.

Chapter 3

Pleasantville

Autumn's multicolored maple leaves settled soggy and wet round our South Seattle home that gloomy October. My family didn't know it then, but we too were living in the dark. The dismal weather mirrored our clouded souls; our hearts were blocked from each other and our minds were stifled. Yet we thought our lives were normal and even, at times, exceptional. To be considered right in the eyes of God, I had to honor my mother and my father. I didn't need to think on my own or ask questions, so for most of my life, I didn't. I followed the rules set by my mother, hoping by doing so that I would gain acceptance from her, from society and best of all, from God. But deep inside, I felt empty and alien and I didn't feel real.

I didn't know that my entire perception of God and the universe could change with time and in response to a challenge. I didn't know that a light so intense could not only shine *on* me, but *in* me. I didn't know that all the answers to my questions were accessible. And I was surprised to learn that God really *does* communicate in mysterious ways!

Before my mom received the phone call that changed our lives in a radical way, my parents tried to do everything right. They wanted to play by the rules—God's rules. Life was considered valuable when done correctly. Joy, my mother, graduated from a Nazarene college located in Napa, Idaho. Allen, my father, earned a Physics Degree at the University of Portland, Oregon. While at the University, he was hired by Boeing to work as a Systems Analyst Engineer and later Mother was hired on as a draftsman. They loved their jobs! In 1960, they bought a large plot of land and Dad started building their dream home. At the First Presbyterian Church in Tacoma, Dad trained to direct a choir and Mom furthered her study of the organ. When their

23

teacher thought they were ready, he recommended that they serve God at a Presbyterian Church nearby. Mom played the organ and piano; Dad volunteered to direct the choir and teach Sunday School. He was immediately voted in by the leaders to function as an Elder. Their religious duties gave my parents passion and a sense of purpose. They were working God's will. What was next, but to start a family? First came Michael in 1965, David arrived in 1967, and the adoption of Jeanette and me from Seoul, Korea, when we were only six months old, completed the family in 1972. We were raised with traditional Christian values. Mom and Dad planned to give us a good home with lots of toys, solid educations, and religious morals. They had good intentions.

As time went on and we children grew older, Mom became increasingly restless. She felt stuck in the house when she craved creativity and adventure. She had given up a precise and artistic job to stay home and raise her children, only because it was the right thing to do, not because she found joy in doing it. Instead of striving to create peace within, she kept busy driving us to various destinations and activities: Mike had trumpet lessons; David played the piano; both boys received tap dancing training; Jeanette and I took ballet and private violin lessons. All of us were involved with swimming, youth group and scouts. For a good part of our childhood, Mom drove us to and from a Lutheran school that was located many miles away from home. Dad worked overtime at Boeing as much as possible to pay for all our lessons and our private schools. We were constantly busy: doing, doing, doing.

Perhaps because they wanted to save some money for our college educations, our parents decided to enroll Mike, Jeanette and me in a public school while Mike was entering high school and we were going into third grade. Because he did not have to work so hard, my 52-year-old father decided to try a new sport, called hang gliding. Against Mom's wishes, he spent Saturday afternoons practicing with a second hand hang glider on the training sites. Mom thought he was crazy or going through some sort of mid-life crisis. Whenever he lugged the hang glider out from under the balcony, carried it up the hill, and then secured it to the top of the Volkswagon bus, Mom got nervous. There was so much more he could do around the house. For starters, he could at least finish putting the front door in. The six of us lived in a house that my father started building in the early 1960's. By the 1980's the exposed wood frame was as brittle as old bones and only a few walls were dressed with sheet-rock and plaster. Dad had planned to finish the house promptly, but his work lagged. The problem was Mom's habit of obsessive shopping. Her purchases filled not just the nooks and crannies of the four thousand square foot home, but every surface that could hold a box or bag. Dad finally gave up; Mom continued buying and filling.

The summer of '84 ended and Dad had not yet reached his goal of "soaring" at "high altitude". Dad hoped that Saturday, October 20th would be a good day for flying. Hopefully the air would get warm. Thermals, heated air that moves upward, were needed so the hang gliders could soar. All that Dad had ever achieved during his six prior high altitude flights were "sled rides". Since cold Fall air would soon prevent him from accomplishing his goal, he felt that Saturday would be his last chance at flying. He felt impelled to reach his goal this year. He was impatient; he didn't want to wait for next summer—he was determined to "soar".

Dad spilled out about twenty sets of keys from a cut-opened, plastic milk carton onto the kitchen table. The keys belonged to an assortment of old '58 to '68 Cadillac, Limousines, and a garden variety of other collectibles, including a '53 and a '54 Jaguar. A total of 14 cars in all were parked in the yard—some of them working, but most of them covered with moss and mold.

"Allen, what are your plans today?" Mom asked.

"I'm going to check the VW's engine. Tomorrow the fellows are meeting me at Dog Mountain. The instructor thinks the weather will be adequate. I want to make sure the VW is running properly." Dad's eyes sparkled with anticipation. "Shoot—where are those keys?"

"They should be in the milk carton like they always are," Mom said. Dad's never-ending activities outside the home caused her to feel lonely and dissatisfied. Even at home, his mind was preoccupied with work, church and flying.

One by one, Dad dropped the keys back into the milk carton. "I can't find them!"

"Allen, why can't you do something with the house instead? Can't you wait until after you've finished the closet doors before going out?"

I could see the light in his eyes slowly dim into frustration. "Where are the keys? I won't have time to check the engine tomorrow. I've got to get the lesson plan ready for Sunday School."

"Allen, why can't you install the carpet today instead, like you've promised?" Mom asked. "Or what about building the dining room balcony? When are you going to start on that project?"

He kicked a box, causing empty plastic containers to disperse onto the floor. "I'll never be able to finish the house with all your stuff in the way. I can't even get in the dining room! How am I supposed to work on it?"

"Well, if only you would work on one project per month, we would have the house finished by now! Instead you waste your time on your vehicles and on your hang gliding lessons! Why can't you at least put in the front door?"

"Get rid of your junk!" he exploded.

"Allen! You'll never know when we might need something from those boxes!" The valuables Mom held close to her heart were packed away until Dad could finish the house. That day never arrived. Their temporary fixes: the front door, the carpet scraps over the unfinished wood floors, the cardboard doors to Mike and David's bedrooms, and the boxes stuffed with usable, second hand finds from the Goodwill caused blockages within their marriage, like heart disease.

Dad stormed down the hall, sliding cans and jars from off the shelves with his hands. By the time he reached the bedroom, he punched a cardboard closet with his fist. "Then put things away! I don't want to see this crap anymore!"

Jeanette and I were shocked at his anger. We had never seen him so mad. He rarely got angry. Jeanette and I followed Mom down the hall, wanting to help her anyway we could. We took turns asking gently if she needed help. Like Mike and David, we wanted to show our support.

"No! Go to your rooms!" She was a strong parent who rarely exhibited vulnerabilities.

Dad hurled *Family Circle* magazines to the left and *Woman's Day* magazines to the right. *Why is Dad so angry? He shouldn't yell at Mom like that!* Little did we know that at one time he used to get upset on a weekly basis over her purchases, but by the time we came into the family, he had stopped showing his anger and had learned to ignore the mess. When this eruption happened, Jeanette and I were pre-teens.

"Allen, stop! Stop! I'm working on it! I have the living room almost cleared away!"

Next went stacks of drawing paper, boxes of felt tip markers and colored pencils.

"Allen those are for the kids! Stop doing this!"

Boxes of model airplanes followed.

"One of those boxes has David's project for school! Be careful!"

To make a final point, he threw six or seven boxes of top designer shoes out of *his* way, and into *her* path. Mom collapsed to her knees to pick up the scattered mess. I hated seeing her that way.

"I don't care what you do, just get all this stuff out of sight!" He stormed out the door. Outside, thick rolls of carpet stacked taller than I was and smelling of mold rested under the carport to greet him. They reminded us everyday that the house wasn't finished. Even though these temporary scraps were intended to cover the floors one day soon, that day never arrived. Our five cats used the carpet rolls as shelter in the winter and to sharpen their claws in the spring. Small wild animals used the rolls as an apartment complex: bees hid their hives in them; two moles kept their children deep within them for warmth and security; and one summer, two little birds used the thick carpet rolls as a safe haven to lay their eggs.

On that day, we sided with Mom and were appalled by Dad's erratic behavior. The house looked messier than it really was, we rationalized, because *Dad* hadn't hooked the Japanese styled doors in the tracks to the closets in the first place. We refused to see Mom's boxed-up possessions as a problem. We thought living around boxes was normal. We had no idea that her possessions would eventually become a major source of trouble within *our* own lives.

Most of the conversations our parents had were when Mom announced to Dad that she had temporarily cleared out a certain room in the house. One month the lucky area might be the sewing room; two months down the line, it could be the dining room.

By late evening, Dad finished his work on the Volkswagon bus and entered the house whistling a happy tune. Checking the engine, attaching the hang glider to the roof and thinking about flying had cast a magical spell on him. It was as if he had forgotten all about the argument a few hours prior.

Mom acted as if nothing had happened. "Look Allen," she declared. "I cleared off the piano today!"

Dad said, "Good job honey! Let's go out to dinner and celebrate!" And off they went for a special dinner at their favorite restaurant, *King's Table*, where no tip was required. They tried the best they could because they had a great future to look forward to—a future that consisted of freedom and travel. Their marriage was a cycle of restlessness that depended on the future for some happiness.

Left at home, Mike, David, Jeanette and I thought our parents' drama was ironic.

"Man, Mom is funny. She just moves boxes around, from one side of the house to the other side," David joked after they had left.

"Or from upstairs to downstairs," Mike agreed. "And then from downstairs to upstairs."

"Yeah!" Jeanette and I chimed.

"If only they would leave it up to us, I bet we could get rid of the boxes in a month!" David said.

"And we could finish the house in two months!" Mike exclaimed.

"Yeah!" Jeanette and I chimed again.

"Wouldn't it be great to live in a clean house?" David asked.

We answered him with our own silent thoughts. *What would living in a completely finished and renovated house be like? What would living free of boxes be like?* At night I would fantasize about living with soft carpets, clean walls, and doors to empty rooms, and I was sure Mike, David and Jeanette did the same. We kept this a secret from Mom though. Revealing our thoughts would be disrespectful. Truths, in our family, were left untold; boxed-up clutter, in our house, was ignored. Excesses were crammed and hidden in the basement, till the basement overflowed. Then new purchases would be strewn on the tables and floors, and Mom would try to find space for them.

Arguments would rise to the surface again. It was a never-ending battle.

Chapter 4

Fallen

In spite of all this discord, no one in my family could have predicted that our lives would be altered in a permanent way and that our lives would take a bitter turn. Sometimes, God doesn't answer prayers and pleadings from our hearts like we expect Him to. My twin sister, Jeanette, and I were twelve years old when we received the phone call on October 20th, 1984 about Dad's injury and we became aware that there would be a struggle. That day, we were in the middle of trying to clean our small, junk-infested bedroom at the time. Cleaning the space was a challenge, but worth it in the end. We always felt refreshed after dumping trash and unnecessary papers trapped under and around the bed into garbage sacks. In a sense, we felt we were reorganizing our lives and awakening a part of our souls from a place of sleep. A cleansing was bound to happen; it was only a matter of time.

The gloom outside penetrated through our dirty windows as we worked silently to tidy up our belongings. The space we used as our bedroom was originally built to be a music room, but since the actual bedrooms went to our older brothers, Mike and David, we had to make do with these cramped quarters. Only after our older brothers moved out would we inherit their bedrooms and have some privacy, we were told. That day was coming soon. Mike had recently earned his GED, David was a senior in high school and we had just started junior high! We were growing up and shared optimism that life would certainly get better.

Like every other part of this unfinished house, our pseudo-room was a compromise. The small size of the room made it hard for us to move around. Our bed, dressers, and toys were stuffed into the temporary arrangement and spilled out into the living room like turkey dressing. Mom had scolded us about our mess, yet the entire house was still filled with her own boxes of clothes, stacks of magazines, full shopping bags and excessive furniture covering almost every square foot. For a mysterious reason, she couldn't part with or throw away any of her possessions.

Jeanette and I wore our hair in identical ponytails. We wore identical dark blue sweatshirts and jeans that would bunch up at the crotch whenever we sat down because of our small size. We wore matching purple tennis shoes with velcro straps from Kmart. But, it was not only our clothes that were so similar: we talked the same, walked the same, and laughed the same. Being together was embarrassing, but it was also reassuring. We didn't mind looking so much alike, but at the same time, we hated it. Life as a twin was strange, but it was also who we were and all that we knew, so it seemed normal.

Jeanette and I pulled our sleeping bags off the sagging mattress and stood the dirty thing on end against closets filled with Mom's precious clothes—most of which were never worn and still had hanging price tags. Our garbage, an assortment of papers and small puffs of dust, flew over the floor like swooping pigeons. Jeanette caught what she could, swept up the rest and crammed the debris into the plastic grocery bag that I held. Similar to the way we deal with life, I thought. Jeanette swept the problems off her; I gathered the world into the memory of my being. She ignored injustices; I buried thoughts inside. Ironically though, both of us only remember a few bits and pieces from our childhood. We recalled that we could barely look into Mom's eyes, *feeling* or *using* our senses was difficult, and we were always on the defensive. Remembering anymore about our past was challenging.

After we finished gathering the rubbish, we gently laid the mattress down, and straightened the two slick sleeping bags on top. *Now what?* We stayed in our room and stood against the bed with our hands on our hips, because Mom didn't like us in other areas of the house. She thought we'd cause problems or steal something from her, as if we were strangers. Most of the time, we were assigned to stay in our room or in the basement where a small area was cleared off for our Barbie Dream House. But we were getting too old for Barbie and Ken!

During school vacations the days were long and boring and we were restless and curious. Dad was always at work so we couldn't follow him around like lost puppies. Once in a while, we kept ourselves busy in the room, with nothing to do but peek into Mom's zippered closet bags full of garments and other treasures. We wondered what everything was and why she never wore all the clothes she accumulated. Nor did she read the stacks of magazines, or even unpack the endless stack of boxes. Although, whenever we wanted to explore sheets of colorful wrapping paper or a box of unused shoes, Mom would appear instantaneously and demand that we admit that we had been prying into her things. They were *hers* after all—all *hers*! And we were not allowed to touch *her* things without permission. On happy occasions, she led us to believe she would get out a treasure or two and tell us all about it, but for now, they were to be kept in the boxes and put away. When we got caught peeking inside a box, she always found out and a spanking on the legs with a skinny stick or *The Little Spanker* would follow.

On the day of Dad's injury, we took the entire morning and afternoon to straighten up the mess in our room. By the time dusk arrived, the maple leaves had finished whispering secrets in the chilly Northwest wind. When the aqua colored telephone rang in the kitchen, Mom answered quickly. She always did. No one else was allowed to answer the phone or to retrieve the mail—It was considered "none of our business" and if we were ever caught eavesdropping, well, that was totally disrespecting her privacy and she'd have to think up some form of corporal punishment to teach us a lesson. Usually, she went calling for *The Little Spanker* again.

Mom mumbled some words into the phone and placed the receiver clumsily back on its stand. Jeanette didn't hear her call out for our older brother, David, but I did. At times like this she sounded like Harriet Olsen, the manipulatively sweet mother we saw on the TV episodes of "Little House on the Prairie". Jeanette and I smirked while watching the show, because in Harriet we saw Mom's annoying traits. Both women insisted that everything be done their way, making demands with an authoritative and pseudo-sweet air. Both shared the same *physical* attributes too: Same facial features, brown hair in an up-do, thick build, and round eyes adorned (on Sundays only) with lavender shadow.

"*Girls! Michael!*" Mom called for the rest of us, "Meet me in the basement. I need to talk to you!"

We scrambled down the untreated wood basement steps, then stood against the bare cement fireplace as if in a police line-up. *Did Mike help himself to cereal from the cupboards? Did Jeanette and I look somewhere we shouldn't have? Did she discover a piece of bread gone from its package? What did we do this time?*

Instead, Mom shocked us with news that sounded serious. "Your father has been injured, children," she said in a trembling voice. "He's in the intensive care unit at St. Joseph's. He fell while hang gliding and his helmet has cracked. It doesn't sound good." Immediately, she led us into prayer. We gave thanks to a God who made us and if we followed His way, was willing to share His kingdom with us. We asked Him to rescue Dad from the darkness and gloom of Satan's Kingdom and to bring us into the kingdom of His dear Son, Jesus, who bought our freedom with His blood and forgave us all our sins.

We wondered where our family was headed. According to our Christian viewpoint, we were God's children who should know our ultimate destination is eternal life with our heavenly Father. This was a test of faith from God. Our religion would sustain us through thick and the thin. Christianity was not only a religion—it was our way of life—we each had a personal relationship with Jesus. Nothing could take away our faith. Nothing. All other philosophies were blasphemous and nontruths and destructive routes to hell. Mom and Dad were rigid in their beliefs, and I was learning to hold on with the same desperate dedication.

With Jesus' help, Jeanette and I would be able to take care of the family problems. We would make Mom proud. Unaware of my prayers and noble intentions, Mom placed an arm around the thin shoulders of David, her favorite son. "David and I have decided that we will go to the hospital first. Then she turned to Mike, now eighteen. "Michael, you keep an eye on the girls."

Although Mike was the oldest child, Mom always seemed to favor David. I could see the hurt in Mike's eyes when David put his coat on in a hurry, without looking at any of us. After Mom and David quickly left for the hospital, Mike did not speak of the recent slight. Instead, he took out a felt-tip marker and drew funny eyes on each of our hands, trying to keep things upbeat. "Okay, I'm keeping an eye on you. Now go do what you want!" He didn't believe in authority, even over us, his little sisters.

Jeanette and I lingered in our freshly cleaned bedroom with Dad on our minds. Did he have a hurt shoulder or leg? Hopefully, it was not more serious. Perhaps Dad's injury would prove that Jesus really does have healing hands. We were taught in church that only the faithful Christians were God's chosen people and that he would shower us with blessings and answer our prayers. I couldn't wait to see God's healing work on our family. I couldn't wait to show off his handiwork to the secular world and then save others from damnation.

I reasoned that at least we had Christ on our side. The concept of God was much more than just a figment of our imagination; it was our reality. My comfort came from the same source Mom's did. She had created much more than a typical family; she had followed her parents' footsteps, using morals that were built using the Bible and Jesus as the foundation. We considered ourselves lucky. Mom and Dad gave us the answers to help defend our religion. First of all, no other religion has a God that will answer prayers. No other religion offers forgiveness to the sinful and amazing grace to the wretched. And finally, no other religion has a "hero" who willingly sacrificed his life for us. Christ was going to take care of our insignificant problems—after all, he had already died on the cross for our sins. Healing Dad would be a cinch. Without Christ's help, we could accomplish nothing. We were nothing without Jesus. We were empty vessels. We were worthless.

Chapter 5

Shadow of an Eagle

A week later, I curled into the cold, molded plastic of a hospital chair. My feet barely reached the floor. "Why can't we see Dad?" I asked.

Grooves formed in Mom's forehead as she tried to contain her frustration. "It's a hospital regulation. You have to be fourteen." She looked around the waiting area next to the Intensive Care Unit to see if anyone had heard my plea. Then she said without moving her lips, "You're only twelve. Stop making a scene!"

Mike paced anxiously and tried to defend Jeanette and me. "Mom, you can understand why they feel bad. It's Dad in there! I'd feel bad too if I wasn't allowed to see him."

Mom, as usual, let the significance of his words disappear into the air without a thought and looked instead to David for an answer. But David didn't have any answers. He silently avoided the conflict by staring at the television screen. An ultra-thin body and boyish appearance made him look years younger, but he could deliver the same intense stare that Dad gave—looking into you or through you. This all-knowing gaze remained fixed on the television.

Mike retreated to a chair in the corner and nibbled on his fingernails facing the white wall. "Fuck!" He said under his breath. Mom's presence could drain the buoyancy out of him, just as it did us. Again, she wrapped a loving arm around David and then the two of them headed toward the curtain. I could read her mind: Poor David, this must be so hard for him. I watched as Mike reluctantly followed without a loving arm around him or emotional support.

"What do you want to do?" Jeanette asked, squirming in the unyielding chair.

"I want to see Dad," I said.

Jeanette did not have to say, "me too." We could read each other's eyes.

The air in the waiting area was warm and stuffy and I wanted to sneak a look at Dad. I waited impatiently, flipping through a *Reader's Digest* magazine, not digesting a sentence or a word. I nudged Jeanette when she started chewing on her fingers.

"Quit chewing your nails!"

"I'm not," she replied. "I'm getting the skin around the nails!"

"Then how come I hear click, click, click?"

She let out a deep, annoyed sigh.

Time froze. I stirred uncomfortably in the chair, like I did during long church sermons, then picked up another *Reader's Digest* to flip through. But my mind could not concentrate on one of its short stories, and the tattered magazine rested on my lap. Meanwhile, to pass the time away, Jeanette had turned to splitting a hair strand into two separate pieces. I noticed she did this, not once, not twice, not three times, but until something was said.

"Quit doing that" I jabbed her side. "You're going to get split ends."

"I don't care," she said with another sigh. "Quit telling me what to do."

"I'm not."

"Are too."

"Am not."

"Yes you are."

When I became tired of saying, "am not," I turned my attention to memories of Dad. I remembered when he took Jeanette and me to the hang gliding training site so we could watch him practice for the flight off the real mountain. We weren't forced to act a certain way. We could run along the hill and swing our arms in wild circles without a thought as to what impression we were giving to others. Dad laughed as we raced about like typical eleven-year-olds. We compared Dad's easygoing nature to Nells Olsen from "Little House on the Prairie," although our conservative Dad wore thick-framed glasses, three-piece suits, and an accumulation of ball-point pens inside his pocket protector to work.

When Dad first started his lessons, Jeanette and I loved the times when he offered to let us tag along. We would find a spot on the grass to lay down the blanket, pop open our Precious Moments umbrellas and set them behind us to keep the sun off our backs. Meanwhile, Dad hummed a cheerful tune while putting the hang glider together. He never complained about lugging that heavy thing around. He told us the joy and freedom at the top was worth the struggle up the hill. We heard people at church saying he must be crazy, but we were enchanted with his boyish enthusiasm, his energy, and his courage. "When I become skilled at flying, I'll take you with me as high as you want to go!" he told us. He wanted us to experience freedom and I looked forward to that and even dreamed of it.

I thought about the times during church services when Dad massaged my forearm whenever I sat next to him. Church was a warm comforting place in his presence. In contrast, church was intimidating when Mom was around. It was not uncommon for her to politely inform my sixth grade Sunday school teacher, (the pastor's wife) that she needed to "borrow" me for a few minutes. Her face told the truth—a spanking was due. I had committed a crime. I had pilfered for some food. As far as Mom was concerned, hunger was not a valid excuse for eating without permission. We weren't daughters; we were like small quick rodents. We were like mice who slipped through the kitchen, stealing from the bread drawer and from boxes of cereal. She called us "thieves". Our hunger probably symbolized a need for love. Mom believed it implied that we didn't appreciate the sacrifices she was making to give us a good Christian home. With a firm grip, she would drag me into the large choir closet located in the far end of the hall, close and lock the door and hit my legs with a wire coat hanger. I squirmed in the hospital chair, remembering the sting of the hanger.

Mike emerged from behind the hospital curtain, pushing the cloth away as it tried to follow him out. He brushed past us and through the glass doors to sneak a cigarette under the rain. His golden red, naturally curly hair bounced with each step. Even though I liked how his glittery strands sparkled in the sun, he never seemed to like the way it knotted up and wouldn't brush out straight.

I thought about the Bible verses I had recently memorized at Sunday School. Matthew 10:39 says, "Whoever finds his life will lose it, and whoever loses his life for my sake will find it." I interpreted that verse personally. Jesus was talking about Dad. At the moment, Dad's life may be lost, but Jesus would heal him no matter how bad his condition was. And if Dad's faith didn't heal him, *mine* would. I had absolutely no doubt in Jesus' capabilities. No doubt. That was how sure I was of my faith. In Matthew 9:1, Jesus said to the paralytic, "Take heart, son; your sins are forgiven. Get up, take your mat and go home." To the astonishment of the crowd, the man stood and walked home. Jesus also healed two blind men. When the Son of God asked if they believed that He was able to heal, they both replied, "Yes, Lord." Then he touched their eyes and said; "According to your faith will it be done to you." Their sight was restored, and afterward they spread the news about him all over the region. The same miracle would happen to our family, and, of course, I would gladly spread the news as well.

Eventually, Mom and David returned from behind the curtain. After quiet talk with a few nurses and the doctor, she finally nodded at Jeanette and me. "Girls, he's doing better, I think. Soon he'll be out of the Intensive Care Unit and you'll be able to see him. Let's go home. We'll come back tomorrow."

Jeanette and I immediately stood, stretched, like synchronized swimmers, and then followed them out into Tacoma's rain. The downpour drummed fast and cold, against the depressing cement, brick building and us. When Mike thought Mom wasn't looking, he mashed his cigarette into the ground, and drooped into the black Trans Am behind us. Mom sniffed the air, but said nothing. I noticed that his clothes emitted a pungent tobacco smell when he sat between us in the back seat. In the front seat, David stared ahead intensely, as usual.

Once home, Mom parked the car and the five of us dispersed into our own separate areas without saying a word. Mike found an efficient way into the house and around the boxes to get to his orange-painted bedroom, then slid his cardboard door closed. The bright shag carpet did nothing to raise his gloomy spirit, but drawing cool designs with his silver markers and playing Led Zeppelin on the record player (at a low level!) did wonders for his soul. The ultimate escape was, of course, to sneak a cigarette.

David stayed by Mom's side while she made phone calls to distant family members and close church friends. His presence calmed nerves and bandaged emotional wounds. Mom put up a shell and kept her feelings locked inside and only David had the key. She was profoundly shaken when she comprehended the finality of her husband's situation. Her pain was written all over her once-rosy face. She needed to contact Boeing's Personnel Office, sell the cars, get the finances in order, call Social Security, and clean up the house before Dad was discharged from the hospital. Anxiety arrived in our home, uninvited. How was she going to do all this alone? Who could she turn to except for God? And God did not talk back with answers. She felt more alone than ever and to make her ordeal worse, she couldn't invite anyone to the home because of the mess. With all her strength, she constantly prayed for God to make the nightmare disappear.

What did we do to deserve this? Why is life so unfair? I also prayed to Jesus to give Mom her husband back! Seeing them miserable made me worried. Why did God allow this to happen when Mom and Dad did their best to raise a good Christian family? Mom didn't know what to do with the pain, so it just settled inside and made a confused home within her.

Jeanette and I wandered into our room and sat at the edge of the bed. After staring out of the window for a few minutes, I decided to get out my little diary and write inside:

Hang gliding is bad luck! Saturday October 20ᵗʰ 1984 Mom got a call from Lion, Dad's hang glider friend. Dad crashed in a tree. He had to get out of the tree by helicopter. Now he's in St. Joseph's Hospital. His shoulder is dislocated and he broke his elbow and bruised his head. I can't see him because you have to be fourteen or over and he's in the ICU. But soon he'll be moved to another room and I'll be able to see him – I think. He lost his glasses too. We are getting tons of calls!

Jeanette turned on the clock radio. After a few moments of fiddling, she found a band called Mr. Mister playing their song on a static-free station. I listened to the words with mute hope. *Take these*

39

broken wings and learn to fly again, learn to be so free. Dad was like the shadow of an eagle. His shadow would remain on the ground for who knew how long.

Chapter 6

Flawless

A few months after junior high started, Dad was taken out of Intensive Care and placed in a regular hospital room on a different floor. I entered his room resolved to be brave and hold back my tears. Even though he was hooked up to machines, he appeared to be aware of our presence, and when our eyes met, he even gave us a frail strange, smile. I couldn't help but notice how foreign he appeared. At the same time though, in a twisted way, he looked the same. A bulky cast protected his left arm to help heal it correctly. Orange, yellow, olive bruises decorated his face and body like autumn leaves. His left eye turned inward, which made him appear cross-eyed. *How are the doctors going to fix that?* To hide it, a nurse placed a black patch over that eye.

Where was the man who dressed in a navy blue business suit every weekday? Where was the intellectual who confidently solved problems? Now his injured head was bandaged and looked fragile and vulnerable. Before his injury, he was involved in military projects at Boeing, trouble-shooting, implementing control requirements and making sure the systems worked together. Dad's job required him to be demanding, exact and organized. Now his brain and body were beyond his control.

A baffled stare replaced his usual cheerful greeting. Like a helpless fly entangled in a web of fat and wiry tubes, he wanted out of the mess and tried to tell us he was going back to work at Boeing as soon as he could. We believed him. After all, Dad taught his Sunday School students that God performs wonderful miracles for all with faith, and Matthew 21:22 says, "…Whatever you ask in prayer, you will receive, if you have faith." There were many more verses from the Bible that said the same thing, and we definitely felt secure in God's hands.

Dad gazed at the colorful poster full of goodwill wishes from the kids in the youth group, assuming that he would fulfill his religious duties in church again and soon. The banner motivated all of us. Shortly, Dad would be active and leading the church with his smile and charm. We were a family of faith. No doubt God would perform a miracle on Dad's broken body and his bruised brain. Christianity would never fail him or his family.

I waited by the wide door of his small hospital room, while the doctor talked to Mom about his condition. *What's going to happen to us?* It was strange to see Dad so broken-up and out of control. My security, my rock had turned to sand. How long would his condition last? He was my favorite parent. Jeanette and I called him "the nice one," who didn't need to check up on us to make sure we weren't snooping around. He actually trusted us. Now there was no one to protect us from Mom when she got tired and angry. Why did this have to happen to him?

Jeanette and I turned to each other for strength. The situation could only get worse; apprehension crept into our bones. It forced us to be thankful for each other; we were twins for a reason. On the flip side, we had hope and faith in using God's strength. *Can our home life get better? Maybe Dad's injury is a blessing in disguise. What's going to happen to us?*

I didn't know how to handle my pain, so I watched what Mom did. I stared at Dad with tears held back and grief deep within.

The doctor talked about Dad's discharge from the hospital in January. After a final overview, he wrote on a chart: verbal speech is present, however incomprehensible... status post-head-injury with altered mental state... upper torso tremor... left arm immobilized...

From what I could understand, there were several things wrong with Dad's body that might never be fixed. He had lost his sense of smell, some hearing, some stamina and balance, some memory, and the quality of his voice.

After the short visit, we headed home. Hospital visits became a regular part of our daily schedule. After a few months, we grew jaded and the visits were less frequent. Mom was getting worn and tired.

Friends were becoming less concerned. This was too much to handle for too long.

Why, why, why? Mom forced a fake smile on her face for the church friends and to us; she had to keep going. But could she for another day? I'm sure she fervently prayed to God at night, in fact, I could almost hear her. Each morning she woke disappointed and upset and not wanting to get out of bed, but doing so anyway, wondering if she could make it through another day. Her painful emotions screamed to be let out as she walked in a royal purple bathrobe from room to room. *God help me! Is there anyone there? God answer me! Will the pain ever end? Why is God neglecting us? I need my life back! I don't care if it wasn't perfect; anything is better than this.*

"Girls, there's a new man at the hospital and it's not your father." Mom told us after arriving home from a support group meeting. "It's like your father is dead."

"But, I don't see him as different," Jeanette responded. "I see him as the same as before."

"Honey, that's an immature way of looking at the situation. You aren't married to him. You can't comprehend the severity of what has happened to him and me. It's like he is dead. I don't have my husband anymore. And to make things worse, now I have to take care of a stranger."

I stood back, fascinated with what Mom was saying.

"After a spouse endures a head injury, it is expected that the marriage won't last. It's common for divorce to happen. At least that is what the statistics say."

"But," we wanted to say, "who cares about statistics?"

As if she could hear us, Mom said, "Girls, you're not grown up. You haven't experienced life like I have. Your father is not the same. The man I married is gone."

"Oh," was all we could say, but we did everything we could to keep from believing it.

My parents didn't know what role to play. Dad's role as a provider was nonexistent and the role Mom was supposed to play as a wife disintegrated and she didn't know how to react. If Dad couldn't provide for his family, if he couldn't fulfill his role, if his body didn't function the way it was supposed to, then what else was he except less? Since the society we lived in placed importance on appearance, then my father literally was inferior; he wasn't considered a husband any longer. My mother, used to being cared for, was now forced into the role of caregiver.

Three months later, Jeanette and I watched the rehabilitation team prepare Mom for the role of caregiver in what they called a care conference. One by one, the physical, occupational and speech therapist entered the room to explain the standard home evaluations required before Dad was discharged.

"It won't be easy, Mrs. Vance," stated the physical therapist with cropped hair.

"I'll do fine," Mom said. She embraced David, seeing the potential in him that I wished she saw in me. "My sixteen-year-old son will help."

The physical therapist flipped off her plaid camping jacket and tossed it over the hospital bed. Though her voice was deep, I realized she was female. "Usually we run a home evaluation before we discharge the patient. It's to help you, the caregiver. That way, we can assess where is the best place to put up handrails—you'll need many—in all the rooms that Mr. Vance uses. Maybe a transfer pole for the bed, so he can get up out of bed without your help. It'll take some hard work and practice for him to regain his balance and stamina…"

My mind wandered. *There isn't any room for all that stuff. Maybe it'll give Mom some motivation to actually get rid of her junk, and then once Dad is healed he can finish the house and everything will be normal—even better than before!*

"An assessment really isn't necessary. But, thank you," Mom said.

"This is how you should let Allen get out of bed independently." The therapist got on the other hospital bed like the Pillsbury doughboy to demonstrate. "Have him roll onto his side with legs bent at the knees. Remind him to push off with his good hand. He can push his upper torso while at the same time swing his feet over the edge of the bed."

Even though she quickly went from laying down to sitting up in proper position, the process seemed so complicated all of a sudden.

"Okay." Mom answered without her former confidence.

A nurse knocked and entered the room to remove Dad's catheter. I tried not to look, but couldn't help seeing her hands do the task—she was so fast. Immediately the catheter was off and his hospital gown down before I realized what had just happened. Mom shot me an irate look. I spun around and looked innocently out the window at the gray slab building next door.

Two nursing assistants complained that Dad was too heavy to lift. They didn't have all day to wait for him to get up, onto the wheelchair, and into the bathroom. They had too many patients to help.

The doctor was the slowest moving of the bunch. He just wandered from one patient to another, as if time meant nothing. A crossword puzzle was hidden beneath his clipboard.

"There's no way Mrs. Vance will be able to handle him alone." I overheard a nurse's aide say while she struggled to get Dad up off the bed and onto the wheelchair by pulling his hospital gown.

The physical therapist argued, "Yes she will. If she uses proper body mechanics, and a "gait belt," she will do just fine. I'll go over to the house to make sure everything is set up properly. All of the staff is here to guide and support."

"Whatever you say," the nurse's aide murmured, then left the room. "You know best."

The physical therapist patted Mom on the back. "Now, to get your husband from chair to standing, he'll need to scoot to the edge of the chair. Then remind him to use his good hand to push forward and up. Remember. Nose over toes. Say that to him while he's doing it because he's going to need 'cues' when attempting to do anything. A great exercise you can do at home is to time how long he can stand and then record it into a log. When he gets to a standing position, you can get your son to start the timer, and then when Allen falters, you help him back down. Your husband will feel good about himself as it'll build up his endurance."

"Okay," Mom and David said together.

"Now, to help him with walking. This might be in the far future, but just to get started, you stand behind him and hold his hips. That way, if he starts to go down, he can use his capable arm to hold himself steady." She turned to a staff member. "Are there going to be railings put up in the hall?"

Mom answered before anyone. "We have a long balcony that runs the entire length of the house. We can practice out there. It has a nice thick railing."

It's too cold out there, I thought, but kept my mouth shut.

"Great! Fantastic! That'll work out just perfectly! Now, when he's up and walking—oh, yeah, make sure the railing is on his right side, you know, his good side, so he can grab it if necessary—he'll need to learn how to turn." She looked down at Jeanette and me. "Right? We don't just walk in straight lines all day long! Wouldn't it be funny if everyone just kept going? Just kept walking in a straight line?"

Jeanette and I snickered, but not because we thought her comment was funny. Even though we were already a month into seventh grade, we looked years younger. No one could guess that we had already started junior high. Our matching outfits told the world that we were immature and childish. Mom still believed that we were much too young to pick out our own clothes, especially during occasions like church and youth group activities. She laid out our outfits, selecting Lisa Frank sweatshirts and matching pressed pink slacks for that day's hospital visit. I thought the clothes she picked were babyish and from the children's department, but I wasn't going to start an argument over it. Anyway, I felt comforted by the fluffy fleece next to my skin; the scattered juvenile balloons, stars, and even the hearts in pastel colors didn't really bother me. She completed the look with black shiny shoes trimmed with little pink roses. When I glanced into the mirror before we left, I felt corny, dressed up like a cute doll. We wanted to grow up and to be taken seriously, yet we looked cute and childish. Of course we couldn't talk to Mom about our wants. She would interpret our opinions as disrespect, so most of the time our mouths stayed closed. Anything to avoid conflict. But I wanted more, I wanted the physical therapist, as well as the rest of the world to know that we were much more than our clothes, and we were much more than just our puny bodies. We were capable of helping Mom overcome this tragedy; we were capable of helping Dad physically heal.

The physical therapist saw nothing but small identical twins and Mom's anxious face. She continued the instructions. "For now, just practice along the balcony or a kitchen counter. You may want to start with two people for safety and to help build Allen's confidence."

A woman with hair colored like frosted flakes strolled in and parked herself next to Mom. Her nametag suggested that she was an occupational therapist, whatever that was; I had no idea. "Hello there, I'm Margaret. I'm going to review a few daily living skills with you."

Mom pondered for two seconds before nodding nervously. "Okay."

I could see that she was overwhelmed and nervous, and I didn't blame her. Who wouldn't be? Each therapist added duties on top of responsibilities, making Mom's once happy life, burdened with care.

"You're going to be watching him do most of the work because, as with all therapy, you are working to get him as independent as possible. Are you currently working out of the home?"

"No, I'm a full time mother. I do have a job on the weekends as the organist for our church. Allen was the choir director."

Margaret scribbled fast notes in a file, and then asked, "Are you going to be working full-time in the nearby future?"

"I can't. I've got four children at home, and now with Allen like this, I won't be able to."

"Okay, so there aren't really any demanding time constraints. Good," she said gently, "because dressing will take some time. I'm going to start with instructing you on the proper technique to get his shirt on. What you'll want to do is remind him that his affected arm goes in first, then he pulls his top up over his head, and slips in the working arm. When taking off the top, it's the opposite routine. But remember... he does everything himself." She turned toward Dad after he had inadvertently bumped into the cabinet on the way to the hospital bed. "Did you hear that, Allen? You can do it. Don't make your wife do all the work." She faced Mom one last time. "Now, I'll go over the proper way of giving him showers with you later, Joy. It might seem a little overwhelming at the moment. As for the other self-care activities, such as brushing his teeth, shaving, and combing his hair, basically, you just need to set up the items he uses and he can do the rest himself. Just remember, when he's at the bathroom counter

47

doing his ADL's (Activities of Daily Living), it would be best if he was standing with his wheelchair behind him—brakes on! Wouldn't want him to slip back and break a hip, now would we? When do you want to go over the feeding regimen?"

"I don't know."

"Okay, we can go over that later, but for now, just to get you set for home, get him some thick-handled utensils, and I've got a rubber mat to place under his plate so it doesn't slip and slide all over the place. It's going to take some time to help him drink from a cup, since that one hand trembles." Margaret stood and smoothed out the wrinkles in her long flowered skirt. "Before I leave, let me give you this." She handed Mom a strange looking cup with a u-shaped form cut out from its rim. "This is called a 'nosy cup.' The cutout will enable him to tilt the cup farther back without hitting his nose against the rim. Drinking from this will keep him from having to tilt his head back, which might cause him to choke."

Mom set the cup down, not really wanting to look at it. The bright color and thick plastic looked as if it was made for a toddler, not for a man of fifty-three.

The sixth or seventh staff member—by now I had lost count, knocked before entering the room. "Hello there, I'm Della, the speech therapist." She shook Mom's hand as if she was the president of some important company and sat down. Her navy blue pantsuit adorned with gold buttons reminded me of an outfit Mom wore to church. "Since Margaret has already given you the cup, let me just warn you not to give him thin liquids yet. Everything needs to be thickened up."

"I know that I cough a lot," Dad contributed, "because I have a hard time separating air and liquid in my mouth."

"Joy, give him thick liquids, like milkshakes," the speech therapist said.

Behind her back, Dad smiled like a Cheshire cat at the idea.

Della sat straight against her chair with both feet flat on the floor; there was no ease in her position. She turned her back to Dad as she talked with Mom. This woman with the blue suit made a good impression and Mom took her comments very seriously. "I've been working with Allen for sometime now," Della said, "and I've noted that he demonstrates significant cognitive problems, and obviously has confused speech. Let's see… what did I write in my notes?" She studied her notebook. "His orientation can go from good to very poor, and he has a limited ability to process what he hears… he has a reduced attention span, short-term memory loss… at the moment he doesn't respond appropriately to social situations, apparently due to his poor insight into his problems. The goal is to introduce a memory log so his confusion is reduced…"

A nurse's aide brought Dad a tray for lunch, set him up for it, fixed his hand around the fork and laughed at what Della had just said. "In other words, Mrs. Vance, get him a journal." Then the aide left the room.

Dad had trouble holding the fork. His arm shook, causing the prongs to stab his cheeks and chin until he eventually found his mouth. Jeanette and I looked at each other. We could hardly bear to watch him struggle. Jeanette took the fork from him, loaded it up with food, and then deposited it into his mouth. When she got tired, I finished the task.

Finally, a social worker trekked in with more paperwork for Mom to sign. "It'll be tough, Joy. You've got more than you can handle, what with four children and all." She caressed Jeanette and my hair. "Your girls are beautiful. Where did you find these two?"

"We adopted them from Korea." Mom expounded on our humble beginnings to the curious listener and toyed with our hair. "Our girls were found on a street corner in a cardboard box. Unlike the boys, we were able to choose these two." She looked at us and smiled.

Our adoption was a fact of life, but still, I felt different, separate, and distant from who she was. Even though Mom gave the message of "want," to anyone who asked, I felt like a burden. I didn't understand why I didn't *feel* wanted. *What's going on inside? What's wrong with me? I shouldn't feel this way. Are these feelings from Satan?*

The social worker gave Mom a hug before going over the paperwork. "Why do bad things happen to good people? Boy, I wish I had the answer."

Prior to leaving the hospital Mom told us to go stand next to Dad so she could snap a picture for the album. We turned on big, bright, artificial smiles causing Dad to grin again. His grin was different—crooked, but I could see his essence. To me, his spirit was flawless.

Chapter 7

Sister Act

From Jeanette's diary:
1984
 I feel sorry for Mom since Dad's hang gliding accident. I hope: 1) She gets a job; 2) She wins a million dollars (I pray every day); 3) Dad will be healed when I'm sixteen. I know for a fact that Mom likes David the best.

Dad was released to go home, one bitter day in January, three months after the injury. At home, tortured by self-piteous thoughts of what could have been, Mom was afflicted with migraine headaches that even aspirin couldn't ease. As she tried to recuperate on the fawn couch with the fleur-de-lis appliqué, someone interrupted her thoughts by knocking at the front door. The large intimidating fence Dad had built around the house years earlier kept the neighbors and solicitors away when our family was proud and capable; now it prevented anyone from helping. But it didn't restrain one curious couple from at least attempting to see how we were doing.

"Who could that possibly be?" Mom wondered aloud, surprised by the disturbance. She squinted through the glass door. Once she realized it was a church couple, she pressed her lips together, gave a painful grin, and opened the door, embarrassed by the scattered packages stacked about, between the counters, and on the floors. She had every intention of getting the mess cleared and put away, but now with so many responsibilities, it was going to have to be put on hold. Jeanette and I wished the clutter behind her would magically disappear so we could invite the couple in and honestly tell them how we were doing, but that would only cause trouble and hurt Mom's ego. Instead, Jeanette and I hid from behind the stuffed boxes off the

51

living room and watched. We were brought up with the belief that as children, we didn't have a right to be seen or heard. Mom's life was considered none of our business.

The couple smiled as Mom opened the door. "Hello Joy. How are you holding up?" It was Mr. and Mrs. Rogers from church. Mrs. Rogers, plump and brunette always wore corsages and fancy hats to church and Mr. Rogers wore thick polyester suits from the seventies and a hearing aid that he continuously fiddled with.

"Oh, fine thank you," Mom lied with a forced smile still on her face.

Could they see the boxes overflowing in the background—evidence of Mom's inability to throw anything away? Probably not, she always kept the kitchen cleared out and halfway decent-looking for the few who ignored the intercom system and passed the front gate. Beyond the kitchen though, the accumulation was impossible to conceal.

"We brought you a hot dinner and some of the get-well cards from the families at church."

Mom's demeanor went from mourning to upbeat within seconds, although she couldn't hide her swollen complexion. "Well, that's sweet! Thank you for doing this. I'm so glad we've got the Lord on our side."

"Is there anything we can do for you, dear?" Mrs. Rogers gently handed Mom a white ceramic casserole dish and a collection of cards.

Mom cradled the dinner close against her waist. "Thank you, but the biggest help would be if you could just comfort me on Sundays."

"Are you sure?" Mr. Rogers asked. "Where is Allen? Can I see how the ol' choir director is doing?"

"Oh well, he's resting now," Mom fibbed. How would she admit to the couple that the former choir director and Boeing Engineer was no longer capable? The truth was too painful for any of us to comprehend.

"We should have called first; we're sorry," Mrs. Rogers said.

Hospital visits were common, but how was Mom going to keep the visitors from coming to the house? The compassionate faces of the polite couple told me they expected to see Dad's speedy recovery for themselves. Instead, they left disappointed but spread the word in the close-knit church that Mom was doing fine and that there really was no need for visitors. They were the first and last to come to the house and we were left to handle Dad, and care for Mom on our own.

After the couple left, Jeanette gently rubbed Mom's feet and I did my best to massage the pain away from her forehead while she recovered on the couch. Mom interrupted the silence by letting us know that our hands were strong. Startled, we looked at our hands, then smiled inside. The comment made me feel like I was worth something, as if my size didn't matter. Perhaps there was hope for me after all. These moments of appreciation and connection caused me to want to give her everything I had. Afraid to stop the momentum, we carefully switched places and continued the task.

I fantasized about making enough money one day to send Mom on a Hawaiian vacation. Hawaii was a place she dreamed of and talked about often. Now it seemed she would never be able to see the place except through photos from her friends' vacations and on television shows. Maybe I should write to Sally Jesse Raphael or Donahue about her plight. I rehearsed what I would tell them in my mind, over and over again. I prayed for an answer that might miraculously turn Mom's pain into peace of mind. These prayers grew more fervent after I overheard her confide in David that it was too hard to even look at Dad. His presence reminded her of what could have been. There was no future for them as a couple, and that there would never be an equal partnership anymore. I wished she had the confidence to open her heart to me, even though I was still only twelve.

By the late afternoon, Mom was up, tired and confused over God's decision to rip a healthy father from his children, a traditional husband from his wife, a top rated-engineer from Boeing and a good Christian man from the church. *What is God's purpose in all of this?* She scattered the get-well cards on the table and then marveled at each one. They comforted her for a minute; however, after that short minute she was back to being depressed. The cards did the same for Jeanette and me, and they also made us proud that we had so many friends who were on God's side.

"Be careful," Mom said, as she arranged the cards for the album. "They're in a particular order. Don't wrinkle them!"

As if the cards were laden with gold with a hidden treasure inside, we opened each one carefully and gently:

Allen,
*   ...You are greatly missed at church—surely hope you are feeling better each day. You have the "Great Physician" healing and caring for you. Your Joy is such an inspiration to us. Her faithfulness is a true witness to your faith that your family always expresses—you can be sure of our prayers...*

Allen,
*   ...Had it not been the Lord who was on our side, then raging waters would have swept over our soul. Thanks be to God, He is on our side! I want to somehow communicate that I am deeply committed to you. I do pray for you, I support you, I love you. In you, I have seen Jesus...*

Mr. and Mrs. Vance,
*   Your lives have been an encouragement and challenge to me. You have steadfastly, day by day pursued to serve our Lord faithfully. Thank you for showing me Jesus. I look forward to seeing you up and about soon...*

Mr. Vance
*   ...May God, who watches over us and hears our every prayer bring to you the many special blessings that only faith in Him can bring... We miss you!*

Big Al,
*   Get back soon, we all miss you. Good choir directors are hard to find!*

Mom tried to clear the hall as much as possible, but like a weeping willow, she did not get much accomplished. The wheelchair still brushed up and against her stuffed closets and scattered bookshelves. After taking a deep and drained breath, she instructed Jeanette and me. "Girls, could you get your Father dressed? I'm just too exhausted and I need for you to help him with his exercises. I'm just not up to doing this any longer. I'm not sure how long I'm going to last."

We didn't mind. Our moral duty as daughters was to help Mom and Dad. We didn't need to think about what would be involved either. We just took action, knowing that we were helping Mom, easing her feelings of burden, and giving Dad his own deserved support system. There was no way we could complain or shirk our chores for it was our responsibility to contribute to the success of the family. We were there for a reason. Helping gave us purpose and a reason for Mom to love and accept us.

From that day forward, we pushed Dad in his wheelchair from the kitchen and living end of the house, to the other end where he slept alone, willing to help both of them by not spilling Mom's secret. She was just too emotionally miserable to spend moments of time with him and we didn't blame her. Anyone who had to deal with what Mom was dealing with would be depressed and emotionally unstable. Her reaction to his injury was totally normal. I wished it didn't have to be this way, but I couldn't change the past. I could only work toward establishing a better future for all of us.

We were a therapist's nightmare as we dressed Dad each morning with amazing speed. The routine went so much faster if we threw the clothes on him, instead of waiting and watching for him to fight with them alone. I pulled his pajama top off—the working arm out first, then the weak one, finally up over his head. Jeanette waited for me to finish and then she was ready with the clean undershirt, slipping it on using the opposite routine: his weak arm through the sleeve, and then pulled the shirt onto his capable arm, over his head and down onto his chest. We pulled off his tired pajama pants and then waited in the hall, still congested with boxes, for him to fiddle with his underwear in private. When he said "Okay" in a new, unrecognizable, higher-pitched voice, we raced into our parents' room to zip, button, and slip the belt into his pant loops.

Dad lowered his head and rubbed his good hand through sparse hair, unable to hide the agony trapped in his soul. "Why is God putting me through this? I'm no good anymore—" Frustrated, he attempted to take off his thick heavy glasses but only managed to get his hand tangled in the retaining strings.

"Maybe God is testing you," Jeanette searched for more, but the right words were difficult and few. "He knows you're strong and capable at handling hardship. After all, the Bible gives us all sorts of verses about overcoming adversity. Suffering is a natural part of being a Christian—"

His face contorted, fresh lines of age appeared, and then after a moment of silence he let out a painful howl, "Aaagh! I'm no good! I'm useless!"

"God doesn't give you more than you can take," I said, as strong as possible, repeating his old Sunday school teachings.

"I can't take any more, I want my old life back!"

He was right, and we wanted the old life back too. "Why me?" Dad asked again.

Jeanette and I didn't have the answers. We changed the subject by switching the wing-tip shoes he wore to Boeing around, and announced, "Hey look Dad, your feet are on backwards!"

He glanced down, then produced a wide-eyed and open mouthed laugh. We felt good and decided to switch his shoes around from that day forward. If humor could bring laughter to the moment, it could save any situation. Now we just needed to find a way to get Mom to smile. If only she'd let us into her heart.

We wheeled Dad to the bathroom and settled him down on the toilet, trying all the while to think up funny little comments to get him to laugh, yet humorous remarks were hard to come by as we worked with him to complete daily living skills. We were lazy at times. Occasionally, we would only hand him the urinal, and wait for him to finish answering the call of nature as he sat in his wheelchair, instead of transferring him from the wheelchair to standing position, like the therapists instructed. Then, after he announced he was done, we'd run back in, pull him up, rinse out the urinal, and lead him to the sink instead of patiently waiting for him to complete the task.

With every look in the mirror, he would wonder aloud why God was punishing him. Why was God not listening to his pleadings and prayers? The mirror became his new enemy. He couldn't look into his own eyes anymore, and the sight of his new body, his new form, his new incapacitated body hurt his self-worth. The reflection was not who he was. He was so much more, and he knew it, but the reflection gave a depressing message. We called the mirror a region of horror, where we became aware of a miserable future. *Why is God doing this to us?* The question stuck in all of our minds like clogging hope.

"Dad, you look fine! Really you do," I said, after noticing he had caught a glimpse of his off-centered reflection in the mirror.

"Yeah Dad, just relax your left shoulder, bring it down a little—you're too tense," Jeanette said.

"Try to look straight ahead. You look better that way."

"I should have died out there on Dog Mountain."

We let his statement fade into the bathroom walls.

"Now, uncurl your fist, you look like you're about ready to punch someone," Jeanette joked.

"Yeah Dad, turn your frown upside down."

A cheerless smile appeared. After eyeing his odd reflection in the mirror again, he turned away and the smile vanished as if it was only a dream.

"You just gotta be positive," Jeanette said.

"You gotta think about the blessing in all of this." I added. "Can you think of a blessing?"

Jeanette combed his salt and pepper hair back and then tried different styles. She parted it on its unnatural left side, then stood back and stared as if she was a professional barber. After we conferred about the way he looked, she combed his hair forward. He gave an exaggerated grin, causing us to smirk. He appeared older and his wrinkles seemed more prominent. It was an obvious no-no. Finally, Jeanette combed his hair back and away from his face. We agreed he looked the best that way and left it.

I polished his eyeglasses with a small amount of store brand glass cleaner and my cotton T-shirt. Jeanette shaved his chin with his ebony electric razor, and after she was done, I trimmed his sideburns. Almost finished with the bathroom tasks, we held his waist and directed him to the sink. Then Jeanette grabbed his toothbrush, slapped some toothpaste on its flattened bristles and watched him as he tried to find his mouth with the brush, using crazy spastic motions. Behind his back, we snickered when his arm flew out of control, causing toothpaste to splatter over his face and shirt. Pretending not to notice, I situated the toiletries on the counter and Jeanette wiped up goo from off the sink, counter and his top, discovering at the same time that toothpaste smudges always leaves a stain on clothes. He brushed his teeth insanely slow once the toothbrush found the way into his mouth. At last, we were done with the bathroom tasks.

To get to the kitchen for breakfast, I pushed obstacles back against the wall to make room for Jeanette and Dad and the wheelchair. At the table, we took turns transferring him to the seat, like the therapist instructed. Then one of us would move the empty wheelchair out of the way—usually next to the formal dining room with its own piles of boxes still spilling out. Mom set bowls of Rice Corn Chex on the table, then retreated to her couch in the living room, too overcome with depression to look at his new lame body and us. This became a family ritual that would last until we moved out.

"Dad, you need to do your therapy today. We haven't timed your endurance since last week. It's time to do that again. You've got to work on dropping that left shoulder and relaxing your arm. You'll be able to stand a lot longer that way," Jeanette said while we took turns stuffing bites of the cereal first into his mouth and then our own.

He sighed, then tortured us with "I should have" over and over again. "I should have checked those wing bolts. I'm so stupid! Why didn't I check them? I should have listened to your mother and never gone hang gliding. I should have worked overtime that weekend."

I pretended not to hear him. "Remind me to put that tennis ball into your hand after we're done with your exercises so your fingernails don't dig into your hand. Last time, you had deep impressions in your hands from your long nails. It looks painful!" I unfolded his palm and noticed hot gray fuzz embedded in the sweaty creases.

After breakfast Jeanette and I coerced him to sing, "Doe Ray Me Fa So La Ti Doe" from the *Sound of Music*, in our own made-up, speech therapy session. We cracked up when he tried to reach the low notes and then the high ones. When nervous or excited, his voice turned as loud and shrill as an ambulance horn, causing us to wince at the jarring sound. Dad grinned after hearing himself. In public, the noise he made was embarrassing and we gave him a hush-hush "lower your voice" motion, taught to us by his speech therapist, especially while he became so excited and loud that heads turned.

Shortly after our private speech session, we became serious again and started in on physical therapy. First, we instructed him to rotate his shoulders, round and round, forward then backward, and then told him to "shake them off" even though we had no idea how this helped. Following the directions of whatever the therapists said, we reminded him to raise his arms high to the sky, stretch his muscles by turning to the side and to the front. Finally, we let him loose by placing the tennis ball in his palm to keep his hand from tightening up.

Every task took painfully longer than usual. Jeanette and I daydreamed about a better future while we walked beside Dad to the bathroom and then the kitchen. Out of fear that he might stumble while concentrating intensely on each step, we hooked our arms around his as he shuffled, each step exposing childlike doubt. "Just put one foot in front of the other," went an old Christmas tune—easier said than done after a head injury! If he fell, he could break a hip or an arm winding up wheelchair bound and incapable forever. To make the situation worse, his left arm curled tightly into his belly like the letter *C* causing his balance to be unsteady. Uneasy, all three of us were ready at any given moment to grab onto the railing.

"It's okay," Jeanette encouraged, holding onto his waist and standing behind him. "At least you get to be home now and we like that."

Dad wobbled to a stop. "Why did I live? I should have died out there on Dog Mountain!"

"There's a reason why you lived, Dad," I tried to assure him again. But I had no idea what the reason was; it just seemed like the right thing to say, and we really didn't mind his new presence. Jeanette and I thought we did well at accepting the situation right away. "What ifs" bothered us—thinking about what had happened to our near perfect family bothered us, but we dwelled on this less obsessively than our parents.

During moments of depression, we knew we were twins for a reason and the thought would raise our spirits. In secret, we gave each other compliments about what a good team we made at making Dad feel better and getting the chores done. We also remembered to deepen our faith in Jesus with every hardship we endured. Bible lessons implied that goodness comes from working hard, holding the fruits of the spirit in our hearts, and believing that Jesus is the Son of God. Dad had not only believed all of this, he had taught it at one time. Now his job was to work hard to recover. One day he would be back to his old self.

Deep within me, thoughts that at least we had our faith in Jesus Christ comforted me. During restless nights, I repeated 1 Corinthians, 2:9 for solace, "However, it is written: No eye has seen, no ear has heard, no mind has conceived what God has prepared for those who love him." During the days I tried to keep the tears from running down my cheeks by not thinking about our lives, but in bed I found it increasingly hard not to mull over and analyze our new lives. *What would life be like if we weren't on God's side? Horrible! "Thank you God,"* I prayed. *"For bringing us into a Christian family! Jesus will one day heal Dad. Thank you God for giving me Christian parents, so that I know the way to eternal life. Jesus won't let Dad be disabled forever! Jesus will give us miraculous healing, and I will pray every night until it happens."* The more I prayed, I assumed, the sooner Dad's healing would happen.

Late into the night, I would imagine Dad walking down the hall. His footsteps were cool and confident, sure and stable, just like they used to be. Then I would realize that it was only David or a wild wish from my imagination.

In the mornings Dad would complain about his ailments. "Three of my fingers are numb. I always feel cold now. Would you give me another blanket? I lost all the peripheral vision to my right, but at least it's better than seeing double."

I prayed to God to fix his problems.

Dad whined, "I do not have the stamina that I used to have. I used to fix the cars, but I cannot any more."

My prayers increased. I wanted our lives to be back to normal.

"I can only smell strong scents," Dad admitted.

"It probably works to your advantage," Jeanette said, causing him to laugh.

"I've lost my voice quality. I can only talk slowly. I tried to speed it up by reading one page of the Bible out loud each day, but it doesn't seem to help. I am going to try it again. I think it'll work now," Dad grumbled. "My reflexes are much slower than they were and I find that I do not have good control of my fingers. When I use the computer, I hit the wrong key."

I prayed some more. I would do anything to receive God's grace. I would sacrifice whatever was necessary to get Dad healed so everyone could be happy again, and then I would yearn, like a folded flower waiting for the morning sun to rise, for the miracle to happen.

Dad worked for many months to calm his voice during speech therapy; he attempted to complete daily living skills independently in occupational therapy; and he practiced walking and maintaining balance in physical therapy. The many months of working to improve his body yielded small successes. Dad would get depressed if he hadn't noticed a change in his body or if he couldn't pick up a pencil with ease. He compared his progress constantly with his former capabilities and then he would get upset when his body continuously told him he might never be like he used to be.

"When am I going to be healed?" Dad wondered again and again.

"Jesus will heal you soon," we promised. Our faith in God increased ten-fold. Our silent prayers were said each morning, throughout the day and after bedtime when the moon came out.

Whenever Mom was too tired, David drove Dad, Jeanette and me to the facility for his therapy. While Dad was at his sessions, the three of us skipped around the hospital, shook the food machines for some loose change or a hanging piece of candy, and peeked into each antiseptic room, forgetting for a moment what life had thrown at us. The trip was exciting and the time went fast.

At home, when we finished helping Dad take his walk around the neighborhood, he usually scanned the yard and wondered where all his "toys" had gone. Mom was in the process of slowly selling his junkyard vehicles: the GMC Motorhome to start off with, followed by old Cadillacs, Limousines, and one of his favorites, the '65 Mustang. As carefully as possible, Jeanette and I would stammer that she was selling them to pay for the hospital bills, even though she had always made it clear to us that the finances were none of our business. As each vehicle disappeared, a part of Dad's soul died. He was a geek at heart and geeks like their "toys"—things that they can tinker with.

Dad was never social, but a social life wasn't needed when he had engines to fix. He found refuge in engines he could take out, build and rebuild. Mike and David watched, learned and followed his odd behavior. Without his cars, Dad's advanced mind was a jinx, not an advantage and now he had all the time in the world to think up the perfect engine. Before his injury, he had never built a super engine that could outdo all others, but whatever he fiddled with was all his. Now his cars—his babies, were gone, like missing children, and all Jeanette and I could do was to pat his shoulder and wish that we could make things better.

After our walk and our consoling talks, we settled him down into the recliner—his new best friend—located in the master bedroom.

"Do you want to watch TV, Dad?" Jeanette asked, attempting to produce a picture by positioning the rabbit ears.

We could see from his worn body that he would rather just lie in bed and die, but he obediently replied, "Whatever you want."

I sat crisscross next to his feet. Jeanette leaned her skinny body against the wooden armrest of the decrepit green chair. "Hey, look Dad, *Cheers* your favorite show is on," she announced brightly and turned up the volume.

The lines of communication between Mom and Dad were nonexistent. They didn't even watch the same television shows. No more confidentialities. No more discussions about what they could do better to keep us under control, no more messages of love for each other, and no more praying aloud while in public restaurants.

When we heard the faint sound of Mom's footsteps scurrying along the unfinished hall, we'd stand up, feeling sudden eruptions of guilt in our stomachs. Unless we were doing our chores, we weren't allowed in any part of the house other than our room. Our hearts would pound while we looked around and wondered what we should say we were doing. Before we could think up an excuse, Mom would enter the bedroom.

"What are you doing down here? I didn't give you girls permission to be down here."

"Nothing." But our eyes told a different story. *When is she ever going to trust us?*

She glanced into the tattered boxes and bags around her and inside the bulging closets as if we were keeping secrets in them, but she was the one who had secrets to hide. "Go to your rooms. You don't need to be down here. You girls drive me crazy."

The muscles around our faces tightened with resentment and our hearts stung at her mistrust, but we obeyed and quickly left the room.

Soon David departed for college, leaving Mom even more bereft, with only Jeanette and me for support. Mike had already moved out and was living with our aunt and uncle, down in Portland, Oregon. In a phone call, he told me that Aunt Patti was really nice and Uncle Bob was "cool." At their house, taking food from the kitchen was not considered stealing—in fact, Aunt Patti *helped* him make a peanut butter sandwich and Uncle Bob liked to build things with his hands. Mike felt accepted and part of a family for the first time in his life. He said, "Now I know whom I take after in this family, I'm just like Uncle Bob!"

We longed to feel accepted, to feel we belonged. We took on more and more of our mother's responsibilities, hoping we could earn her love.

Chapter 8

School Daze

A year later, Mom still treated us with suspicion. We were thirteen and in the eighth grade. Our parents still thought we had a long way to go before we were properly trained children. Dad believed that children should be raised like dogs. Just tell them once and make them obey, and if you have to spank them, then do it. If the child does not go by the rules by the age of twelve then it's too late. A parent can't do anything except show disapproval.

Mom's crossed arms and built in frown told us that we cared too much about our appearance. Why did her daughters spend so much time in front of the mirror? We were too young to worry about such frivolous things and we were too immature to fix unwanted features on our faces with make-up. What was going on with her daughters? I didn't tell her that I was actually spending hours examining every *ugly* quality about my face in the mirror: my Asian eyes, my high cheekbones, my thick eye brows, my crooked teeth, my olive skin, my pugged nose. I wasn't loving myself, that was for sure! I was actually killing my spirit with my miserable thoughts. Even though Dad, our chores, and homework were Jeanette's and my top priorities, Mom assumed our thoughts were consumed by our appearance. We were such a disappointment. Her only solace was to think about David, but he was off in college. Mom had been adamant. She refused to let Dad's injury hinder him from getting a solid education by enrolling in a prestigious University. After a year of unanswered prayers and numerous trips to the hospital for Dad's physical, speech and occupational therapy, David left for the East Coast to attend a polytechnic institute, causing Mom to mourn over his departure as if it were a death sentence. His room remained untouched, except for the occasional dusting here and there. I wondered why it was no big deal when Mike left. Mom did like David the best!

"I wish David hadn't left," Jeanette worried. "Now Mom's mad all the time."

"How are we going to make it through five more years without him?" I asked. Mom eavesdropped on our trouble-making conversations while we tried to read her mood. *Is she mad today? Is it safe to approach her with a question? Can we ask for a sandwich? No, it's never okay to ask for food! Asking for food is completely disrespectful.* We spied on her while she rested hopelessly on the couch in the dark confines of the living room. *When will she ever be happy?*

With David gone, our lives spiraled out of control. *Who will make Mom happy now? When is the miracle—the miracle we are promised by the church, going to happen? Aren't we worthy? Do we not pray enough? What does God find wrong with us?* Both Jeanette and I knew that we weren't capable of turning Mom's pain into pleasure with only our presence, like David could, so we prayed for her, we prayed for Dad and we prayed for ourselves.

Mom changed her mind about giving David's old room to one of us. We weren't surprised when she stuffed Jeanette and me and our things into Mike's old room. "David will be coming home from vacation every once in a while and he'll need his space," she justified. I shrugged at her decision. On the surface, we really didn't care if she kept her promises. Since the room was our birthday present, I appreciated her efforts in turning over Mike's room to us. Even if it was the same crusty rug and orange walls, faded with age, Mike's old room accommodated us fine. At least we had privacy.

After that, she rearranged our old room off of the living room, which was intended to be used as a music room, into her own separate quarters. She bought a brand new canopy bed, plush rug and window treatment decorated with lavender lilacs trimmed in lace. She set up an arrangement of dolls, ornaments, and treasures on a small nightstand. The space looked like a giant doily from a J C Penny's catalog by the time she had finished. I caught her on several mornings sitting on the edge of the bed and gazing at the things around her somewhat satisfied with her creativity, but still unhappy.

Some months later, she finally reshuffled the cramped master bedroom. Warped boxes full of clothes and possessions were moved into a corner so a new recliner would fit in front of the small television set. Every morning and afternoon, she would set the channel, adjust the rabbit ears, and then leave the room for her side of the house.

Jeanette and I kept Dad company as much as we could.

"I have always liked stuffed animals," he confided. "And now I have my bear since Joy has decided to sleep in the music room I will sleep with the bear every night. I guess she has trouble getting any rest if she tries to sleep with me. As a child, I always liked stuffed animals and had several that I took to bed with me. Now I have the one bear that you gave me and he keeps me company most of the time. The bear provides personal companionship at night."

"That's nice," Jeanette said.

"My Auntie Lee and Auntie Dorothy used to make stuffed animals for me and give them to me for my birthday and on Christmas. They used to stuff them with foam rubber and they were very nice. They made me Mickey and Minnie Mouse, Pluto, and Clare Bell the cow. I used to put them in a circle like a nest when I would go to bed. Now I sleep with my bear, Pugsly, every night."

"That's nice," I said.

Dad had become almost childlike since his injury. "I tried various things to keep alert today. I still have trouble throwing Pugsly where I want him and I tried to practice that some. I also practiced standing on one foot. I stood behind the chair and tried one leg for a while. That is part of the fine motor control. I still do not release the bear at the correct time so it does not go where I want him to go."

When Dad wasn't trying to improve his motor control skills, he watched the television programs until Jeanette and I arrived home from school to take him on his daily walk and exercises. The walks were quiet. He was too short of breath to spit out words. Each step required concentration. After the walks, he'd complain about the secular ways of the world. Jeanette and I nodded in agreement.

*   *   *

During the first semester in eighth grade, I was able to make a friend. A new girl in school named Shanie. She wasn't a Christian, but by this time I was learning to accept non-Christians, even if they weren't God's chosen. I still had questions about them though. I wondered why her parents' chose not to teach her Christian beliefs. How could they not teach Shanie that Jesus died on the cross for our sins? Christianity gave my family hope while we faced our challenges. Fritz Ridenour, author of *How to be a Christian in an UnChristian World* told us there are only two types of men "One man holds the Naturalist point of view. For him, the universe consists of nothing but mass, energy and motion. The other man is a Supernaturalist. He is a Christian, who believes in the Bible as the revelation of God" There are no in-betweens. Dad agreed, "You're either *for* God, or *not* for God." There is nothing in the middle; there is no middle road. You are either a Christian, Supernaturalist and God's chosen or you're a non-Christian, naturalist, and a refuser of Truth. There is no middle ground according to Christian authors like Fritz Ridenour, David Wilkerson and James Jauncey. Their books and many more filled Mom and Dad's collection.

Shanie was "not for God". She was a free spirit who ignored my nerd-like reputation. She was nature's child and her mother's name was Sunshine. I felt sorry for her, not because she chose to hang around me, but because she wasn't a Christian. Instead, Shanie wrote me notes in class spilling all sorts of exciting gossip, calling me her "little sis." She described tales about boyfriends who lived in Seattle, wild parties she attended and exciting shopping escapades at the Zebra Club, the *only* place worth shopping because of the latest trends. Even if some of her stories were tall, unChristian like, and a little exaggerated, I didn't care. For the moment, I even ignored what I was being taught from the Bible. I enjoyed school with Shanie around. Too bad she was going to the fiery furnace for all eternity after living such a fun and exciting life and admiring the way of the pagans. My mind got so confused about the world. So many kids were going to hell. I imagined all of them being swallowed up by God's damnation.

Even though Shanie treated me with respect and called me her li'l sis, she too, would swim in the lake of fire. It didn't matter that she helped a Christian in need. It didn't matter that she pushed me around from class to class while I sat, like a dork, in Dad's big metal wheelchair after I had sprained my ankle in gym class. Mom didn't see the point in wasting money on crutches when we already owned a perfectly good wheelchair at home. Because of my faith, I reasoned that I could overcome adversity. At the same time I thought it was strange how Christians must live in hell in order to get to Heaven. Non-Christians, on the other hand, lived in a "worldly" heaven, and then ended up going to hell—unless, of course, they invited Jesus into their hearts and asked for forgiveness after experiencing pleasure or right before they died.

I finally got my big break in eighth grade. Literally. The students clad in matching red PE outfits sat in rows on the bleachers for our individual volleyball test. Each student took a turn in front of the entire class, either fighting against or taking total control of the volleyball. In my case, I fought against it. During the test, Mr. Thompson tossed the ball to one of us, then we were supposed to take control of it, by bumping, setting, spiking, passing and serving it over the net and back to him. *Take control of the ball? How are we supposed to do that?* I had never controlled anything in my life—let alone, a volleyball! Man, I hated the thought. I hated anything that had to do with physical strength, balance and coordination. When I worried about throwing the basketball into the hoop, hitting the softball with the bat, or kicking the soccer ball, classmates told me that at least I was probably good in gymnastics. Well, I wasn't good at gymnastics either, I could barely touch my toes and I would trip before I even found the balance beam. However, I could run and I ran fast. Attempting, maybe, to run from problems, or toward a great future.

Amy, up first, graced the gym floor with her elevated, already developed presence. She flowed with the ball as it came flying toward her. She bumped. The ball flew over the net and back to Mr. Thompson.

"Great job!" He praised. Then he went into a spiel about how he hoped we were watching Amy. "Notice her body position. Her trunk leans forward and her back is straight with about a 90 degree angle

68

between the thigh and the body. Her legs are bent and her body is in a partially crouched position, with the feet shoulder-width apart."

Yes, the boys were watching all right, but not because she was the poster child for hitting the ball correctly. The boys drooled and whimpered, jabbed each other and grinned at the sight of her.

Mr. Thompson tossed her the ball again. She followed it with blue eyes, then raced after it with the grace of a dove. She set—soft and easy.

Jeremy, one of the popular students assigned to spike, stood tall, proud, and of course, with shoulders back. He paced back and forth like a lazy but cool lion on the prowl. When the ball flew over the net, he slammed it down the other side. He nodded at Mr. Thompson, and then bowed to Amy and the class. Damn, he was good. I hated him.

Mr. Thompson clapped. "Wonderful! Spiking is the most effective play in volleyball, and when done properly, is extremely difficult to return. It depends a great deal upon the ability of a teammate to set it up properly. Amy did just that. That's an A in my book."

Both Amy and Jeremy sat next to me; Amy giggled; Jeremy flirtatiously messed up her hair.

"Jeanie, you're up," Mr. Thompson announced. "I would like to see you do a basic bump."

My heart raced and my body trembled and I was too timid to tell him that he had pronounced my name wrong. I quickly realized that I hated being in the spotlight. I hated everyone's eyes on me. My hair was still straight and stringy, when all the other girls wore curls and sky-high bangs. My shorts hung low around my waist, exposing scrawny, scratched up and hairy legs.

I struggled with the proper body position: I stood straight but felt awkward; next I squatted like a crouching tiger; finally I clasped my hands, and was ready to hit something... hopefully the ball. Mr. Thompson must have thought I was doing a weird foxtrot because he asked if I was done dancing yet. The kids on the bleachers snickered at his comment. When I nodded my head, he tossed me the ball. My eyes followed it; my mind tried to remember what Amy had done. I struggled to race after but hit empty air instead and managed to trip over my foot on my first step to the side. Before I knew what had happened, I was on the ground with a shooting pain in my right ankle.

The students sat, chatting and tweeting amongst themselves, apparently unaware of my injury. I wanted to rise to the surface and spit fire like a hidden dragon; instead I fell to the glossy gym floor again like a puppet tied to strings. When I tried to stand again another sting detonated inside my ankle. *I'm a total idiot. I'm being crucified like the prophets in the Bible.*

"Jeanie, go ahead and go to the nurse, if you feel the need," Mr. Thompson said nonchalantly.

I limped to the nurses' station, embarrassed that the entire class had seen me incapable. At least I was humble and Christ-like. Again, I questioned the world I lived in, but at the same time I wanted to be an important part of it. Why didn't schools teach some good old-fashioned Christian morals? Empathy and compassion. My friend, Shanie, admitted that she didn't mind pushing me around the halls; at least she had an excuse to get out of class a few minutes before the bell rang. Eventually she moved before I could convert her to Christianity and share the "Good News".

Eighth grade ended with a few popular girls refusing to sign my yearbook and the word FAG written across my yearbook pages helped to complete ninth grade. I wouldn't admit this to anyone, but yes, after a couple years of being seen as strange, I was guilty of hating some of the kids at school. I wouldn't mind seeing some of them suffer. What if my life had started in 1982 instead of 1972? What if I didn't have a twin to confide in? What if I didn't give a damn? What if I lived in middle America? What if I was a white boy who had access to a gun? "What ifs" could be dangerous!

"What ifs" could also get people thinking. What if the students were taught the consequences of bullying as it affects the community as a whole? I'm not saying I was bullied, but I was disregarded by the "cool" group, and I *had* seen some incidences that warranted a teacher's reprimand. I had seen contempt for diversity and pride at its worst. What if students were taught the rewards of respecting each other and the benefits of working together instead of constantly competing?

Except for a few accepting friends, I found nothing meaningful in Junior High. There was nothing to look forward to at school. I was an outcast. I didn't belong. I spent lunch-time in the library pretending to read and watching the clock closely for the time to disappear. I didn't belong with the "cool" group or to society as a whole and I didn't feel a sense of belonging with my own mother. No one wanted to be my friend. Kids disliked me because of who I was and for what I *didn't* look like. I had nothing special to offer at school or at home. No one found value in my presence.

The future was bright. The future always seemed brighter than the moment. High school *had* to get better. Of course, I wanted more! Life would not go on like this forever! Jeanette and I did what we could to improve our looks and fit in at high school. We spent our baby-sitting money on make-up even though Mom gave us looks of disappointment and disapproval before we left for school. How could her daughters be so concerned about their appearance? She failed to remember that *she* was just as concerned over how we presented ourselves at church. Once, long ago, she became irate at Dad for not changing out of his jeans before an evening church service. Even though he enjoyed the thought of going to church in jeans, Mom couldn't smile at his lack of concern. We were Cadillac Christians after all, and Cadillac Christians went to church with respectable clothing, like navy blue suits and flowered dresses. We should look our best for our God. Doesn't God look down and smile at his children when they're clean? Isn't cleanliness next to Godliness?

On some hot high school issues, Mom loosened up for Jeanette and me. She reluctantly gave us permission to hang a poster on our closets, as long as we used a special non-stick material. I taped up a poster of Jon Bon Jovi, a wild-haired '80's rock singer on my side and Jeanette secured Richard Dean Anderson, otherwise known as McGyver, a television star on her side. They were secular idols and it bothered Mom. We placed a mirror and a shelf holding make-up, bought from baby-sitting jobs, between two freestanding closets. Our cool cousin, Cindy, from Portland, Oregon, sent us curling irons for our birthday. Still no friends were ever invited to the house, no telephone calls were allowed. Mom just didn't understand the point of telephone calls. We had rules concerning where we were allowed in the house. All the rooms were off limits—her possessions, even though still in boxes, were just too important and too valuable to be disturbed.

Before going to bed each night, we braided each other's hair into six or seven braids, not recognizing the striking resemblance we had to the snake-haired mythical creature, Medusa. In the morning we unbraided the mess and then faced a small mirror to apply bright colored make-up to our faces. I made sure Jeanette looked presentable before we left the house. *Man, here I go again. Following the ways of the world. Shame on me!* But I tried to talk some sense into her anyway. "Jeanette, you need to back-comb your bangs some more to get them higher."

Jeanette attempted with a brush. "Like this?"

"Higher!"

Jeanette ratted with vigor. "Like this?'

"No." I said. "First spray your hair, then use a thin-toothed comb to get the height. After that, blow it dry with the hair dryer. It'll get it to stay up all day. Then spray it with firm-hold Aqua Net hairspray."

"It's too much work!"

"Just do it!" I pushed. "You'll look great, I promise."

Mom watched through the crack of the opened bathroom door in horror at my attempts. When she couldn't stand my obsessiveness any longer, she let her presence be known. "What do you think you're doing? You should wait until you're in college before fiddling with yourself. You girls are just too much."

I rolled my eyes at her comment. *What does she know?* Our thick Asian hair had a mind of its own. It didn't want to be curly, that was for sure. Our hair did not want to have anything to do with the style worn by rest of the world. During our walk up the neighborhood hill, across the field and track, and finally to the school, we discovered that moist Northwest air melts Asian hair. And cheap mascara, eye-liner and blush would rather drip down our faces than stay put. Our hair, make-up and the weather joined forces so Mom and God could prove they were right and we were wrong. We deserved to be punished for disobeying the rules.

God punished my wants and desires by stunting my growth, as well, and all the prayers in the world could not change His decision. I had only a half an inch to go in order to reach five feet. Before I could begin my second round of prayers, He zapped me with shrink-wrap.

For the rest of my life, I would be the size of a twelve-year-old girl—*before* puberty!

I was tempted by the ways of the world. *What the hell is wrong with me? I am a Christian! I should know better. I should know that obedience is imperative if I want an everlasting life with Jesus.* But I longed anyway. I *wanted* the riches from the earth, risking a life in hell by doing so. I ignored the Bible verse, "The Lord is my Shepherd, I shall not want." *What is happening to me? Who am I going to turn into? A life without Jesus is like committing suicide.* I was constantly confused about hell. I thought about hell all the time. I imagined what it would be like to burn forever and ever and ever—for all eternity. *Why would God burn billions of non-Christians for not believing that He exists? Why would he kill us for not using Jesus as our savior?* Christian books only gave partial answers, the rest of the answers, we were taught, would be put to rest with faith. I couldn't ignore the nagging questions, even if they were brought to me by Satan. Faith and a belief in someone better should have given me a sound mind. Why then, did I still have questions? I reasoned that by believing in Christianity, I had nothing to lose. So if I lived a Christian life limited with the rules, at least I would be saved from the burning fires of hell. I'd rather be limited than hell-bound.

Mom tolerated our questions. She didn't understand where they were coming from, but she knew that God was on her side, so no worries. Her face told another story; it displayed a magnitude of worries. We were *strong-willed children.* We were not cooperative children. Dad had no idea what was going on. He sat in his room watching television, reading his Bible and asking God over and over again to perform a miracle on his body so he could go back to work and church again.

Tenth grade would soon start and Dad was still disabled. We were confused. *God, I want patience and I want it now! When is God going to perform a miracle?* Keep the faith! Ignore the questions. Ignore our feelings. We have to keep the faith! We already possessed the faith—so much faith—our faith was much larger than that the mustard seed they talked about in the Bible.

Chapter 9

American Beauty

High school became an opportunity to turn over another new leaf and make new friends. Jeanette and I kept our old friends too, like Jenny and Ly. And just as anticipated, we found new friends along the way. They mostly consisted of "leftover and left out" Asians who didn't belong to any group: like us, Anne was adopted; Belinda was half-Filipino; and Quynn was Vietnamese. All of us had a common bond. Dreams of a future in creativity kept us bonded and excited: Jenny excelled in photography; Ly designed and sewed amazing outfits; Belinda was a natural in drama; Jeanette could draw faces that looked like models from magazines; my passion was interior design. We deemed ourselves artists.

We were well-liked by our friends. They found us mischievous and fun to hang with because we liked to joke and laugh a lot. Jeanette and I kept updated with fashion and music and trends by watching MTV and VH1 on the sly on Tuesdays and Thursdays while Mom was at square dance lessons. We wanted to keep updated with the kids at school. We gossiped on the phone and even had a few of our friends over at the house sometimes. We weren't concerned about the problems of the world. Instead, we wrote immature notes to each other, stole toilet paper, rebelled in insignificant ways. We referred each other to low paying summer jobs. Once in a while, Jeanette and I entertained our friends with stories about the weird conditions we lived in, just like they protested about the rules made by their own parents. Everyone had problems. Everyone had growing pains. We weren't ashamed of Mom's cluttered boxes as much as we were intrigued by what they all held. Dad's injury had become a part of living.

According to Mom and Dad, life had dwindled to almost nothing—no meaning or purpose. They wanted to know why God let this happen when we were a family of faith. With David gone, all Mom did was park herself in the living room with a cup of International Delights flavored coffee and stare into the television with the remote control in hand. She watched and watched as if the actors from *The Young and the Restless, As the World Turns*, and *Golden Girls* could comfort her better than we did. Her sad situation motivated me to *live* my life when I grew up. I would find comfort from *real* people, not the fake ones seen on TV. I felt sorry for her. One day I would be able to surprise her with a trip to Hawaii. How happy she would be if she went on a vacation. Hopefully she would forget about this dreadful life that God had given her. Most of the time she blamed God quietly; on a few occasions she blamed Dad aloud for hang gliding and putting the family through this mess, and then she blamed Jeanette and me for being a burden and preventing her from being able to live life fully.

Mom spent her days in the West wing of the house while Dad passed his time in a Lay-Z-Boy chair over on the Eastside, doing nothing but being. Before his injury he would joke: *don't just sit there, do something.* As luck would have it, he had become the motto: *don't just do something, sit there. Doing* was completely out of the question. Jeanette and I stayed in the middle of the house and dealt with our parents' emotions like shock absorbers. The memory of how things used to be made my stomach turn. I had always thought we were a typical family. Now Dad waited for each meal and needed help to be put into bed each night. Dad's sitting around made Mom nervous and stressed. *How can Jeanette and I solve this? What can we do help?*

"Go ahead, girls. Go to Ly's house this New Year's Eve. There's nothing here at home to look forward to anymore," Mom said. "I don't know how much longer I can keep this up."

Ly and her family lived in an olive-colored three-bedroom house. A chain-link fence around the premises provided whatever security it could offer. Ly's father, Mr. Ngov, drove a VW bus the same color as their house. Even though Ly's home was small and opened to the street so pedestrians could see her mother cooking "strange" Cambodian meals in the yard, I felt unusually comfortable there.

Most of the time her mother would speak in her native language with an English word thrown in occasionally. After she watched Jeanette and me eat bowl after bowl of nothing but rice and soy sauce, she would ask Ly questions about our strange behavior. Ly would give us a quick translation. "My mom wants to know why you only eat rice." Her parents thought *we* were the weird ones.

I shrugged my shoulders. I didn't know why. Until then, I took the comment "Asians only eat rice" literally. I really did think that Asians *only* ate rice. No one told me that, comparable to the bread in the West, rice in the East was just a staple food eaten with an array of main courses.

The garage at their house amazed us. The walls were old and peeling, the floor was an outdated vinyl, but it was transformed into a sewing room filled with fabrics from all over the world. Rolls of bright pink, aqua, and orange fabrics, trimmed with gold, black and white silks, and bolts of cotton blends lined the walls. Ly's older sister sat at one of the two sewing machines making a dress.

"We've been sewing since we were very young," Ly said. "If you ever want me to make you something, I can. My mom does it all the time for American ladies who can't find clothes that fit in stores."

"Wow!" Jeanette and I were amazed. We scanned the beautiful fabrics, and soon found ourselves in love with the ornate texture, pattern and vibrant hue of each roll of cloth. I had never seen such bright, rich colors. I wondered if the country they came from was always so colorful.

After school we spent time at Ly's house as much as possible. Unable to read a word from the pages, we studied the photos from Asian Magazines intrigued at the models and products that were sold. Until then I didn't know that Asia had movie stars, pop idols, music videos, and beauty magazines. My parents didn't feel the need to discover the unorthodox beauty found in other cultures. Did they even know that beauty came in different packages? My limited notion of beauty mandated Western blond hair, blue eyes, and long legs. The message I got from Glamour and Elle magazine was that there was no hope for me to be considered beautiful. My facial features were clearly Asian, yet I knew nothing about Asia. Who knew, if behind our backs, Ly, her sisters, and mother looked at one another, puzzled at our strange ignorance of Asian culture? On the surface, they accepted us. They sewed, gossiped, laughed and watched Asian soap operas as if we were part of the family.

Jeanette and I followed Ly into the master bedroom where she picked up tweezers and started pulling out single hairs from her eyebrows, a concept that was totally new to me. *Her mother actually lets her do that to her face? Geez, my mom wouldn't.* Just recently, Mom became upset when I accidentally walked in on her while she shaved her legs in the bathroom. Even attempting to ask if we could use make-up at such a young age would be against God, and against Mom. I wouldn't want to disrespect them.

Ly interrupted my thoughts. "Hey you two, you should think about tweezing your eyebrows before we go out tonight."

"Why?" Jeanette asked.

I looked in the mirror and noticed thick hair over my eyes and even a few stray hairs above my nose. I had never even considered doing something so extreme to my face.

"Do you want me to do them for you?" she asked, hunched over the master bathroom sink.

"No thanks," we immediately said. I instantly noticed other flaws, but I was taught that if we changed anything on our faces, we were really disrespecting God. We should appreciate what He gave us, regardless of whether we liked the attribute or not. Our God-given features were not for us to judge. Yet as I studied myself in the mirror, I noticed that everything about my face was still crooked and my body was scrawny and straight, not really developed yet. *Why did God make me so ugly? Why didn't God bless me with halfway decent looks?*

Jeanette and I had no idea what to expect that New Year's Eve, since we were fifteen years old. Little did Mom know that Ly's father had bought her older sister a sleek new car, which could easily maneuver us down the wrong road. Ly and her sisters weren't Christians. I had been taught in church that if I set a good Christian example, I would have a better likelihood to pressure or at least influence her family to join the family of God through Jesus. Ly and her older sister weren't interested in being converted. They were ready to check out a club located in Seattle's Chinatown, and since Jeanette and I were spending the night, they invited us to tag along. Before Dad's injury, Jeanette and I had only visited Chinatown's typical tourist attractions, like the Japanese gardens and the standard Americanized Chinese restaurants.

We followed Ly and her sister down the basement steps of a decrepit building and into a club called Modern System. Thick smoke permeated the air, making the room seem mysterious, but alive. Asian guys dressed in shiny metallic suit jackets, baggy slacks, and long dark overcoats walked by and eyed us up and down. Asian girls wore their bangs ratted up high—higher than any girl from school. I was impressed. The sleek, sultry sounds of *Modern Talking*, a popular European new wave group, spilled out into the air—not the typical top forty hits played on the radio.

Because I was an adoptee and an Asian minority living in a predominately "white" world, I was rarely proud of who I was. I was led to believe that my Korean skin was inferior and less. Except for one black model, Iman, who broke into the modeling world, television and magazines only used white models to sell their products. American beauty was "white" beauty. I was not and would never be linked to American beauty. I had never seen a black male on magazine pages, and seeing a desirable Asian male on display was impossible to imagine. I'd seen only one Asian male in a teen-movie and that was the nerd from *Sixteen Candles,* which was released when I was in eighth grade. In tenth grade, I was shocked to learn that my white friend had a crush on Dustin Nguyen, a Vietnamese actor on a program called 21 Jump Street. He was the only Asian I had ever seen on TV. A white girl in love with an Asian male? I suspected that she pretended to like him whenever I was around, since I was an Asian too. No one ever told me that half way around the world male and female Asian models existed and were even considered pleasing to the eyes.

It wasn't until high school that I learned there was a whole "nother world" out there. A world of Asians who were actually proud of who they were with strong ties and deep roots. They had loving and supportive families who taught them to be proud of the culture they came from.

I had no cultural roots. Like the frayed end to a shoelace—the part with nothing to hold it together. If I was to learn about my roots, *I* had to take responsibility—it wasn't forced upon me like it was on other Asian teens who complained about it, but were anchored by it. In order to know where I could go, I had to first figure out where I came from. Keeping myself together was my duty, and no one else. Until high school, I had refused to keep the tie going. I was unaware of the beauty in the Asian culture. I mistakenly thought the white community that I had grown up in and wanted to be a part of would accept me more readily if I rejected my Asian brothers. My impression of Asian guys was completely wrong.

Sadly, when it came to boys, I had crushes on a few white boys in school. Starting in first grade, I developed a crush on a little blond boy. I even went as far as to kiss his hand and swat his behind. By the time I reached junior high, my infatuation with white guys blossomed into crushes here and there. I believed what society told me; my Asian brothers were less important. One particular guy of Thai descent let it be known that he was interested in me. I refused to have anything to do with him. I saw him the way the other kids saw him, instead of seeing him for who he really was. I didn't see his essence or his spirit. I wasn't aware of his value because my own self-esteem was so low.

At the dance club, I felt *real* for the first time in my life. It wasn't obvious that we were minorities and no one knew that we didn't belong. Teenage boys checked us out for the first time in our fifteen years. Jeanette and I checked out the teenage boys with excitement in our eyes. *Thank God* I chose a black and white miniskirt and black sleeveless turtleneck to wear. I looked halfway decent. I looked like I could belong.

A Vietnamese guy dressed in a metallic white shirt, thin black tie, loose wool pants, and a solid businessman's overcoat asked me to dance. I found him so intriguing. "Dance?" Was all he had to ask before my heart jumped and I answered, "Yes"!

As we were preparing to leave the club, James walked up to me again. "Do you want to go out sometime? Maybe the mall?"

"Sure!" I didn't stop to think.

"Phone number?"

I immediately scribbled down the number on whatever we could find—a paper napkin.

That night, I learned that my Asian brothers and sisters were just as guilty about conforming to the American way. They judged appearances, they compared cultures, they were conscientious about their clothing. Gangs and pride were also members of their world. *PRIDE. People Rejoicing In Dangerous Ego.* But this time, I was a willing part of it. I *wanted* to be included in the mess—at least, now, I belonged to something. The Vietnamese girls thought they were better than another cluster of girls because of a certain facial feature or particular style; and the Vietnamese guys thought they were better, because they drove certain cars. Generally, the cultures did not mix or cross boundaries and they did not hang out together. The comparisons, the divisions, and the disconnections just kept going and going. It wasn't until I entered the world of diversity that I learned all Asians were definitely *not* the same.

On the way home from the dance, I promised myself that there was no way I was going to let Mom's weird behavior risk a chance relationship with this guy. I decided that she had no choice in my decision to date James. I wasn't going to share with her a word about him. Instead, I confided in Dad, telling him all about the experience because it was safe to tell him the truth. He smiled. Mom would have attributed his smile to his head injury. During a sneaky phone call, James and I made arrangements for a date. On a Friday evening, he was to drop by the house and pick me up. I nervously waited by the front door for the headlights to his car, then planned to make a sudden dash outside as soon as I saw anything that resembled movement.

Mom watched me stare out of the glass front door. "Where did you meet this boy?"

"At the skating rink." My answer was a partial truth. I *had* seen him at the skating rink while with the youth group from church, but at the time had thought nothing of him. For some reason he looked different emerging from a smoke-filled atmosphere. The chance meeting at the dance club was a happy coincidence.

"How old is James again?" she asked.

"Nineteen."

While I waited for my date's arrival, Mom set Dad up like a stuffed scarecrow in between boxes of her stuff and the bare cement fireplace. He wore taped up thick black glasses and, because of the cold in the house, a bulky washed-out ski jacket and red plaid scarf. "Jeannine, it's very important that James comes in to meet your father."

"Why?"

"Because then he'll know that you come from a good Christian home. He'll be less likely to take advantage of you."

"Whatever," I said under my breath. I knew what she was *really* thinking. This way, if he truly loved me, he wouldn't be intimidated by our unusual circumstances or by Dad. I rolled my eyes. *Who does she think I am? I'm not stupid!*

When she saw the headlights to James' car, she walked out the gravel driveway to meet him. I reluctantly trailed behind her feeling ashamed and embarrassed.

"I would like you to meet Jeannine's father," she said. "You're welcome to come inside."

James, dressed in black from head to toe, exited his black Honda Accord like a young Batman of sorts. Mom appeared weaker than I had ever seen her, but as usual, she was still in control and knew exactly what impression she wanted to give. He and I followed her into the crowded living room where the biting cold glare from the huge plate glass windows obscured all but a silhouette of the back of Dad's head. As we made our way around to face him, the low winter sun shone brightly on Dad's face.

As if savoring this moment, Mom said, "This is Jeannine's father. Allen, say hello to James, Jeannine's new boyfriend."

Dad's smile was lopsided. Gold-capped teeth sparkled. His upper body shook out of control.

God, get me out of here! I gritted my teeth, took James by the hand and quickly led him out of the house.

"Jeannine, James is too old for you," Mom shook her head in discouragement every time I was ready to leave the house. "And he doesn't come from a good family."

I rolled my eyes again, even though she was probably right. His family still lived in Vietnam. He didn't have two solid parents to guide him in the right direction, like I did. Whenever James wanted to take me out, Mom invited him inside the house to say hello to "Mr. Vance." It was the proper thing to do. *I hate being proper! I want to be a free spirit.*

"Why are you so intent on dating this Vietnamese boy? Why don't you date Korean adoptees?" She wondered aloud. That way, we would be dating inside our nationality and complying with the scriptures of the Bible. The problem with her idea was that there were no Korean adoptees at school and most of the Korean guys were fighting amongst themselves for a chance relationship with popular white girls.

Should I limit my dating choices to one type or one group? What if I was attracted to a non-Korean guy? Should I block my heart because his skin color was not like mine? Should I block my heart because he came from a world unknown to me? Questions about my dating choices followed me to sleep. It just didn't make sense. Mom wouldn't understand my point of view or my curiosity, so I silently listened to her sermons and gave her the impression that I agreed with her decisions for my life.

Chapter 10

Heart to Heart

About a month after I had started dating James and after many awkward greetings with my parents later, he told me that it was nice knowing me, but we just didn't belong together. I agreed, but blamed it on Mom; she freaked him out on purpose. She didn't want me to have a life.

Danny, the guy Jeanette met at the dance club and was still dating, introduced me to his friend, Sean, who happened to own a black Trans Am. He had recently returned to Washington State after working on one of the fishing boats in Texas. His stature intimidated Mom—he had tan skin, a buff body, and was taller than most Asian guys. Right away I was attracted to his solid build. I was going out with this guy, whether Mom liked the idea or not. I wasn't going to comply with her strict rules any longer.

On February fourth, Sean picked me up to go on a double date with Jeanette and her boyfriend Danny. They came from Vietnam, a country I was totally ignorant of and intrigued by. Sean shook Dad's hand the moment they met and said, "Nice to meet you, sir." He gave Mom the same respect. Mom crossed her arms and frowned, displaying an abundance of disapproval. Obviously these boys were going to take advantage of us.

We left the house in Sean's Trans Am and stopped by Albertsons, where he bought Peach and Strawberry coolers on the way to Redondo Beach. He put his black leather coat around me as we wandered along the dock and drank from our bottles. I stared into the seawater, now black against the late evening sky and waited for him to start a conversation. A few motor boats glided by causing the water to ripple and sparkle at us. I didn't care what Mom thought anymore. Sean didn't say a word while on the dock, causing me to wonder why he was so quiet and if he ever talked. To fill the awkward silence, I asked about his parents.

"They're still in Vietnam," he answered.

I wondered what that must be like. How lucky he was to live in a foreign country without parents telling him what he could and couldn't do. I envied him. He stopped walking and leaned against the big rock formation along the dock, called Redondo's Archway and wrapped his hand around my own. I was caught off guard by how big and coarse his fingers felt.

"Where do you work?" I asked.

"Today was my first day at a garment factory." He squeezed my hand tightly as if he didn't want to let me go. When I reached for his other hand, he readily gave it to me. "How many brothers and sisters do you have?" I asked, facing him against the rock formation.

"Three brothers and three sisters," was all he said. I leaned into him, not caring if anyone saw and not worried about whether what we were doing was right or wrong. My body said *who cares if I'm too young to be so close.*

My head told me, *What the hell are you doing? You shouldn't be doing this!* I ignored my head and followed the careless directions of my body. It stepped outside of myself and pressed against him. He felt warm and powerful against the cold winter surroundings. Sensations ran through me like I had never known before. I wanted him, but my head told me it was wrong. While he held my hands, my mind and body continued to give me mixed messages. Then he bent down and planted his lips onto mine. He felt so strong and capable, I wanted him more than ever—I didn't give a damn what Mom would say if she found out. I wanted to be free from her claws.

Snap out of it! My head finally won and I reluctantly pulled away. We continued to walk in the chilly winter air along the dock and drink from our bottles, not saying much of anything, just thinking about the moment.

Even though I was a little tipsy from the peach cooler, I could still think and that's what I did. I thought about my roots and the foundation that Mom and Dad tried to build. Mom would be so outraged if she had discovered my heart had fallen out of sync with hers. She would be lost if she knew I was about to enter a world that didn't hold Jesus dear. And I would be a pure disappointment to myself, as well. Jesus and all that came with Him *were* my roots. I shouldn't follow my heart. After all, what do I know? I'm a mere mortal, a mere empty vessel, a sinning creature. I shouldn't allow a material man to take my heart. I finally concluded that Sean could have my head, but only Jesus could have my heart.

After an hour of analyzing the situation and guilty bliss, Sean looked at his watch. "It's time to take you home. Come on, we better get going."

I reluctantly followed him back to his Trans Am and motioned Jeanette and Danny to do the same. Once at home, Sean and Danny parked outside the gate and waited in the car until Mom opened the door to let us inside. I stood next to Jeanette, shivering from the cold and impatiently waiting at the doorstep. "Why can't Mom just give us a key to the house like any normal parent would do? I feel like a total stranger."

"I feel like a salesperson," Jeanette said, staring into the hideously crowded kitchen and dinette area. The interior and its contents seemed so surreal, as if they weren't a part of who we were. The contents inside were untouchable and off limits.

Mom emerged from amidst her boxes in the living room and strolled in a leisurely manner to open the door. Her face was angry and I couldn't stand the sight of her—I wanted to run away and hide. She looked desperate, as if all the hope she had for us was gone, as if our futures were damned by evil. Once she closed the door behind us, she plopped back on the couch, alone and depressed. Our happiness was her pain. We felt ashamed for being gone, but staying home was torture.

At home all I could think about was Sean. I turned up the clock radio to block out my wild thoughts but the music blared what was trapped in my head. Bono from U2 sang, *I want to run, I want to hide, I want to break down these walls that hold me inside. I want to reach out and touch the flame, where the streets have no name.*

"How old are Sean and Danny, and where are their families?" Mom asked before Jeanette and I left the house with them again the following weekend.

"Nineteen," we lied. The answer worked for about a week. Every time they came to the house, Mom would eye them up and down skeptically. Finally the truth came out, they were really twenty-one, and both their parents lived in Vietnam. They had been living on their own since 1980 when they arrived in America. And no, they didn't come from a good Christian family, but there was nothing Mom could do except tolerate the situation.

"Why would you choose these boys... I mean they're not boys; they're men. Why would you choose these men over your own family?" She asked.

We didn't know. All we knew was it felt good to be with them. We didn't have the answers to her questions and even if we did, she wouldn't have listened to us. Maybe it was because we didn't feel unconditional love at home. Maybe it was because in order to be respectful, we had to hide our true feelings. Maybe while we were with Sean and Danny, we could be ourselves without getting punished or causing problems.

"Can't you see what this is doing to the family? It's tearing us apart," she pleaded. We ignored her and turned up the radio. Top-forty hits played until Jeanette and I fell asleep at eleven at night, making it almost impossible to get up in the morning. But who cared? Mom felt hopeless over our salvation. I felt hopeless over her lack of understanding.

Out of resignation, Mom finally set a 10:00 P.M. curfew. She retired. She couldn't save us from our rebellious ways. I didn't understand why she was so set against us finding some happiness. Sean was like a gift from heaven! God had sent him to me to give me hope of a higher better future. My prayers were answered. Now, I had a reason for living. After all, he was someone who left home for the unknown and was able to survive. Unfortunately, Mom only saw him as trouble.

On further dates, Sean surprised me by bringing gifts of oranges, chocolates, and cookies from Chinatown. He didn't have second thoughts about pampering me with dinner at Vietnamese restaurants and buying me outfits from new wave clothing stores. He even came to the house with a brand new outfit for me to wear at the Chinese New Year dance in Seattle. I loved going to the new wave concerts;

everyone was dressed so modishly, and the atmosphere was alive, a feeling I sought. At home, I felt controlled and unwanted.

"You don't think my family's weird?" I asked on a lunch date at a Vietnamese café called Saigon Bistro, located in Seattle's International District.

"No, I've seen 'Different Strokes' on television. Your family is kind of like that."

My mind flashed to scenes from the comedy show. The characters solved their problems easily and everyone was happy in the end. It was definitely not the real world and it wasn't my life.

"What about my house? Don't you think it's kind of strange? So full of crap and stuff?"

"Not really. It's a little strange, but it's pretty normal at the same time. I've noticed that here in America; people have a lot of stuff. It's normal. In fact, haven't you noticed that no one parks their cars in their garage? They put their stuff *in* the garage, and park their expensive cars outside."

When the waiter approached, Sean ordered lunch in his native tongue. I waited for him to finish before responding. "Isn't that how it is in Vietnam?"

"No, back home we don't buy stuff just to look at it. Everything we have, we use. Only the rich own a car; everyone else rides motorbikes."

"Weird!" I tried to imagine an empty house with only a motorbike for transportation. His culture seemed so fascinating. I wanted to learn more! However it didn't take long before my thoughts turned to Dad again. They always did. "Well, what about Dad? Don't you think he's a little weird."

The waiter set coffee in a small metal container atop a mug holding a spoon-size amount of condensed milk on the table. The coffee dripped down from the contraption, emitting an intense aroma. "Not really, he seems pretty normal to me. After all he had a head injury."

"What about Mom then, isn't she strange?"

"No, I don't think so. I think she treats you guys differently because you're adopted."

I thought long and hard about what he said, but I didn't want to believe it. Our adoption was never a secret. Listeners usually gave us looks of pity when we told them that we were found on a street corner, but being abandoned never bothered me or caused any emotional damage, at least, not on the surface. In fact, to illustrate my ease about our dirt-poor origin, I tried to make the listeners feel comfortable with jokes. "Isn't everyone found on a street corner? Isn't everyone delivered by the stork?" Being adopted was really no big deal.

My thoughts about our adoption changed after experiencing the home-like comfort and camaraderie I had with Sean. It was the first time I felt wanted for who I was. I didn't have to conform in a certain way to be loved. I realized that being adopted was like being pulled from our roots and planted in soil completely foreign to us. The home environment was difficult to adapt to. Even as young children, we could sense that we were different. I felt like a Korean radish expected to blend in or at least go unnoticed in a western tossed salad. I wanted desperately to be a cheery cherry tomato or a loud crunchy crouton—not a somber, out of place, yellow radish. The tossed salad didn't need me; in fact, it tasted fine without me. I wasn't needed or wanted in this mix. Jeanette and I were outsiders from the very beginning; we didn't even belong to our family. As adoptees, we would never admit this. Instead we fuzzed out our senses and lived in denial, pretending as we went along in life that we were normal and felt a sense of belonging. When people called our parents, "step-parents" or "sponsors," on automatic pilot we'd play the game of life by saying that our adoptive parents and brothers were our *real* family and our birth parents were only birth parents, nothing else. We maintained that we held the same feelings of affection for each other and experienced the normal situations that all families shared. That's what adoptees are supposed to say. But was it normal to feel like a worthless burden to our own mother?

"You know, we've been more like charity decorations to Mom than anything else. Our adoption in the family was to make Mom and Dad look important. They just played by the rules; there was no heart in their decision to adopt us. Well, maybe there was at that time, but I don't feel it now."

"I don't think people should adopt. It's impossible to ignore your feelings," Sean said. "I mean, how can they love their adopted kids as much as their *real* ones? You know you can't fake something like that."

"Yeah. Television shows make adoption look so dreamy, but they really don't talk about what happens when the kids grow up. I mean, I'm not against it—that's for sure! It's just that there needs to be love involved. One thing still confuses me. Why does Mom treat Mike badly? Like David, he's my parents natural-born kid," I asked. "Mike doesn't feel like he belongs either."

"I don't know, I'm just telling you what I see." Sean poured the coffee into a tall glass, then gently pushed the iced drink towards me. "I don't have the answers, but I can see that your mom treats you differently because you're adopted."

This guy was like no one I had ever met before. It was as if, by instinct, he could read my parents without really knowing them. He wasn't a big talker. Was prudence taught in the Christian church? No. So I didn't value it. I thought Sean was quiet and I still wasn't sure if I was in love. One thing I knew for sure though. Sean was proud of his Vietnamese roots; I needed that. I was never proud of my roots or myself.

The waiter approached with our order of rice noodle spring rolls. As the gaunt man left to take the order from the next table, Sean said "*Com ca*" then turned to me and whispered. "You know Jeannine, you shouldn't be ashamed of who you are. You can't help it. You were adopted. I know what you mean about feeling out of place. I've felt like that ever since I came to America. So far, except when I'm with you, I haven't felt at home. I could never pretend that I belonged in high school. I'm not good at pretending or hiding my feelings."

"Try fifteen years of pretending. I've felt like an alien all my life. I've never felt like I've belonged. Most of the Korean kids don't really include Jeanette and me much because we don't speak the language, and most of the white kids think we're just Chinese geeks. But, I'm used to it now; it almost feels normal."

"Do you want some soybean milk? It's really good. You should try it. I'll order it for you. Have you tried the Vietnamese sandwiches? I'll order some to go so you can take a couple to lunch tomorrow."

"No, that's okay, you don't have to."

He left the seat to order soybean milk and sandwiches from the cashier, anyway. I munched on the remainder of the meal. According to Sean, food wasn't forbidden or considered a sin, like at home. I liked his world better and Mom couldn't comprehend why.

On his return to the restaurant table, he asked, "Do you want to meet my two older brothers?" Breaking me out of my trance-like state.

"Sure."

We left the restaurant and arrived at an old apartment complex invaded by masses of tough juniper and stubborn scotch broom. Inside, the filmy vanilla interior felt damp and cold, but the atmosphere and occupants were beautiful.

"This is my brother Un Lam and his wife, Christina." Both were in their twenties, dressed from off the pages of Vogue magazine. Not one strand of hair or article of clothing out of place; nothing bought from outlet malls. "And this is my oldest brother, Un Duc, and his wife, Chi Oanh." Sean pointed to the other couple, and I noticed the woman's thick, shiny, long, black hair, beautiful eyes, and remarkably long lashes.

He pointed behind a white leather couch. "This is my five-year-old nephew, Phong." The little boy was the cutest thing I had ever seen. He quietly sat on the floor playing with a toy truck. I fell in love with him immediately.

"Jenne, take off your shoes," Christina said.

"What?"

"Take off your shoes."

I looked down at my feet. "Why?"

Oanh nodded in agreement. "Jenne, take off your shoes." She pointed to a pile of expensive shoes next to where I was standing.

Oh, everyone wears socks inside. Strange. My shoes seemed cheap and obnoxious when I slipped them off. My white socks had turned gray in the wash and my black patent shoes bought from Payless were scuffed and dirty.

Christina rose from her chair and patted the white leather sofa trimmed in black. "Jenne, sit here."

"No, that's okay."

She took my arm and guided me into the supple cushion. "Jenne, down."

I stood up feeling nervous and ogre like. "No, that's okay, I can stand."

"Jenne, sit."

"Okay."

Oanh left her seat for the small galley kitchen. "Jenne, did you eat yet?" She lifted the lid to an enormous steaming pot, pulled out a deep ladle of beef broth and filled a bowl served with white noodles.

"Yes." I patted my stomach.

"Come, sit at table. Eat."

"No, that's okay." I remembered the chicken and pork sandwiches in the car. I had more than enough food for the day. I should feel guilty for eating when I'm not hungry.

"Jenne, come eat."

I patted my stomach again. "No thanks, I'm full."

Oanh set a gigantic bowl of hot soup on the table, then arranged bean sprouts, bits of lime, basil leaves, and sliced chili peppers onto a small plate. She positioned plastic bottles of thick soy sauce and red chili sauce next to the bowl. "Jenne, come here. Eat."

"No, really I'm fine." The aroma of basil and Vietnamese cinnamon caused my mouth to water without its usual control.

"Go," Christina insisted.

"But, we just ate..."

Oanh grabbed my arm and led me to the table. "Eat."

"Okay," I complied.

She handed me chopsticks and a deep spoon.

"Um, do you have a fork?" I asked, feeling insecure. I remembered using chopsticks once or twice as a child, but we didn't really use them; we just studied the directions from the packages.

"Sure." She handed me a fork, then watched me try to shove long, stringy, rice noodles into my mouth.

"Where are you from?" Duc asked, in a Vietnamese accent.

I didn't know what to tell them. I was more confused than ever about who I was and how I fit into the world. Instead of answering, noodles dripped from my mouth and soup splattered on my chin. While I rotated between eating the soup with the fork and the spoon and making a mess in the process, Sean answered in Vietnamese for me. When I picked up a paper napkin to wipe my chin, both chopsticks flipped onto the floor.

"Christina is from Korea too," Sean told me. I looked to her, impressed by her poise and her stylish outfit bought from Nordstrom. She was so well put together. Not like clumsy and insecure me. My mother dressed me in clothes from secondhand stores even though we could afford namebrands. In traditional Korean societies twins were considered bad luck. I couldn't escape the cast even in America. My American parents didn't do much to build my self-esteem. They ignored the fact that I was different and that the society I lived in would perceive me as so. By the way Christina presented herself, I could see that her parents built her self-esteem. They had given her a strong sense of self-worth; they taught her to be proud of her Korean heritage. I was stunned by her confidence. Like most individuals, she had strong roots. I, on the other hand, had nothing to hold onto, consequently causing me to feel ashamed of who I was.

"Put some of this in." Oanh pointed to the unfamiliar vegetables.

"No thanks."

"Do it. Makes it taste good." She grasped a bundle from the plate and plopped it into my bowl, then dribbled in thick sauce and watched me eat. "Do you like hot?"

"Um, no thanks."

She poured thick red chili sauce into bowl. "Eat. Good!"

"Okay." I did exactly as she said even though my stomach felt heavy and ready to explode. I didn't regret it one bit though; I relished the unusual spices and herbs. I was hooked on the spicy food, the Vietnamese way of life, and their generosity.

At home, Mom was still unhappy about our choices. She turned on the television and made Jeanette and me watch *Sally Jesse Raphael* and *Maury Povich*. Then she lectured us about the defiant teenagers. "Look at those teenagers. They look like prostitutes. If you don't stop your disrespectful behavior, you're going to end up just like them," she warned. We deserved to go to boot camp, but the best she had was a talk with our school guidance counselors, youth group leaders, the Presbyterian pastor, and anyone who would listen. They didn't know what to do with us either. "Try enforcing more rules and following through with threats," they suggested. They thought we were turning into disobedient, teenage rebels who were ready to protest if anyone got in our way. Why didn't they see that we wanted love and respect more than anything else? Why did they demand respect based on the decisions they made for our lives but refuse to value or listen to our own? *Do they really think they can earn our respect by enforcing strict rules? Did they think we're incompetent participants in our own lives? Do they consider us so naïve and worthless that our voices should be left buried in our throats? We don't care what they think and we're not going to conform to their strict standards!* Strict rules and regulations only made us angry. Why couldn't they see that we were capable of making sound decisions? Why couldn't they see that we wanted to give back to society what we were given?

The high point came during the summer after tenth grade when Jeanette and I were given the opportunity to go on a mission trip to Mexico with the church youth group. A group of about fifteen teenagers from different Presbyterian churches planned and then built cement houses for the local residents who were currently living in cardboard shacks. I enjoyed myself so much that I seriously thought about becoming a missionary after graduating from high school. The feeling of making the children laugh even though we didn't speak the same language put me in high spirits. I enjoyed the freedom of not worrying over superficial issues such as what to wear and how to look. Mexico seemed rich in spirit compared to what I was used to. I also liked the warmth and authenticity of its people.

We kept our ideals and dreams and our truths to ourselves and sometimes confided them to Dad while we groomed him for the day. Mom would listen by the entrance to the bathroom wishing that we would share our feelings with her. But talking to her wasn't safe. We didn't have a right to our feelings. According to her, we were still children who should be seen and not heard.

Jeanette and I listened to Mom spill the latest to David, who was away at college. "I don't know what I'm going to do," we heard her complain over the phone. "They're just horrible and full of lies. I've tried getting them involved with church, counseling with the youth group leader, but they just don't listen. I've got to make it for three more years... three more years, until they graduate. What will the

93

twins be sneaking next? What's after rock and roll? Sex, smoking and drugs?"

Was Mom right? Sometimes my head gave conflicting messages from that of my heart. I was concerned and confused. My head told me that I should not get serious with Sean because he did not share the religious beliefs that had been my foundation. My head wondered if God would forgive me for going outside of Christianity. Christianity was not just a religion—it was who I was. In contrast, my heart told me that my feelings for Sean were meant to be. We liked each other too much to simply say good-bye. So we continued going out, getting to know each other more and more with each date.

Chapter 11

Dear Diary

From my sister's diary:
2-4-89 (age 17)
   I woke up at 4:00 A.M. and heard Mom crying in pain because of her gall bladder. I stayed awake wondering what I should do. It's weird, because Dad had the same problem and recently had surgery. At 5:00 A.M. Mom was at our bedroom door calling Jeannine and me. I instantly paid attention because she never called us like that. She said she needed one of us in case she fainted. She was very disoriented. She didn't know what time it was or what she was talking about. She said she hoped she'd make it through our high school years and even talked about dying.
   She called Mr. Reynolds at 9:00 A.M. and told him to take her to the hospital. (She thought it was 6:00 A.M.) After she left I told Dad (they sleep separately since his accident). He was up in his chair with his hat and the scarf that I gave him, and a blanket. It's so cold in the house. I asked him how long he'd been up, because he looked dead tired, and he said all this stuff like "I brushed my teeth and combed..." Then I interrupted him and said, "Mom is in the hospital." His face changed. "What?"
   Mom got home around noon and said she wanted one of us home all the time to take care of Dad. So Jeannine and I are going to take turns. I think maybe I'm too mean to Mom. I better loosen up about her, I don't want her to die! It's freezing. Jeannine and I made sure the fire kept going, fed the animals, and fed Dad his meals.

Went to church and during prayer requests, Mr. Reynolds told the pastor to pray for Mom. After church, a lot of people asked if they could help with anything. I thought it was such a nice gesture, but no one came to the house. Friday 5:30 A.M.: Mom is going to get her operation and she is scared and irritable.

3-13-89

Yesterday Mom had her gall bladder operation. We spent the night at Ly's house because Mom wanted us out of the house when she was gone. I don't understand; David is home from college so he can keep a watch on us. Plus we're sixteen, and juniors in high school! Mrs. Reynolds called and told us that Mom is doing okay, but is a little nauseated. Dad was mad because he had to stay at the Healy house. Jeannine and I could have taken care of him, but Mom doesn't think we can. She doesn't want to burden David.

5-30-89

Mom is in New York for two and a half weeks to visit David at college. Jeannine, Dad, and I have to stay at the Healy House, the adult family home. It's a big nuisance. The caregiver drives us to school in the morning and we take two buses to get back. It sucks. We get up in the morning, feed the dog, get Dad up and dressed and fed, and get ourselves ready. What a nuisance! I also have a miserable cold.

6-25-89

I am seventeen years old and my boyfriend, Danny, is twenty-three. I am finally done with my junior year and now I have one more year of high school. Maybe everything will get better for me. For the last three nights, without telling Mom, I've been spending the night with Danny.

Before our seventeenth birthday, Jeannine and I walked into the house after spending the day with Danny and Sean, and I could tell Mom was upset. Went to Dad's bedroom to give him a T-shirt for Father's Day. While we talked to Dad,

Mom asked, "What's the plan?" I said, "I guess Jeannine and I will move out." I knew that is what Mom probably wants. Then Mom said, "Okay, I'll pack your things and you can pick them up in the evening." So we left.

Mom is so strange, she packed only some of our stuff, but I don't care. She can have whatever she wants. I had everything organized at Sean and Danny's apartment when we got a telephone call from Mom asking us to come over for cake and ice cream. She put Dad in the T-shirt we gave him that said "100% Daddy" on it. It almost made me cry. Mom wanted us over so we would feel guilty for moving out. I miss Dad sooooooo much. I always have him on my mind. He must be so sad now that he's all alone. He knows Mom doesn't love him anymore. I only wish I could visit him, but Mom said that when we want to stop by we have to call first. Such a pain. I don't want to do that. I just want to visit him. I miss him.

I started a job at a dry cleaner's. The owners are both Korean. I get three-fifty an hour and I work four hours each day after school on weekdays, and five hours on Sunday. Every white person that comes into the shop automatically thinks I'm the owners' daughter. It's irritating. They say, "Tell your mom to sew the button on my shirt." At first I'd say she's not my mom, but later I don't care and don't even correct them. The owner has three daughters, who all used to work in the shop. The customers always ask me how my sisters are doing. I say, "You mean, Jeannine?" They get all confused and answer, "Jeannine? I thought their names are Kim and Lisa."

7-1-89

I haven't called Dad yet or visited him. I feel so guilty. I LOVE YOU DAD! It's been seven days since I last saw him. I am so worried. I know he's lonely and suffering.

7-13-89

Jeannine and I decided to go to the store to buy something to eat. We were in the magazine section when I felt someone's eyes on me. It was Mom and she was just staring at us. Weird. We said "Hi," and quickly left the store. We felt like strangers, like she wasn't even our mother.

7-21-89

Two days in a row, I rode my bike home to see how Dad was doing. Wednesday I saw him in his room watching TV. I waved frantically because I was so excited to see him. I was so happy but so sad at the same time. I wanted to run into the house and hug him so much. Through the kitchen window Mom saw me waving and she slowly emerged and asked what I was doing. Like I was crazy or something. I said I was waving to Dad. All she said was "Oh."

Today, I went over again and saw Dad in the kitchen eating dinner all by himself. I secretly cried to myself. He watched TV by himself too. I tried to get his attention without Mom seeing. (She was in the living room, but I kept myself hidden just in case). I think he saw me. God, every time I go over there I torture myself but I just want Dad to know I love him and I haven't forgotten about him. How else can I let him know? Mom says I can't visit him unless she is there, but my relationship with her is completely over. It's obvious that she doesn't love us and I don't feel like I know her. Sometimes I feel like crying and often I do, especially at night when there is nothing to think about except Dad. I just want to ask someone to trade lives with me.

7-22-89

Jeannine and I continue going to the house to catch a glimpse of Dad, just to make sure he's all right. We found out that Dad tried to escape from home to find Jeannine and me. He walked without assistance all the way through the neighborhood, up the steep hill and onto the main street. I bet it took him hours! I'm surprised he got so far! When He sat down to rest, two men thought he had fallen, so they got out and asked him if he needed any help. Mom was heading home, when she saw that Dad was out of the house. She stopped the car and approached Dad. When Dad saw her he started crying, "Don't let her take me!" Mom then explained to the men to ignore his pleas and because of his severe head injury, which affected his problem-solving skills. Mom just installed a lock so Dad can't go outside. Mom said that Dad's behavior is normal for someone who is "head injured." Things are getting pretty desperate. I can't stand Mom any longer. I wish she would change and give Dad some freedom!

7-23-89

I moved back home. I called Mom and asked if it's too late to move in. At first she said yes, but then I cried. I couldn't help it. I missed Dad. She asked why I want to move in and I said I felt guilty for leaving my parents, especially since David's in college. She said I could come right over. When Dad saw me he cried. I am so glad to be back home. I ask Dad how he knew I'm Jeanette and he says that Jeannine is stronger. Then he says it's not always good to be too strong because it can hurt someone. This coming year I'm going to be a senior and then I'll be able to move out with Mom's approval.

12-28-89

Jeannine moved home right before Christmas. We're taking on our usual chores but we spend our weekends with Danny and Sean. Mom doesn't like it. She knows we spend all our time with them. Now she hardly talks to us, but I don't care.

Graduation
6-15-90 (age 17)

Mom is diagnosed with breast cancer, and she finally told us she has been keeping it a secret. Jeannine and I are taking care of Dad due to Mom being emotionally unstable. We are graduating this month. I am pregnant and I got the positive tests results back on my eighteenth birthday at Planned Parenthood.

It is also David's graduation from Stanford University. He has a master's degree in Engineering. He followed in Dad's footsteps, and Mom is proud of him as usual. He will be moving back home and can now support Mom emotionally. Mom is extremely happy about that. She doesn't trust us and she doesn't want us to see her vulnerable. I think that is why she kept her cancer from us for so long. We have been taking care of Dad as much as possible, keeping him company, taking him for walks through the neighborhood, and continuing with our daily chores of dressing him and attending to his needs. We also bring him treats to lift his spirits and try to make him laugh.

I am living with my boyfriend again. Mom offered Jeannine and me an opportunity to stay home while we go to a community college. I guess she doesn't want to pay for a good college like she did for David. We're not worth it. I'm not going to take her up on her offer. There's no way I'm living in Mom's hell house. At least Danny is happy, and he plans to support the baby. He even went out and got a job to prove he is serious. The scariest thing is going to be telling Mom about my pregnancy. I told Danny that that is his duty. I'm keeping it a secret all through prom and graduation. The baby is due January 24th!

Danny and I agree it's time to tell Mom that I'm pregnant. We went into the house and I immediately excuse myself to visit Dad. Down the hall, I could hear Danny excitedly tell Mom, "You're going to be a grandmother!" in a proud father-to-be-type of voice. Mom tried to hide her disappointment. She tried to convince Danny to do the "next best thing" and get married as soon as possible. She said she might even chip in a hundred dollars. Danny patiently listened to Mom's sermon, but deep inside we knew we both don't want to get married. But if we don't, I might be damned to hell, so maybe I should start convincing Danny that we should.

Mom has talked about the option of giving the baby up for adoption because of my age. She doesn't think I'm capable of giving the baby an adequate home. That is totally out of the question for me. I am totally capable of loving a child. I think the teenage mother scare adults use to keep us from having sex is just a ploy. I am not going to feel guilty or ashamed. I wonder if she'll ever figure out that I found love elsewhere because there wasn't any at home.

Now I go to the Department of Social and Health Services (DSHS) for money and food stamps. I loathe it with a passion. Using food stamps and cashing government checks is painful and humiliating. Danny and I moved into a one-bedroom apartment where the majority of tenants are low-income people. It's kinda' funny to watch everyone who lives here line up at the mailboxes on the fifth of the month to wait for their checks from the government. It's embarrassing and I want to get off as soon as possible. I hate DSHS. I never know if I'm going to be able to pay rent on time—or pay rent at all! All the stares from people in line at the grocery stores are unbearable. I just want to crawl into a hole and hide. It's humbling. At least during this time of "hell," I'm learning to be compassionate for the less fortunate.

Thanksgiving
1990 (age 18)

We were all invited to the Reynolds as usual for Thanksgiving. I'm seven months pregnant. When entering their home, Mom looked at me with hatred for being the family disgrace. When I got near her she spat, "When are you going to get married?" Then throughout the whole dinner she made sure she stayed away from me. Mom cares too much about outside appearances.

I'm attending a class for young mothers, since they claim teenage mothers are at a much higher risk of using drugs and alcohol. While pregnant, we meet once a week and after we have our babies, a nurse visits our home twice a month for the first year of our child's life.

1-26-91

I just got off the phone with Mike. He asked if anything happened yet, if the baby came out. One minute after I hung up, my water broke. We are headed to St. Francis Hospital as soon as we see if we won the Lotto.

1-27-91

Mom and David stopped by while I had my contractions. I gave Danny a look to let him know that I wanted Mom out of the room. David only stood back observing and appeared speechless. Right after they left, Ly came in eating a McDonald's hamburger. She asked if I want a bite, and I threw up from the smell. I sat in the hot tub to decrease the pain, which helped a little. Jeannine sat with me throughout the whole twelve hours, while Danny slept in the rocking chair. At last I started pushing hard around six in the morning. Finally, Dustin was born at 6:45 A.M. and he is the best gift ever. Danny is being the best father he can be.

Chapter 12

Entrapment

Throughout our senior year in high school, Mom successfully hid her fight with breast cancer from her daughters. We were the only two people in the world who didn't know. We could only imagine how horrified she must have felt when she learned of her disease. It wasn't until *after* we had graduated and moved out of the house that she decided to let us in on her private life. When we asked her why she didn't share her anxieties, she told us it was because we were too immature to understand the severity of what she felt. We were too juvenile to handle the topic of death.

A part from being worried about her chances of beating the cancer, she was swamped with worries about Dad and us. What if we preyed on her vulnerabilities and took her for all she was worth? She turned to David for comfort, especially since he had recently graduated from Stanford with a Masters in Engineering and was, thank God, finally home for good. Mom invited *him* to live with her among her favored belongings.

She was also eaten alive with worries concerning our perception of Dad: *Why don't we understand the severity of his head injury? Why do we confide in him when he's "not all there"? What if he "spills the beans" about their own secret past?* To make our complicated mother/daughter relationship worse, every time she tried to convince us that Dad was incompetent, we politely changed the subject.

Mom and David sorted the family mess all by themselves. Later Mom revealed what they had planned for the rest of us. Since Mike and his new girlfriend, Angie, were living in a camper at the house, she could, as Mike put it, *kill two birds with one stone* by buying a RV for Dad to live in, and then rent two spaces in the nearest Indian reservation. This way, she could get Mike off her property at home.

She paid for his three-hundred-dollar monthly lot; in exchange he was responsible for Dad's care. Mike agreed to the terms even though he had never cared for anybody disabled before in his life or even given Dad a bath. He told Jeanette and me that the lot was a dive, and that there were drugs and alcohol all around. He thought he was getting gypped, but he didn't protest. Dad didn't know about the deal until it was time to move.

Family arrangements and finances were kept a secret. Even though we were adults, we didn't need to know what went on and how much Dad made. We never asked either. Mom eventually confided to us her fears of going without. "Girls, your father's retirement and social security barely cover the expenses. I'm forced to live out the rest of my life on a limited, fixed income. You have to understand that he's not like he used to be. I don't know why your father is complaining. He has everything he needs," Mom said the day she let us in on her plan. "Your father is now living in a RV. He has a shower, a toilet; I've packed sack lunches and dinners to last him a week. David will fill his refrigerator every week and bring more propane tanks. I need peace of mind while fight my disease. I don't have a husband to take care of me. I'm too ill.to care for him. And David needs to *live* his life."

We disliked the arrangements, but refused to cause any more friction by fighting her decision. I nodded as if agreeing with her idea. My silence kept the peace, but for how long? A volcano was about ready to blow. I was an adult, after all, but looked nothing like one. Again, the body I lived in deceived even my own mother. She couldn't see me. She couldn't see that I was capable. She couldn't see that I possessed the strength to take care of the family troubles. Couldn't she see that Jeanette and I were almost nineteen? Adults and able to help out? No. She saw us as a threat. Our concern for Dad confirmed her fears. We were against her.

The Dodge RV was a heater on wheels. It was way too confined a space for Dad to live in for the rest of his life! The pink trim led me to believe that Mom had originally bought the place for herself. *How long does Mom expect him to live in this tiny place?* Dad sat in a mini chair next to the door with his Bible on his lap and prayerful thoughts in his head. Five highlighter pens surrounded him like a security blanket. He had assigned each color a different meaning while he read the Bible, and highlighted each passage. Red was used to mark the bad things God promised Israel, green was used for the good things God promised Israel, blue was used for the things man did or would do, yellow was used for things of general interest, and finally, orange was used for the things that would happen in the future. His Bible was a chaotic jumble of color.

One by one, the pens fell to the floor whenever he moved. I watched him pick each marker up, painfully slowly, and place it back into his chair. Finally, all five were close at hand again. His life had dwindled down to zero. *How long will marking pens and a Bible comfort him?* Dad talked about the Bible and his Christian faith with anyone who would take time to listen. Since Mike was around, he told him his thoughts.

"There are events and processes in God's work. There are five events and one process: salvation, where a person is saved and will go to heaven; baptism, where a person is immersed in water and symbolically dies and comes to life as Christ did; filling of the Holy Spirit, where the spirit of God takes up residence in the believer; gifts, where God gives the gift to whom He wants and when He wants."

Mike nodded. "Hey, Dad. You should see this guitar I'm building now. I found a piece of driftwood on the beach. But you should see it, man! The rings in it are just beautiful!"

"And the last event is the Resurrection, which is still in the future and where all of the believers will be raised to everlasting life," Dad continued.

"I'm almost done with shaping the body of it. Man, you are going to be amazed when I'm finished!"

"Michael, do you know which process in God's work I most identify with?"

"It's almost as if the rings are in the shape of a heart."

"I can identify with becoming holy or perfect."

"Dad, do you still have your guitar?"

"Michael, Did you know there are four categories involved in learning? Heredity, understanding, attention, and repetition."

"What?"

"I don't intend on repeating them, Michael. You aren't listening."

They quickly ran out of things to talk about and the silence grew uncomfortable. Dad became resentful toward Mike for not sharing his Bible-based ideals. He feared that Mike was still following the wide, destructive path. On the other hand, David was making the *right* decisions, even though they were no longer confidants like in the good old days. He came by to fulfill tasks for Dad, but sharing scripture wasn't on the agenda. Mike wanted Dad to appreciate his interests, but Dad was too interested in the Bible to talk about what he believed to be frivolous things.

Dad compared himself with Job from the Bible. He talked about how God's grace makes up for unfair circumstances and turns a nobody, like him, into a somebody. I thought that God did the exact opposite, but didn't let on. Dad was also confident that God would give him what he needed at the moment. *Then why doesn't God do something now?* I felt guilty for having so little faith. *God please forgive my wicked thoughts. Forgive me for doubting your love for us. One day, I promise to match Dad's faith.*

Jeanette found the promised sack lunches inside the small refrigerator. Each one was marked for the day of the week. Frozen dinners were mysteriously placed in the freezer, seven in all.

Mike's refrigerator was still empty. He rode his bike to the nearest store—a mini-mart owned by a Native American family. I felt bad for him. He deserved more, but there was nothing I could do except watch this ordeal. During my visit, I drove him to the mart so he could buy a few groceries, using the twenty bucks I had on hand. Upon entering the small place, we saw a table with pairs of jeans on display. I could see in his eyes that he wanted to buy a pair for his girlfriend. I offered to pay for them, but wished he would buy himself a pair instead. That was Mike. He was more willing to give to someone else than to take care of his own needs. We went back to his place with jeans for Angie, two single cigarettes, a few candy bars and a six-pack of beer.

Dad's face dripped with sweat and his arms were damp and gummy when we returned. His Bible was still open for solace and his markers repeatedly fell out of place and onto the floor. It was a lost cause. When he picked up the last fallen marker, the others would spill onto the ground again.

"Girls," he admitted, "I've finished reading the book of John for the red pen cycle but I did not mark any red in the Bible because God did not make any threats to John. Jesus did most of the talking in the book of John and I only use the red pen when God makes a threat. In fact, it was so innocuous that I did not even pick up the red pen off the floor against the wall. In fact, the only thing that I highlighted was John 3:16 and that was with the yellow pen so I did not need the red pen at all. I did read the book of John even if it did not require much highlighting."

Jeanette and I promised to visit him twice a week and take him to church on Sundays. His strong faith in God was our solace. Wouldn't Jesus whisk away all his problems? After all, this was what Dad taught his adult Sunday School students for years, and not only did *they* believe him, *we* did too. Many books written by Christian authors kept him company during that time: *The Passover Plot, Men Who Knew Christ, Billy Graham and Seven Who Were Saved*. Dad was a huge fan of Billy Graham. The Southern evangelist proclaimed the Bible meant exactly what it said. Take it literally. To know God, one's inner self must totally surrender; we must immerse the ego in total submission to His Word. And with that condition, God reveals Himself as a living and enriching being. The miracle of Jesus is constant proof. During Graham's revival meetings, he told of wonderful miracles performed if we prayed and believed and really trusted. As soon as we present God with a problem, we'd get an answer. There was a catch though; answers would come *only* if our faith was real. No questions about it. Graham was so sure, he proclaimed excitedly that God had ordained him to be a preacher. He stated to his followers that his faith was *real* and that was that! No one could take his faith away. Look at what his strong faith had earned him—he was a prophet for Pete's sake! Dad's faith was as strong as Graham's. He not only intellectualized the Bible; he immersed his soul into it. When was he going to get his reward?

At the end of our visit, I told him to think positive thoughts.

"It's very difficult because I do not always feel positive," he replied. Once outside, we spied on him through the crack in the hospital-pink curtains. His head stumped down to his chest and the movement of his shoulders confirmed to us that he was not happy with the situation. We dashed back in to do what we could do to make him feel better.

Jeanette moaned on the way home, "There's got to be something we can do."

I agreed. Dad was depressed and I hated seeing him that way. So we concocted our own little plan: we would share Dad. Yes! Dad could stay with one of us on rotating weekends and, out of respect for Mom, he could stay in the camper during the week. Our hearts raced with excitement. Now some of the family stress would be eliminated. By sharing Dad, Sean and Danny wouldn't bear the entire weight of the family responsibility. Now all we had to do was figure out how we could mention this idea to Mom without causing her to feel left out or manipulated. We discussed the idea of asking her permission first. *Wait a minute. We're adults and living on our own—we shouldn't need to ask permission any longer.* If she needed help or wanted emotional support we would give our support to her as well.

Fall was approaching and the days in the camper got long and cold. After church, we dropped off Dad in his small place. Settling him into the mini, built-in recliner, I wondered if Mom had visited him yet.

"No. She had to go to chemotherapy for her cancer," Dad answered. "But David did come by, though, and filled my refrigerator."

I scanned his new home. To me, it was a prison where no life could flourish, not even a potted plant. The only sound of civilization was the deafening roar from the nearby highway. *Where the hell was God?* Mom was doing the best she could under the circumstances, but uneasy feelings of doubt, fear, and anger welled up from deep inside me. They weren't strangers. I had known these feelings for many years. They were at me consistently, playing games with my head and causing a war within my soul. Finally I said, "Dad, you need to write Mom a letter. It'll give her a chance to understand your feelings." My heart accelerated. "Maybe she'll see how depressed you are."

Dad nodded in agreement. "Jeannine, please get me a stamp and an envelope."

"Sorry Dad, if I get those things for you, Mom will suspect that the letter was my idea. I don't want to get into trouble." I reluctantly refused, then exited the motor home feeling guilty for not doing more to solve his problems and for leaving it up to him to get stamps.

Chapter 13

Walks to Remember

From my sister's diary:
9-18-91
   The nurse and social worker from my prenatal classes visited me. I finally got up enough courage to tell my nurse what was going on with Mom and Dad. I told her I feel like Mom is neglecting Dad, and that I don't have a very good relationship with her and can't really communicate with her. I told the social worker that Jeannine and I still have respect and empathy for Mom's situation. We visit her often and let her know what we've been doing and tell her not to be afraid to ask for help or if she needs anything to call us, and that we will be right over. My nurse advised me to call Adult Protective Services. So I called anonymously.

Mom called me on a chilly September evening. "You know, you've just ruined our family," she scolded. "A social worker came by the house today. The State has the power to take everything away." She dripped resentment with each word, but I remained calm and pretended that I didn't know what she was talking about.

"And that horrible letter! That was you girls' idea, wasn't it? Why would your father deceive me after I've taken care of him for six years? Six years! This is why I can't take care of him any longer. He betrayed me by writing that letter. I've done so much for him! It's his head injury. It's affected the judgment portion of his brain."

My heart fell. The solution I'd conceived had only made the situation worse. I wondered what Dad had written that would cause Mom to be so angry. Evidently, she thought of me as the enemy. "I don't know anything about the letter," I equivocated.

"Is this what I get for bringing you girls up in a nice home? I've taken you to Girl Scouts; you've had ballet, violin, and swimming lessons. In fact, you have been given just about everything you've ever wanted! I can't believe you're doing this to me!"

I had not wanted all those things. I had just wanted to be loved and accepted. I didn't want to be considered the enemy anymore, but my mouth wouldn't open to say how I truly felt, and it wouldn't open to say that I wanted her to be happy too. I promised myself never to fill my future children's lives with meaningless activities. I refused to teach them that getting ahead in this rat race by staying busy and competing were important. What was the point of being considered "better"? What harm would be done if we raised kinder or more accepting kids? Why not put value on *care* and *concern* for others? Why make life a competition? Why put that type of stress on a child? I would *see* and *value* my own kids as equals. I would teach them to find happiness by appreciating what they had and to strive for peace by appreciating others. I would inform them that they have the potential to change the world for the better.

"That social worker could take everything away if she thinks we're not living up to the state's standards. Your father and I could lose everything. Everything!"

The last thing I wanted was for her to lose everything. She felt that losing the house and all her belongings to the state would be worse than death.

A familiar, unemotional voice broke into my conversation with Mom. "It's obvious you're doing this for money."

Mom must have asked David to use the extension and to eavesdrop on our conversation.

"Money?" I yelled. David hit a nerve. I looked around the house where Sean and I lived. It lacked overstuffed boxes that reached the ceiling and mountains of clothes, shoes, jewelry and accessories. We could actually throw things away, without heartache. "If I wanted money, I would be on Mom's side. She's the one who's got control of all the money!" I was furious at his suggestion, and regretted that I couldn't say more in my defense. It was Mom who wanted control! It was Mom who kept the finances a secret! It was Mom who confided in David, but didn't think it was appropriate for Dad to confide in us!

But what made me the angriest was that she assumed we valued money like her. I was nothing like her!

That night Dad convinced his friend to drop him off at my house after Bible Study. When I saw him at my door, I couldn't turn him away.

"Dad, you can stay in our spare bedroom for the night." *Here I go again—deceiving Mom by following Dad's wishes.* As I settled him into the spare bedroom, I couldn't help but to think how much she would hate me for conspiring against her, even though I still hoped for a healed relationship.

Late in the night, I heard Mom knocking at my front door, "Jeannine, open up!" Somehow she knew Dad was there.

I tried to collect my thoughts, but they seemed sluggish. *Should I open the door and lie? Should I pretend to be asleep and wait for them to leave?* No, Mom could smell lies a mile away. *Would Mom eventually give up and leave?*

Pound, pound, pound.

Shoot! Sean was at work and wouldn't return until two thirty in the morning. His brother's family would see her crazy behavior from their side of the duplex.

Pound, pound, pound.

Geez, I wish that I had normal Asian parents, like Ly does. Anguish settled in the pit of my stomach. Halfheartedly, I touched the door handle, but Dad interrupted my frantic thoughts. "Jeannine, whatever you do, do not open the door!"

I tip toed to the spare bedroom and whispered through the door, "Dad trust me. Don't worry, it'll be okay… I'll talk to her."

Pound, pound, pound.

Maybe Mom's heart would soften after we talked about the situation; after all, I was her daughter, not an enemy. I cracked open the door before Sean's family heard the commotion. She shoved her way in.

"Where is he? Where is he?" She asked.

My heart sank. *Damn it! My mouth won't open!* Mom didn't wait for me to speak. She knew just where to go. Like a trained canine, she ignored the dark living room and sniffed her way into the spare bedroom.

"Grab him, David!"

David obeyed. Dad screamed, cried, did whatever he could do to fight them off. Mom pushed; David pulled. I watched in quiet horror, too distressed to say anything, and without the confidence in myself to argue with what they were doing.

Within a few minutes the three of them were gone, and there was only silence. I stared at Dad's empty Velcro tennis shoes left next to the bed and his abandoned reading glasses, wondering what I should do. I called Jeanette, but she felt just as helpless. Both of us definitely did not have the answers.

I tried to get my mind off what happened by turning on the television and sitting down. Obviously, Mom was in God's favor and Dad, Jeanette, and I were the undeserving souls suffering God's wrath. For some reason, we didn't deserve goodness. Our thoughts, insecurities and opinions were rarely taken into consideration. Why did she adopt us anyway?

As I mindlessly flipped the channels to the television, a hated childhood memory surfaced. Jeanette and I were about nine or ten.

Mom asked us to do a favor during the church service. "We're putting on a special event this evening," she said before slipping leather heels on, and then fiddled with the strap. "An organization is going to come to the church to talk to the congregation about saving the hungry children from the poor countries."

"Okay," we answered simultaneously and waited for her to continue.

"What we need you to do is walk up the aisle and hand the invitation to the pastor during the service, and then the pastor will read the invitation out loud to the congregation. You are going to be special messengers."

We looked at each other, "Okay." *That sounds nice.*

"You're going to have to wear a costume," she said, grabbing her Bible, then searching for the organ music.

"Okay."

"Who wants to be the boy and who wants to be the girl?"

"I don't know," I responded.

Jeanette shrugged her shoulders.

"Jeanette, how about you be the girl, and Jeannine, you go ahead and be the boy."

"I don't want to be the boy."

Mom pulled out one of Dad's dingy undershirts from a bag. "Jeanette, we need you to wear this."

Jeanette studied the flimsy material. "That's all?"

"Yes, it's long enough." Mom sighed, as if she wasn't expecting her to refuse. "It'll keep you covered, if that's what you're worried about."

"I don't want to. Do I have to?" Jeanette examined the shirt and noticed holes and grease stains. "What about these holes? People can see through them."

"Quit complaining. It is for a good cause." She searched the bag and pulled out Dad's stained dirty clothes. "Jeannine, you need to wear these overalls and your father's work cap."

Relieved that she didn't pull out another skimpy undershirt, I kept my mouth shut.

She checked her appearance in the mirror, then reached into the bag once more. "Now, once you get these on, you'll need to walk up the aisle, slowly, and hand the pastor this note. In fact, it would work even better if Jeannine limped a little or used some crutches." She snapped her fingers. "Shoot, I don't think the church has crutches. Jeannine, why don't you crawl? Yes, that's perfect! Jeannine, you crawl."

"I don't want to crawl. This is humiliating," I whimpered, but inwardly thanked God. I would rather crawl than wear one of Dad's skimpy undershirts.

"Why can't Michael or David do this?" Jeanette asked, wadding the undershirt into a crumpled ball.

"Because it'll have a more profound effect on the congregation if you two do it."

"Why?" I moaned.

"It's not proper to ask so many questions. Just do it. It won't take long." When she stood, she looked radiant as usual. She was ready to leave for church, but we weren't.

Changing into the pathetic outfits in the downstairs church bathroom, Jeanette and I prayed frantically for Mom to change her mind. Our determined prayers went ignored. We found ourselves in the back of the sanctuary ready to follow her instructions. During the service we did exactly what she told us to do. I crawled down the aisle next to Jeanette in her torn and skimpy T-shirt. The time it took us to move up the church aisle, dressed as beggars, seemed forever. Everyone sat silently while we performed our embarrassing act. Church members stared at us as if we were wounded animals or a charity case. As I crawled up the stairs to hand the pastor the letter, I realized I hated who I was. I hated my body and my olive colored skin. Jeanette did too. I could see it in her slouch. We wanted to be like everyone else. We didn't like being charity advertisements to the church or to our family, but beggars can't be choosers.

Ten years later, we still felt like beggars, particularly when we went the following Sunday, to plead with the pastors at the Presbyterian Church for answers about Dad's plight. *What does God want now? What do we have to do to win His approval, or at least gain His attention?* Not even the pastors had the answers.

"God has a plan. It is up to you to have faith." The junior pastor said. "Please, do not question God's will. Have faith. Remember it is not up to God to be on your side. It is up to you to be on God's side."

The senior pastor added, "This is an opportunity for you to honor your parents. Remember, honoring your parents is a commandment. Put your trust in the Lord; take it to the limit."

What happens if, by honoring one parent, we're dishonoring the other? This question dredged up another memory. Once while in grade school, Mom had driven one of the Cadillacs into a nearby ditch in the neighborhood. Dad told Jeanette and me to stay with them while they tried to sort out the mess; Mom told us to "go home and wait". They screamed back and forth to each other about the reasons behind contradictory commands. Jeanette and I started walking home, heard Dad's call, and headed back to the car. Then Mom ordered us back to the house and we went. We did this "back and forth" dance until we realized we had better do what Mom said. Now, years later, we were still in a quandary. Whom do we honor and obey?

Two weeks after Dad's abduction from my house, Jeanette received a surprising call from him. I heard that he was finally back home but living in a motorhome next to our house. I decided to visit

Dad, even though Mom would consider my action disrespectful. My heart beat at a frantic rate soon after I spotted the camper parked in the secondary driveway to our home, at the end of the cul de sac. *Dear Jesus, please make sure Mom does not see me,* I prayed. I hid my Nissan Sentra as discreetly as possible. The sharp red color burned against the giant green fir trees that stood as still as soldiers. I prayed again for Mom to be at the rear end of the house so she wouldn't notice the bright color through the thick black fence. My heart pounded. Suddenly the Northwest wind picked up and blew fiercely, causing the stiff fir trees to transform into rebellious hula dancers. I discreetly closed the car door, and tiptoed to the camper.

"Dad! What happened? Where have you been?"

"Joy put me down in Portland. I've been staying with her parents so the state can't bother us," Dad said.

I was relieved, but surprised. "Grandpa? He's ninety-one! How did he take care of you? Someone should be taking care of him!"

"I've been staying in the motorhome on the property. Last week, David and your mom came and brought me back." Then, not wishing to talk about it any more, Dad changed the subject. "I got up this morning assuming that David was going to reconnect the electrical power so I could resume writing on the computer, but he said he couldn't connect it because it required some sort of adapter to connect the cord to the outlet in the motorhome. As a result, he needs to purchase an adapter before he can connect it."

"Well, I'm glad you're doing okay, and at least Mike and Angie are here too, if you need someone to talk to. It's just weird that Mom and David live in the house, and you and Mike have to live in separate motorhomes next to the house."

"I guess Joy got the letter I wrote, and that is why she and David picked me up. David was driving my green Jaguar. Joy was mostly concerned about the social worker and the possibility that the State would take the house away and then she would have no place to live. She has questioned me repeatedly about what you girls talk about with me during the week that I've been here, but I haven't told her anything. I intend to live with Jeanette."

"We have to stay on her good side, so she'll consider letting you live with her."

"I slept in the sleeping bag, but without my bear, Pugsly. I particularly miss him."

I was surprised he was still attached to the stuffed bear I had bought him years earlier. "Don't worry. I'll get you another one if you want."

"I hope Jeanette still wants me to live with her because I am counting on it. Joy will probably be upset and say all sorts of unkind things, but I intend to do it anyway. I don't expect my action to be very popular with her, but I hope it will be with Jeanette."

"Don't worry. Jeanette still wants you to live with her. We plan to talk with Mom about the idea. If Mom saves money while you live with us, then I'm sure she'll agree. We have to make it sound as appealing as possible."

"I often wonder what she did with the money she got from the sale of our lake properties and all my vehicles. I don't see any of them anywhere. She even spent the inheritance I got from Auntie Lee. All of it!"

"Yeah, I don't know either. Of course, she would never tell me anything."

The camper door burst open with a bang. Mom appeared angry. She growled, "What are you doing here? You get out right now... and don't come back until you set up an appointment through me!" She slammed the door shut and I assumed she headed back toward the house, but she was really on the other side of the door listening to me.

Hateful words erupted from my mouth as soon as she left. "I hate her! I hope she dies from her cancer! All our problems would be over!" She was forcing me to take her on as an enemy. Mike and Angie stared at me with huge disbelieving eyes. How could I be so cold? It was easy. It seemed that Mom rarely cared for and respected my feelings.

This thought brought back the pain I felt when she took me to the store to purchase my first pair of glasses.

I could see out of my right eye, but only if the object was held two inches from my face. My left eye was getting worse by the minute. I had kept this a secret during elementary school. While taking the eye exam, I would slowly move the eye guard to the left so I could see out of both eyes while I called out the letters. When I reached eighth grade, the nurse detected that I was cheating. When she told me to keep my left eye covered, I finally admitted that not only could I not make out the large E at the top, I could not see the white chart. The vision in my right eye was 850/20. The left eye too was losing vision quickly.

When it came time to pick out frames with Mom, the sales lady went over her spiel about a "Two for One Deal" going on at the store. Mom frowned at the idea. She just kept saying, "Wait a minute. In order to get that so-called "Two for One Deal," I'll have to pay for that extra feature. So that doesn't make it such a great bargain, now does it?"

"Yes, but your daughter will have two pairs of glasses instead of one."

"Yes, but I'll still be paying more… for that extra feature," Mom said, without a smile.

I picked up the red large-shaped frames, put them over my face and looked in the mirror. Horrors! I had turned into the stereotypical Asian geek straight from a comic book or from some racist movie! My right lens was an inch thick. It was so thick, my eyeball looked like a fake black pearl. I could see myself clearly in the mirror for the first time in my life. Two sets of teeth hung out of my mouth like white dandelion puffballs. This was more than I could bite. "There's no way I'm wearing these to school," was my immediate reaction. Mom glanced into the mirror with me. "You look fine," she said and pulled out her purse to pay for the frames.

My shoulders drooped at the finality of her words "You look fine." I was stunned and silent. I *didn't* look fine and my feelings meant nothing to her. I wished she had asked me how I felt and had empathy for my pain and my insecurities. I wasn't a nerd! I told myself that I should consider myself lucky because I was living in a good American home. Anything is better than the streets of Korea. How appreciative I should be for receiving God's grace; he had restored my eyesight! On the other hand, He had also punished me with a comical appearance—an appearance that caused classmates to turn away in amused disgust. Being unhappy about God's decisions with my life was a sin. I had no control, except of course to accept God's grace and His decisions for my life.

118

I followed Mom out of the store cringing under the weight of the big thick red glasses. Details. There were so many details in life that I had missed without glasses. I didn't know I was blind, until I could see. I noticed that the maple trees were no longer a green mass, they actually had individual leaves on them, and flowers were no longer only colorful fuzz, they each had personality. In the mall, I noticed each piece of jewelry, each fabric headband, each rhinestone barrette, and each beaded necklace. I could see people too. Each person had a separate face; they weren't just washed out shadows. I could see what kind of mood they were in: if they were mad, in a hurry, happy, or avoiding eye contact. My early years had been a blur. For years I had traipsed around blind and ignorant, trying to make sense of what I saw. In spite of my clearer vision, I still grumbled to myself. "If only Mom had bought that special feature. If only she cared about my feelings."

As I sat in Dad's motorhome, I realized that I'd outgrown my obsession about how I looked, but I still cared about how my mother perceived me. I did not want her to treat Jeanette and me—her "two in one deal" as outsiders.

. Finally, in October, we heard rumors through Mike that Mom had finally located an adult family home for Dad to live in—and that it was our fault. We had ruined Mom's life, maybe even her reputation. She was on a fixed income and now she was forced to spend more money than necessary for Dad's care, she complained. Worse, her assets might have been taken away. *Thank God! Dad won't have to spend the winter in the motor home. Maybe God does answer prayers.*

The adult family home was located in an older, but prestigious housing development 20 miles south of Seattle, Washington. Dad lived in his own room. He had all the basic necessities: a recliner, bed, Macintosh computer given to him by a neighbor, encyclopedias and the Bible. When he wasn't studying the Word of God, he was typing Christian thoughts on the Mac, with one working finger. We added little things to the room to help him feel at home. I bought a fake slug carved out of wood, lacquered to look slimy, and set it by his window; Jeanette brought him religious books and edible goodies; David came by frequently with items for his Macintosh computer and other knickknacks.

Dad assumed Mom's infrequent visits meant that she was still uncomfortable with his disabled body. He was right. In spite of this, he insisted that we keep the faith. A miracle was bound to happen. While waiting impatiently to hear from Mom, he read from a set of encyclopedias to fill time, and continued looking for answers in his Bible. Dad's faith in Christianity grew tenfold. I was amazed.

In a phone call, Mom told us, "I just don't understand why your father doesn't feel like he belongs. Your father is not the same, girls. You have to understand this. He's had a terrible head injury. The doctors say he'll never fully recover. The judgment portion of his brain was affected. I really should show you girls your father's hospital records so you can, once and for all, comprehend the severity of his head injury. He can no longer make sound decisions for himself."

I held my tongue; Jeanette let Mom's words bounce off her. Neither one of us had the courage to tell her how we felt. Voicing thoughts caused disruptions within the family. Telling her our truths would only cause pain.

"Girls," Dad announced from inside the small foreign-looking room, "This is just a temporary arrangement. I'm slowly healing. I can feel it. I'll be home soon and I'll be able to take care of your mother."

"Well, at least you're safe and warm now," Jeanette said, ignoring his comment.

"And you're fed three times a day. Geez, Dad, you're spoiled!"

Dad had time on his hands. *So much time!* He began using this time to write letters to Mom, hoping to win her attention and her affection:

2-2-92
Dear Joy,
The following are the ways in which you have demonstrated that you no longer love me, even if you refuse to admit it or are not knowledgeable of it:
One day in the RV, I had no heat or food.
You have taken me out of my own home.
You no longer get my opinion on important issues.

You don't bother to tell me when you are going out of town.

You stopped taking my 2:00 P.M. calls.

I missed church all the time I was at home.

You spend as little time with me as possible.

You no longer consider my activities as important as yours.

You did not send me to my mother's funeral.

You are only interested in saving your face; mine is expendable.

You were concerned that the social worker would force you out of the house, so you got me out of the state.

You don't mind separating me from my toys as long as yours are unaffected.

You only consider me as an income.

You only come to visit me when it is convenient for you.

You have apparently rearranged your priorities and I am a low one.

I may be injured and have reduced tactile capability, but I am not stupid. The injury did not reduce my mental capability. Also, I am improving and someday I may be able to function again.

Allen

2-10-92

Dear Joy,

I guess that in the end your lack of love is my fault. I should have been more aggressive when I had the chance. It is probably too late to do anything about it, but I want you to know there will never be anyone else.

As a human I am motivated to get even, but as the Bible says, I am at fault and I am willing to accept the blame. I am sorry I have let it go so far, but you have to remember I am only human and I do a lot of dumb things.

I didn't do a very good job of complying with 1 Cor. 13. Most of my first letter was a list of what I considered to be your faults, and I am sorry about that. How could I have been so stupid? I guess I was trying to get revenge instead of demonstrating love. Anyway, I want you to know that I accept the total blame for the situation and there will never be another.

Allen

Chapter 14

Runaway Bride

My four year relationship with Sean was not perfect. We still had a ways to go before we would fully accept the differences between us. Yet, he held no doubts that I was the one for him. From the very first date, Sean was attracted to me. The attraction motivated him to work harder at his job so he could support us. He made a modest income, but he knew that by working hard we would reap rich rewards in the future. Sean was fair and honest and he wanted a life with me. I respected that. His unconditional love freed me from the box I was in.

Surprisingly, Sean knew I was pregnant before I did. He could feel the lump in my stomach, and knew it had nothing to do with my family troubles. "Jeannine, I know you're afraid, but the timing is perfect. After the baby is raised, we'll still be young enough to travel the world."

"But, I'm going to hate the looks people will give me when they see me pregnant and then a mother. They're going to think I'm too young to be a mother."

"Who cares what other people think about you? Why do you care so much?"

"I don't know. Maybe you're right. I mean, look at Mom and Dad. They waited until they were in their forties before they started a family and look at us now. We're far from perfect."

"See what I'm talking about? Age doesn't matter. It's how we feel that matters. We're going to be great, loving parents. We've been together for four years already. Four years! That's a lot. You're not in high school anymore. You're nineteen and I'm twenty-five. And we're finally out of the apartment."

My initial conflict about being pregnant came from feeling the disapproval from society, God and worst of all, from Mom. *I'm an adult! Why do I feel like a child who had done great wrong? Is it because my nature is sinful?*

"Jeannine," Sean said, "If you think we should get married, if that would make you happy, we can, you know," he said. "I'll buy you a diamond ring too. You can have anything you want."

"No. I don't want or need a diamond ring. Having stuff doesn't solve problems. The problem is I'm not sure if I'm ready to have this baby." I kept the remaining fears to myself. Sean wouldn't understand my concerns.

The first months were miserable. I suffered bouts of morning sickness, worried about Sean not being a Christian and heartsick about not being able to call Mom. More than anything, I wanted her to approve of our marriage. Worse was the thought that she would be disappointed in me, because a baby out of wedlock was a sin. Insecurities about telling her that I was pregnant gnawed at my conscience. *She's going to think I'm as worthless as Jeanette for getting pregnant so young, but if I don't tell her, she'll never forgive me.* Mom didn't want me to grow up so fast; she feared that I would make the wrong decisions and she believed I was too young to get married. She wanted me to have the life that she had made for herself. A Christian husband would lead to happiness, security and traditions. If I made the wrong decision, who knows what would happen? It never occurred to me that I was fine the way I was, and that my dependence on her approval cost me happiness that I could have immediately claimed.

Sean tried to reason with me. "Jeannine, listen. Is anyone ever ready to have children? My mom had ten children. None of us was planned. That's life. We just need to learn to work with the situations that come our way. When the war broke out, my mom didn't plan for her three oldest sons to leave home either. Don't let surprises scare you. No matter how much you try to do things *right*, something wrong or unexpected will always happen. You have to adjust your mind to it. You have to keep going. That's how I survived when I came to America."

My fears were irrational. Sean had recently been promoted to a management position in a large company. He loved me and intended to support me forever. Wasn't *that* considered love? But was his love

124

real? A young person's emotions, according to some religious zealots, were dangerous and ungodly. *How does one differentiate real love from fake love?*

More challenges presented themselves: there was a religious clash in terms of upbringing. We were, in the eyes of God, unequally yoked. Love outside of Christianity did not have a solid foundation and was doomed.

Those who didn't know Sean, saw him as serious and a bit unfriendly. He was systematic, orderly, and dedicated to his work, always on time and followed tasks through with a dependable, steady and persevering quality. Supporting me was his priority. I, on the other hand, was full of ideas, but rarely followed through with them, especially after discovering how much work was involved. Sometimes, so many ideas swirled about at once, that I ended up accomplishing nothing. I was a talker; he was an avid listener. He complained that I immediately trusted people and then got easily disillusioned. I complained that he forced people to prove themselves before he gave them a chance. A long time would pass before we figured out that we were the yin and the yang, and that together, we were actually very well balanced.

"It's very important for us to get married in the Christian church and I won't have it any other way," I demanded.

"Okay. If that'll make you happy, we can do that. I love you."

All I could manage to sputter was, "Me too." I didn't say *love* very often. I had very few memories of Mom giving me a hug or telling me she loved me. Even then, I sort of just echoed the words, but without the passion it deserved.

Though I didn't show my affection to Sean very often, I felt lucky that he loved me. Deep down in my soul I knew he would make a dedicated spouse. Could I be as dedicated? Somehow I needed to convert him to Christianity so our marriage would be right in the eyes of God.

"I left my family when I was fourteen. Then I found you, and I felt like I had found a family again. A family I belonged to," Sean confided. "If I lost you... it would kill me."

I was profoundly moved. His words left me mute.

"It wasn't easy. I came over on a small boat without my family. In Vietnam, my dad got hit by a grenade and lost sight in one eye. My parents didn't want anything like that to happen to us. That's why they sent us over here for a chance life in America. It was hard for them to let us go. On the boat, we went without water for days and we couldn't drink the seawater. I thought for sure I was going to die. There were many boats and we even got robbed by pirates. Many people even got raped and then killed for their belongings. Then when we got to Malaysia, I thought I had it made—everyone on the boat did. There was so much hope for a new safe future without the risk of being shot at for being in the wrong place at the wrong time. But once I arrived in America, I realized that I didn't have anything except my clothes. I didn't even have a bed to sleep on. Thank God I found my two older brothers. They came here before I did. We ended up sleeping on mattresses that we found in garbage dumpsters. At least we had a place to stay. Another Vietnamese family let us stay in their garage."

"That's awful."

"I don't regret any of it. It was hard, but it made me strong. Look where I am today. You know it takes hard work to make a living. A good, rich life doesn't come easy. You know, you may think I'm too serious, but I've got—"

"Courage and strength." I said, although many more words came to mind. He was also loyal, honest, and tenacious. Yet, as much as I respected him, those traits wouldn't get him into heaven. What he really needed was a personal relationship with Jesus and it was my moral duty, as a Christian, to convert him.

Unaware of my missionary zeal, Sean continued to share his life story. "Then my brother enrolled me into junior high. I didn't even speak English."

"God, that must have been hell."

"I learned that the most important thing was to understand the language. Once, while waiting for the bus in the junior high school parking lot, a boy yelled at me. He said, "Stop staring at me!" I had no idea what he was saying. I couldn't figure out the word 'staring' so I just concentrated on remembering that word so I could ask my brother later. The guy pushed me down and my arm broke. The other

126

students just stood there laughing. They thought I was the stereotypical Asian nerd."

"Weren't you furious?" I remembered how hideous adolescence was. Going through it without parents to fight for you and in a totally alien environment, without the ability to speak the language would be terrifying. It was mind-boggling.

"Yeah, but there was nothing I could do. When stuff like that happens, you can't change it. So you just have to live with it and work around it. I didn't even tell my brother until later that night when my arm swelled up."

"No wonder you're never the first to laugh at anything. And you rarely start a conversation. You don't talk unless absolutely necessary."

"What are you talking about? I laugh. I talk."

"What I mean is you're observant. You watch people first, before you interact with them, before you get emotionally involved."

"I wouldn't say that."

"Well, some of my friends think you're too serious because you don't really smile very much."

"I don't?"

"Not really."

"I smile." He gave me a forced grin.

"I'm not saying you *have* to laugh, talk or smile. I'm just saying you don't do those things very often."

"Thanks a lot. Is that supposed to be a compliment?"

"What I'm trying to say is that people misunderstand. There's nothing wrong with not showing emotion. It's just that other people might not like you because of it."

"Jeannine, you really care too much about what other people think of you."

"No, I don't." I picked up the telephone receiver and whispered, "Shhh, I've got to call the pastor. I don't want him to think that we're a young immature couple who wants to get married."

Sean rolled his eyes.

When the pastor got on the phone, I asked him how soon he could marry us.

He stuttered for a moment before answering, "In view of the tremendous importance of marriage, all couples must attend a series of marriage counseling sessions."

Counseling? What if he finds out Sean isn't a Christian? I was too afraid to ask if he would still marry us because, deep inside, I already knew what the answer would be. "How long does that usually take?"

"Usually a few months. And it's not possible to perform a wedding until all the sessions are completed."

Shoot! It'll take too long. By the time we're done with the sessions I'll be huge! "Oh, well. See we wanted to get married on Valentine's Day."

"I'll tell you what. Since it's a small church, maybe I can shorten the process. Valentine's Day is a busy time of the year. In fact, I've got three weddings booked on that day already. The sixteenth is open, though. Perhaps, I could fit you in then."

The date sounded great, so I immediately agreed.

"Sean, whatever you do, do not slip up and tell them I'm pregnant!" I emphasized after the phone call.

"Duh!" Sean mimicked my American slang. "Oh my God! My Dad was Catholic and my Mom is Buddhist! Like, don't worry! I know the rules."

"Obviously you don't or you wouldn't have gotten me pregnant." I prodded him playfully. Secretly, I prayed for our marriage. *God, please make me strong so I can lead him to You.* "You better keep your mouth shut about us living together, too. I hope you know we're living in sin."

"You might be, but I'm not. And why are you worried? Didn't you tell me that I never talk, smile or laugh?"

"No, I didn't."

"Yes, you did."

"Did I?" I remembered our earlier conversation and I felt like an idiot. "God, I hate it when you use stuff I've said against me. I just don't want the pastor to find out I'm already pregnant. I don't want him to think I'm a sinner. Okay? Is that too much to ask?"

"You *really* care too much about what people think of you."

I was filled with anxieties. Was I stubborn. When was I going to learn? When was I going to quit being so egotistical? When was I going to realize it is better to love than to be right and follow the rules? My Christian roots declared that we were at war with the secular world. Anything or anyone outside Christianity was considered wrong and dangerous. If Jesus' name was not in the mix, no consideration should be granted. All other countries, cultures, and concepts would lead us astray from the lighted path. My moral duty, as a Christian, was to continue walking the path my parents cleared for me. In order to honor them, I must follow their footsteps. I didn't dare throw away old ties and start anew. It did not occur to me that I could break the chain of pain. It did not occur to me that I had the right to do so.

Sean was not aware that there was a battle to be won. He had never sung:

> *Onward Christian soldiers going onto war,*
> *with the cross of Jesus going on before!*
> *Christ the royal master leads against the foe.*
> *Forward into battle, see his banner go!*
> *Hell's foundation quiver at the shout of free.*
> *Brothers lift your voices, loud your anthems reign.*
> *At the sign of triumph, Satan hosts a fleet.*
> *On dance Christian Soldiers onto victory!*

Those were words that had echoed across America, sung by many generations. Many battles were fought for God and in Jesus' name. Was God's ego so huge that he stood on the sidelines and cheered for the team who used his name the most? Did he jump up and down in joy whenever a team gained victory over another? Or did he know the value in all the participants? I was a willing participant in the game called WAR. I was one who agreed that we Christians were right. I failed to see the tragedy from the murder of 6 million Native Americans for the belief in WAR.

The mandatory Christian marriage literature finally arrived by mail. I skimmed through it and noticed something that could prevent us from getting married. It said: "In view of God's clear command not to be 'unequally yoked together with unbelievers,' we will not marry a believer with a nonbeliever. See 2 Corinthians 6:12-18; Amos 3:3;

and 1 Corinthians 7:39. Also, we will not marry couples who are not Christians and only in unusual cases, will we marry couples who are not members of our assembly."

Thank God, I was a member of the Presbyterian Church, but somehow Sean was going to have to pretend he was, at least, related to the Christian Church somehow. He needed to lie in order to be accepted. How ironic! Religion had its grip on me and wouldn't let my fears go. Religion was right! All of us were natural born sinners and it was my responsibility to convince Sean of this sad fact by making him lie.

He listened to what the pastor had to say and attended a couple of sermons. During the sermon, the pastor talked about a life before Christ, when we are born with stony hearts that only want to sin. When we accept Christ, the hard shell, the part of us that likes to sin, is discarded. Jesus secures our freedom. What if Sean didn't grasp the importance of being saved? What if Sean couldn't see that by being tied to religion, we were really free? We sat up on the balcony facing the pastor and listening to all the rituals. I closed my eyes and hoped the vibrant hues from the large stained glass windows and the angelic melodies from the choir might inspire my soon-to-be husband to turn his soul over to the Lord, Jesus Christ. If the music couldn't suck him in, then just like the pastor had forewarned, his heart was made of stone.

My nervousness brought on a wave of morning sickness. Sean squeezed my hand and wrote a note saying that if he could, he would give me his strength and energy and infect himself with my nausea. It meant a lot, but he still wasn't a Christian, so I prayed for his conversion. *Please God, touch Sean. Make the pastor's messages ring true within his soul. Make him understand the importance of being saved so he won't burn in the everlasting fiery furnace.*

We listened to more sermons addressing the importance of choosing Jesus over Satan, because Jesus was Freedom. "Careful," the pastor warned. "Satan has us by his leash. All other religions are wrong and can lead us astray." More lectures suggested ways to be friendly to non-Christians.

The junior pastor invited us to his office for our premarital counseling session. He greeted us with a big smile. "Just call me Pastor Abraham." He extended a hand first to Sean and then to me.

"You have a Bible name," I replied.

"Yes, you're right. My parents named all their children from the Bible." He laughed.

"When I was a child I was called Abe, but once I started serving the Lord, well, let's just say, my associates were impressed by my offerings."

"Oh," I said. Sean hadn't heard the Bible story where Abraham's faith was so strong, he almost killed his son, because God told him to.

Pastor Abraham misunderstood Sean's lack of emotion and joked. "Oh, no, I didn't sacrifice one of my sons. Let's just say the sacrifice came out of my pocket book... I'm named after my grandfather and father, too. They've spread the good news for many generations. Welcome." He pointed to two plump chairs near his desk. "Have a seat! Get comfortable!"

Sean shook his hand again and said, "Thank you, sir."

His respect for authority reminded me of the day we were pulled over by the police. My friend and I shared the front seat, another girl scrunched in the rear of the car, where the seats had been folded. We must have looked like a bunch of no good teenagers cruisin' the streets in a rebellious red 280Z. When the officer approached, I was surprised by Sean's civil manner: "No sir. Yes sir." Typical American teenagers would be full of attitude and excuses.

"So, let's see the ring!" the pastor sang.

"Oh, it's just a gold band. I didn't want a diamond. I really don't understand the need to wear so much money around my finger, and plus it might catch on things." I twisted my fingers into knots. "I'd rather get a tattoo around my ring finger to signify my love." I nervously added, "A tattoo can't get lost or stolen."

The pastor placed his hand on his chin and looked at me. After soaking in the information, he jabbed Sean like they were ol' football buddies. "Most young ladies want to have the carats. How'd you get so lucky?"

No advocate for excessive banter, Sean remained quiet. I filled the silence. "We're quite nontraditional. Sean is the only guy I know who doesn't like football and loves to shop and I guess I'm the only female who doesn't want a diamond ring."

"Let's get down to business, shall we?" the pastor declared, and folded his hands suggesting prayer. "Let us pray."

I nudged Sean to follow. "Dear Heavenly Father, thank you for sending your beloved son Jesus to be here with us as I guide these kids into a holy relationship with You. Help them to realize that Jesus' way is the road to salvation. Amen."

He talked about the Christian war against Satan. In order to win victory, we must never lose sight of our prize, Jesus Christ. Marriage is one area where many of the greatest battles are fought. We must be on God's side in this battle. Although the policy concerning marriage may not be popular in the secular world, Christians must never make any concessions or exceptions to God's principles. Satan will do everything in his power to destroy this relationship. After a moment of thought, he advised. "We should not laugh at the devil. He is a creature of vast superior intelligence, brilliant reasoning, and lofty. Following him may sound like fun, but..." the pastor chuckled. "Eventually, it's hell!"

Sean didn't laugh as expected. My soon-to-be husband didn't move a muscle; no, he hadn't heard the *Good News*. He didn't know that very few were going to heaven and the vast majority were going to smolder in hell forever.

I nodded to the rhythm of the pastor's words, hoping I could explain it all to Sean in the car. Perhaps my fantasy of converting him would be realized soon.

Unfortunately, Sean didn't understand the importance in the messages even after our many discussions. He said that I was free to believe whatever I wanted, but Jesus wasn't for him.

"Jeannine," He added. "My father was Catholic and my mother was Buddhist. Both were good and loving. If Christianity is so great, people would see the greatness and you wouldn't need to force them into it."

"But Christianity isn't about logic. You can't see the truth of it until you're actually immersed in it," I tried to explain. I wasn't going to give up. This was about his salvation. If we didn't believe, we would dwell in hell forever.

"Jeannine, I'm not trying to pull you out. If you need it, that's fine. But I don't."

"What's your purpose then?" I asked.

He thought for a moment. "My purpose is to experience life, peace and happiness."

"The only way you can have those is through Jesus." I had to convince him in a "fast food" type of way, that Christianity was the wisest choice. The wedding date was approaching.

"I wouldn't say that. I'm happy now. I don't need Jesus to be happy." Smiling he added, "Look at you. You've got Jesus in your heart and you're one of the most miserable people I know."

I quickly became defensive. "How would you know? You've never immersed yourself in Jesus. You don't know what true joy or freedom is."

He remained calm during my frantic attempts and told me not to worry. We were just fine. He didn't see the need for his salvation, which caused me sorrow.

I managed to keep my concerns regarding what my new role would be like as a submissive wife to myself. According to the beliefs of the church, the husband was supposed to be the head of the household. I wanted to know why women had to obey their husbands. I wanted to know why women couldn't be Christian leaders. I wanted to know why women were considered less. I thought the entire concept was unfair. I didn't think the pastor would understand my curiosity. During our dating days, my worst fear was that Sean would mold me into a submissive housewife. I overreacted to little incidences that seemed unequal, like who should do the household chores when both of us were working. These questions caused tension between us, which could cause future trouble. I didn't want to be a stereotypical Asian wife. I didn't want to "obey" my husband like the Christian vows assumed. I wondered if I would be able to say, "I will love and obey" during our ceremony.

In spite of this inner turmoil, we managed to pass all the marriage sessions. Luckily for our baby, Pastor Abraham was a generous talker and Sean was a big listener. Sean's lack of faith went undetected and our newborn baby was not considered a bastard in the eyes of the church. During the ceremony, like a good little girl, I submissively said "I will love and obey" even though my heart was not in it and I wondered why I had to say it. As luck would have it, Sean was not brought up with a chauvinistic attitude towards women. He had watched the movies portraying powerful female fighters. He would tell me that the only thing he expected was for me to be happy. In order to improve our relationship, I needed to let go of the resentment I felt being cast as submissive. Instead of being loud and obnoxious concerning my thoughts and ideas, I needed to accept reality, and then treat myself and my new husband with compassion and understanding. After our marriage on February 16th, Dad shared our marriage news with Mom through a letter:

Dear Joy,

When Sean's parents arrive from Vietnam, Jeannine and Sean will have a big wedding, and you and others will be invited.

In spite of everything that has happened, I still love you and always will. You will always be my Punkin. I made a promise to you and GOD, and I intend to keep it regardless of the discomfort of the moment.

I am sorry for my injury and my lack of support of you, and I appreciate all your effort. I am sorry that I now have to live separately and am unable to care for the house and cars. Try to forgive me.

Allen

After reading his letter, Mom called me on the phone. "Jeannine, if you had at least told me, I would have paid for your wedding dress," she said.

"I'm sorry," I answered.

Sean didn't understand the importance of apologizing. He said, "Why does your family treat each other like crap and then think its all okay just because you say two words? Whatever you do, don't say 'I'm sorry' to me. Just treat me nice."

I didn't see the significance in his comment. All I could do was think about Mom; she probably had had dreams of a big wedding for her daughters, like those shown on television. Creating an ideal family, with happy celebrations and traditions had been her motive underlying our adoption. She told us several times after Dad's head injury that it made her sad to think that he would not be able to walk us down the aisle. I, on the other hand, never fantasized about that image. Being unable learn about parenting skills from Mom bothered me more. At least I had *The New Student Bible* to give me answers.

To make our relationship worse, I told David, out of spite, that Sean and I would eventually have a big celebration and invite all the people we *didn't* like. That comment killed my chance of winning Mom's affection. Now, I was really the enemy. Mom was right. I was going down the wrong path. Through the rest of my pregnancy, I prayed for forgiveness. Despite my worries about my sin, God gave us a healthy, beautiful daughter. She was born September 21, 1992, and we named her Vanessa. Her birth helped me to discover the joys of identifying the similarities between us, the fun part of being a parent. Already, I could see that our baby had Sean's features. She was the most beautiful thing I had ever seen. I could finally understand why Mom had a special connection with David and not with Jeanette and me. We looked nothing like her; we didn't possess any of her characteristics and we were not from her being. Why she didn't have the connection with Mike continued to confuse me.

I thanked God for answering my prayers with an easy delivery and a healthy baby daughter. Strange, how God answers some prayers and ignores others. Now I wondered if He could ever heal my relationship with Mom, heal her cancer and heal Dad's head injury.

Except for a few bumps here and there, Sean and my marriage was smooth. Sean worked full time in the garment industry, slowly moving up the ranks. He supported the idea that I find a job. Both of his sisters-in-law owned acrylic nail beauty salons that seemed very successful. His older brother encouraged me to go to beauty college while I was in high school. "There's big money in this business. Very little schooling!" he said. I believed him after watching how they lived. They always offered to pay for things as if money flowed effortlessly into and out of their pockets. They had built their fortunes from nothing.

Once I graduated from high school, Sean paid for my education at the *American Beauty Academy* and I received an Esthetician's

License. In 1992, I found a job in a successful full service salon called *Shear Magic Hair Design* as the only nail technician. Kristin, a hip thirty-year-old, owned the salon and understood the complexities of being a working mother. Her two sisters were hairdressers and their mother helped out by answering the phones and taking care of clients while four other hairdressers and an electrologist worked together to build up the clientele. The owner's mother operated a gift shop inside, which filled the salon with warmth. Souvenir items included fruit-smelling bath salts, silk flowers, greeting cards, coffees and teas. I enjoyed going to work each day and being surrounded by fragrant smells and flowery decor. I felt lucky to find such a warm, caring, family-owned business to work in, and also had fun socializing with my clients. I was given the freedom to decorate the manicuring room any way I wanted, and to work the hours I needed, which came in handy while Vanessa was in preschool and when scheduling Dad's various dental and doctor appointments.

By working in the salon, I learned how the real world worked. I realized, for the first time, that the relationship I had with my mom was not normal and that her thought processes were somewhat limited. Maybe her way of thinking wasn't necessarily right. While observing the owner and her sisters at work, I saw for the first time what a sense of family really meant. The family who owned the salon wanted the best for each other. Their mother nurtured each daughter, using unconditional love; even during times of disagreements. She was considered a safe person to go to whenever a problem occurred. Once in a while, I wondered what it would be like to have a trusting mother, or even a mother who prodded and teased. Jeanette and I had yearned for that mother-daughter bond. Instead, Mom had felt duty-bound—as if we were burdens, as if we were her crosses to bear. I wasn't jealous of their happy family unit, but I *did* want what they had: a sense of belonging, a sense of unconditional love, and a sense of home. I rarely felt that way with my family. If Jeanette and I hadn't been adopted, Mom's life might have been a lot easier. She must have felt boxed into a corner because of us and we were boxed in because of her, longing to love, yet unable to reciprocate.

Chapter 15

Happy Days

From my sister's diary (1992)

Jeannine apologized to Mom for not inviting her to the wedding and asked for forgiveness. We're on good terms now. Jeannine and I feel it is time to ask Mom a question that has stirred in our minds for a very long time. We invited her out to lunch and asked if Dad could live with me while I attended college. We told her that it would benefit the entire family. Mom would only have to pay half as much as what she was paying at the adult family home, it would help pay for my college, and Dad would be with family. Mom agreed with the idea! And Dad will be moving in the next month.

I'm filled with mixed emotions, worried about my relationship with Danny, being responsible for Dad, being a good mother to Dustin, working to make ends meet, and succeeding in school.

Dad moved into our three-bedroom apartment. He is very happy—in fact, all of us are. His small bedroom is cozy and nice. I'm pleased he's finally with family. Jeannine visits twice a week, and helps with meals when I'm busy. Every Sunday we take Dad to church. On Mondays, Dad's friend takes him to Bible Study Fellowship (BSF), and I hired a second-year Occupational Therapy Assistant student to give Dad a bath and take him out for a treat, on Saturdays. I feel good because Dad has constant stimulation and his schedule is set up nicely. I even taught him how to wash his clothes and make his coffee. I enjoy his company, and sometimes when he's gone to BSF on Mondays I go into his room and stare at his chair because I miss him.

I talk to him whenever Danny and I get into fights. Dad has a good attitude, though, sometimes it irritates me when I go into his room upset from an argument and he looks at me and laughs. What's so funny? I want sympathy! But I only get laugher. Why did he see the situation as so funny? This kind of thing is what upsets Mom, but I think it's better to laugh and take things lightly than to cry and get all depressed; it's part of his survival. Mom says it's due to his brain injury and impaired judgment. Occasionally Dad gets depressed about losing Mom, but I try to be there to talk to him and make him feel better.

Dad, Jeannine, Danny, and I discussed the money situation. We think that Dad should have some spending money for personal items. I'm sick of using my money! I'm barely making it, myself. He needs toothpaste, shampoo, and he wants some Bible software.

I'm deathly afraid to go to Mom with the idea. I'm too scared to even put Dad's own letters to her in the mailbox. She has control over me and I can't explain why. I'm twenty for God's sake, and I should be over her control by now. It's going to be difficult to tell her Dad needs a little spending money. She's going to hate me. She already disapproves of my unplanned pregnancy and our unmarried status. I feel like a bad child.

Over the phone, Mom tries to reinforce to me again and again that Dad's head injury has caused his impaired judgment. She says that he can't take care of any sum of money, especially without supervision. I agree with her just to keep the peace and stay out of the middle of their problems, but I feel guilty for not defending Dad. I have a completely different impression of him. He just wants attention and some control and independence back in his life. He's lost almost everything, and now he wants some money for a few necessities. *Is that too much to ask?*

School is beginning and I started my Occupational Therapy program. I flunked my first Anatomy/Physiology test. I'm so depressed, doubt runs rampant in my mind.

I decided against quitting and studied my butt off. School is tough, but God sent me two school friends to help me along the way—Amy and Angela. They make school bearable. Most days during lunch break, I drive twenty minutes back home, fix Dad lunch, and rush back to school, barely making it to my next class. I also go home, clean house, take care of Dustin and Dad, and study for hours. It's putting a strain on my relationship with Danny.

I learned some Occupational Therapy hands-on treatments that I practice on Dad. He's my guinea pig with such things as transfers, bed mobility, adaptive equipment, and dressing techniques. I also use his computer for completing assignments, and sometimes Dad types them out for me. I told him it's a therapeutic exercise.

Dad always encourages me. I want to open an Adult Day Center (ADC) for people with disabilities—one that the clients can run, and make major decisions so they will feel important, like they still have some control over their life. I think many disabled people feel as though others don't trust them to make important decisions. I want to change that. Dad says I can do it. I even drew up a floor plan of the facility and showed it to my college pals. Jeannine and I were thinking of names for the business and came up with "Happy Days—walk-ins and roll-ins welcome!" We even found the perfect vacant building next to Jeannine's work. When I visit her, we peek through the windows and imagine all sorts of things. There's plenty of open space for wheelchairs and activities, but we're a little concerned about the huge heavy doors. It'll be hard for people in wheelchairs to open them by themselves.

We're excited and passion stirs every time we discuss the idea. Can I make enough capital to realize my aspirations? The idea of an adult family center never leaves my mind. I think it will be the fastest and easiest way to get started. I keep this idea in the back of my mind daily during and after school. Jeannine and I work on the business plan whenever we can get together.

Dad was finally given his Power of Attorney back. The attorney even came to the apartment while I was in school. Mom found out. When I got home I saw Mom crying and leaving Dad's room. She asked me why he was doing this to her—she took care of him for all those years. I did my best to console her, but I don't want to get involved. I stayed as neutral as possible, but it's difficult, because I love both of them and I want fair treatment.

I guess Mom felt my sincerity. She invited us back to the church we grew up in for the annual church picnic. Mom and David are still faithful members and Mom continues to play the organ every Sunday. Mom's favoritism toward David is still obvious, though. She told David to go to KFC to buy a bucket of chicken. Jeannine and I went with him and when it came time to pay, Jeannine and I divided the cost. During the potluck, Mom, David, and I were filling our plates. I happened to see Mom scanning ahead to see what was left. There was one piece of KFC chicken left. Suddenly she cut in front of me, grabbed the last piece of chicken, and plopped it down on David's plate.

Mom did let me see her vulnerable side, though. She told me she was losing her hair because of the chemotherapy. Apparently Highline Hospital has a program for cancer patients where they can get a free wig. I ask if I could go with her and to my surprise she said yes. When she picked me up, she wore her familiar blue scarf that she used to wear when her hair was up in curlers.

We stopped at the hospital. They had a small selection of wigs that are badly out of style. She tried one on, but was disappointed. On the way out of the hospital, we were referred to a salon that sold wigs. We stopped at the salon, and Mom explained to JoAnne, the hairdresser, that she has cancer and wants to buy a wig. JoAnne said that she didn't usually do this but she prayed out loud in the reception area. Then she took us to a private room, with a huge mirror, and brought out several wigs. Mom was a little hesitant about taking off the familiar blue scarf and upon seeing her discomfort, I averted my eyes so she could have a little more privacy while removing it. Once the wig was on, I commented that the wigs looked and felt real. JoAnne taught Mom how to adjust the wig to make it look as natural as possible. I brushed the wig to make the hair look fuller. I was as positive as possible, but I feel sad for Mom to have to go through such a traumatic experience.

An old neighbor gave Dad a little Macintosh computer, and Sean found a printer for him. Dad writes Mom letters all the time and always makes me mail them. I feel guilty for doing this because each time she gets a letter, she feels like Dad doesn't appreciate all that she has done for him. She can barely open them, and I heard that she usually gives David the task. David thinks Dad is harassing Mom, and so he doesn't visit very much. Dad feels neglected and writes more letters. The cycle will never end.

9-18-93

Dear Joyce,

Living with Jeanette is so much better than living at the adult family home that I am unable to elucidate.

I am sorry I wasn't a better husband. I didn't realize I was doing such a poor job. At the time I wasn't aware of my deficiencies and I didn't discover it until the injury. At least the injury was not a total loss. I learned a lot about God and people and it gave me a good excuse to get to know my children better. I even got good on the computer but I'll never learn to type with more than two fingers.

I should have paid more attention to you, and I should have never gone hang gliding. You tried to discourage my flying, but I thought I knew what I was doing. Boy, was I wrong.

My condition is slowly improving and I don't know how far it will go, but it's like growing up again. Most people only get to do it once, so in that regard it's advantageous. It's also frustrating because I keep comparing myself to how I was. I am confused about why I am still alive but I will continue to try.

I am repeating Bible Study Fellowship (BSF) and I am in my third year. I enjoy every week. I use the computer to write my BSF lesson.

I was sorry to hear about your mother passing away, and your father must be very lonely. She had been with him a long time.

Allen

3-12-94

Dear David,

Another week has passed and you neither came nor called. You have probably assumed many responsibilities at church and are too busy now to see me but I want to tell you something, as I think you are smart enough to understand. You, and no one else, set your priorities. I enjoyed our history together and I have good memories of it. I doubt that I would change any of it, but it's over, and Joyce has replaced me with you. I worry each week about your visit and that's stupid, so I want to relieve you of any further obligations toward me. I have found other computer assistance, and no longer need to depend on you. You will always be my son even if I never see you again, and I wish you the best. You are well educated, smart, and have a good job and I'm not worried about your financial future, but from now on I will assume you will neither come nor call.

Dad

Chapter 16

Sudden Impact

5-23-94

Dear Joyce,

I am writing you a letter because I don't speak very well. It makes you uncomfortable to be around me, and it gives me more time to think about what to include.

I read a lot and I am becoming pretty knowledgeable.

I have concluded that you don't know yourself very well, nor is it possible. You were raised to be cared for, as that was the modus operandi of your parents; and since I am no longer able to take care of you, it is natural for you to turn to one who can and David is a logical choice, but it hurts. I am not criticizing, just stating a fact. We had a lot of good years together but they are over and we must go on with the rest of our lives. I remember the good years in the north end, the trip to Idaho, raising the children, and living in Huntsville. We built a lot of good memories together and it was worth it. I probably wouldn't change a thing but that does not eliminate the pain I feel now. My condition is slowly improving and I keep changing—for nothing in life stands still, but evolves.

Allen

Summer was approaching. Soon June would make an inviting appearance, although, hope for happy June days seemed like a lost cause. Jeanette and I shared our birthdays—June 21st—with Mom and Dad's wedding anniversary, the first day of summer and sometimes, even Father's Day. On June 21st the family gathered together, usually for dinner at a local restaurant. On that June day, Mom couldn't pretend any longer. She couldn't suffer through another family get-together. While eating her meal, she turned away, disturbed, every time Dad attempted to put a fried piece of cod or a French fry in his mouth with his wobbly right hand. He was a constant reminder of how her life had spun out of control after his disastrous crash. Mom was a God-fearing woman, but God had given her too much to handle. She was afraid she might suffer a nervous breakdown if there was another family gathering.

After the reunion, we entered Dad's stuffy room. Something was up. Even though his back was toward us, we could read his body language while he worked on the computer. He was either concentrating deeply or was tense about something. His hand was clenched around the mouse, both shoulders were hunched and his knees wouldn't stop jiggling.

"What's wrong?" Jeanette and I said together.

Dad turned around and faced us. "Mom wants a divorce!"

Thank God, they can finally be free from each other!

"Stupid! I will not go along with it! She has all the security she needs with me! What else does she want?"

"But Dad," Jeanette said, and pointed to his chest. "What about you? Do you have what you need?"

"I don't need anything! I made a promise to God and I'm not going to break it!"

Malachi 2:16 says, "I hate divorce," says the Lord God of Israel. Jesus said much of the same thing in the New Testament of the Bible. Many other texts in the Bible taught the evil of divorce, causing Dad to want no part of the wickedness.

I disagreed. My thoughts were focused on his potential freedom. What could be wrong with that?

Because Dad was the older son, he had been considered the "top dog" even as a child. In fact, in the old neighborhood, he was called the 'leader of the pack'. Sleeping on the top bunk symbolized his status, although he was a softy at heart. He surrounded himself with a collection of stuffed animals. He never had to prove himself to his parents or try to earn respect. His parents, who were not religious, taught honesty by being honest, the importance of being forthright, by being forthright, and the importance of discipline by being disciplined. Grandpa treated Grandma well and to Dad's knowledge,

144

no battles were fought within the home. All feelings and forms of self-expression were allowed. Even though his younger brother held different interests, he was considered no less valuable. There was no reason to compete against one another. Competition was not an issue within his life until he married Mom. She wanted the best life had to offer and earning the money to make her happy took work. The more he made, the more she wanted.

Mom was also the older of two children. She and her younger brother fought for attention from their parents—Nana in particular. Nana, rigid in her belief systems, believed that it was better to be right than free. It was better to live a life of religious dedication to the Lord than to be at peace. Nana refused to question her beliefs about who God really was and led a life of conformity, self-righteousness, guilt, inhibition, fear of God and dogmatism. In her home, there was no emotional freedom, healing, joy, love and peace of mind. For years, Mom tried to gain her mother's acceptance by conforming to the rules. Now, it seemed, Mom was letting go. Finally, she was moving on and I was happy with her decision. Surprisingly, the tables had turned. Now Dad was the rigid one. Now Dad was set on conforming to the "right" way.

Jeanette's mind was on another matter; she had her own bad news to give. She hesitated before making the announcement. Finally, she said it. She was starting her full time internship. Soon she wouldn't be home much to care for Dad.

"So what?" Dad retorted more abruptly than we had anticipated. "I don't need anyone to take care of me. I'm fine. I still think fast, even though my body does not move fast."

Jeanette had already done some research and found a place for him that was close by and provided many amenities. Three meals were served daily; housekeeping services, exercise sessions, group outings and Bible study clubs were available. Of course, we'd take him to church each week, as usual, and visit him during our lunch breaks. The catch? It was a retirement facility, but we called it a "bachelor's pad". We teased him and said we wished we could move in.

Time slowed at a slug's pace as we waited for his response. Meanwhile, he stared into the white walls, attempting to comprehend the new information. After a moment of silence, he shrugged in defeat. "I'll do whatever you say."

We patted his back and changed the subject to church and Bible Study. After an hour's visit, we left him alone to think. We promised to come back in the afternoon with a chocolate milkshake and a pack of chicken McNuggets, his favorite snack. As we walked to my car, we exhaled a sigh of relief. We agreed: God made us twins so we could help each other take care of Dad, and at the same time, not feel too overloaded with the task.

"I think the divorce is a step in the right direction," Jeanette shared after getting Dad situated in his new place.

"Me too."

Our relationship with Mom slowly improved too. Perhaps, she was seeing Jeanette and me as adults. We were, after all, twenty-one years old. She even invited us to watch the fireworks Fourth of July on her friend's boat. Her friend happened to be a slow-moving blond man in his sixties with a tiny dog serving as a sidekick. We acted as if their friendship was perfectly normal, even though it was strange to see her with someone other than Dad. "Maybe she's beginning to trust us." I said, joyous about the prospect of a healed relationship. "Maybe this divorce thing will actually bring us together."

Jeanette wasn't so sure. "Did you notice Mom's face when her boyfriend complimented me on my potato salad?"

"No."

"She gave me a scowl as if she was jealous that he liked my cooking."

"Weird. It's like she doesn't even consider us her daughters."

Jeanette laughed at a thought.

"What's so funny?"

"Did you see Mom with his dog?"

"No."

"She was nice to the dog when they were together, but when the man wasn't around she scolded it." She stopped laughing. After a moment of thought, she added, "Kinda reminds me of when we were kids."

Hope bloomed. Maybe the divorce would motivate Mom and Dad to lead separate happy lives. Jeanette and I agreed we'd rather have two happy and divorced parents, than two miserable married parents. Finally, even though they were breaking God's rules, an opportunity to start over again presented itself, like Good News, to our family. Unfortunately, Dad only saw problems: a divorce was against the Word of God and he wanted no part of it. He was going to fight it all the way.

Chapter 17

Real World

Jeanette was ready to show off. She had just started a job at a nursing facility as a Certified Occupational Therapy Assistant. Finally, a *real* job! When I visited her place of work a familiar pattern presented itself where families dropped off loved ones and then some families seemed to forget about their relations. Jeanette refused to forget about Mom and Dad. Both, at age 65, were not in good health and needed care. Mom's cancer had spread throughout her body. Jeanette made it her personal goal to make both parents feel loved and cared for. She wanted to provide a safe-haven for both of them. Our parents' advanced age and declining health were what inspired Jeanette to work in the health care field. But Mom refused to see her heart; instead she obsessed about Jeanette being an unwed mother.

Jeanette's daily experiences at the nursing home motivated her to plan a solution for our parent's future care. She could help solve potential problems by either opening an adult family home or an adult care center. She would give people with disabilities and older adults the respect they deserved and freedom to make decisions for themselves. Seeing people unhappy and boxed and imprisoned in wheelchairs inspired her more and more to make a change within the industry.

I supported Jeanette's idea. We were meant to work together. God had been preparing us all along to take care of people and to make them happy. We interpreted Dad's injury and Mom's cancer as a sign from God to work His will and share our care and concern with others. We were twins for a reason.

When Jeanette and I approached the front desk, the two receptionists did a double take. "Hi Jeanette. Boy, who's that? She looks just like you," the older gal said.

The younger gal added, "This is spooky."

"Hi, you guys. This is my twin sister, Jeannine."

"Oh… I've always wanted to have a twin sister. Is it fun?" The younger woman asked. She flashed long, neon, artificial nails and ratted up bangs. I assumed that she had especially enjoyed the '80s. I was a fan of the 80's too, but because I worked in the beauty industry, I needed to change my look to keep up with the times as best I could.

"Did you guys switch places in class and stuff like that?" The older woman asked.

"Sometimes we did," Jeanette said and we exchanged knowing smiles. "But I flunked her volleyball test in ninth grade—"

"And that was the last time we switched classes," I interrupted.

"Jeanette, she talks like you!" The older gal shrieked.

We laughed; it was a comment we had heard often.

"Spooky—she even laughs like you!" The younger woman added.

Embarrassed by the attention, we stopped laughing. Jeanette entered a code to get into the wide, sterile hall where the residents lived. Before the door closed slowly behind us, the older receptionist remarked that our gait was the same.

Bleach and cleaning alcohol unsuccessfully covered the stench of urine, feces, and body odor. Aged ladies lined the hall in wheelchairs. Some called out as we passed, "Help me! Someone please help me! Is there anyone around?" Others ignored our presence and conferred with imaginary companions, as if in another time and place. I overheard staff members whisper, "Oh, my God, there's two Jeanettes," while we walked down the corridor.

"Honey, are you ready to go into the garden room for the big game of banana bingo?" a nursing assistant asked. "If you're the lucky winner, you'll earn yourself a banana or a bowl of fruit cocktail."

A lady with sunken cheeks jerked awake, like an infant startled from a loud noise, when the nursing assistant suddenly pushed her wheelchair. I peered in each room imagining ways to make the residents happy. I had read about a nursing home that used animals as therapy in a *Reader's Digest* magazine. "We could really make a change," I said.

Jeanette nodded in agreement. "I know, I think about it all the time."

"Hi, Mr. Kay. It's Jeanette. How are you doing?" She asked her first therapy patient who reclined restlessly in bed. "This is my sister, Jeannine."

"Just push my table closer to me," snarled the elderly man. "Damn it! Where's my call light?"

Jeanette handed him the remote. "It's right here, Mr. Kay."

"What about my reading glasses? Are they on my table?"

"They sure are!" She waved them in front of him.

"Damn it, Jap, quit waving that thing in my face! I'm farsighted. That means if you're going to shove something in my face I won't be able to see it. Go stand over there and look for my clicker!"

"Hold on, let me look." She ignored the racial slur and scanned the room. "Mr. Kay, how about a little therapy today?"

"Damn it! How many times do I have to tell you people? I don't want therapy. I'm too old to work!"

"You can't go home until you get better. I can't help you if you don't help yourself."

"I know what you can do. You can start by getting me a glass of water. Make sure there's ice in there. Last time they gave me water with no ice. Look in my water pitcher and make sure there's water and ice in it. If not, go fill it up for me. Those damn nursing assistants never give me fresh water."

Jeanette picked up the water pitcher and left the room at his request. "I'll be right back."

I sat on the edge of the vacant bed next to him, feeling stupid and wondering if I should start some small talk. Before I could, a woman dressed in passion fruit orange entered the room, brushed past me and gave the man a kiss on the forehead. A strong wave of lilac perfume forced me to sneeze.

"Darling, how are you?" she asked the man.

"I'm still waiting for some damn water with ice," he growled. "That's all I ask for, and I never get anything when I need it. The service around here is no damn good! I've been through hell and back, and I deserve to be treated with respect. I swear, I'm going to sue!"

The lady searched the room, looking for something to complain about. Towels were spread over a chair; clothes were scattered about. She glared at me with fiery green eyes.

"Why aren't these towels folded and put into his drawer like I specifically requested yesterday?" She let out a frustrated sigh.

I turned, hoping to see a nursing assistant, but discovered I was alone. "Oh, um I don't work here..."

She squinted to get a better view of me. "What? You're not that little Filipino girl who was working here yesterday?"

"Um, no, my sister is getting water for Mr. Kay right now." *And she's not Filipino*, I wanted to say, as if the lady would care.

"This place is not providing good care for the residents," she snarled.

"I know," I agreed. "You know what this place needs? Animals. Pets are so therapeutic."

"Are you kidding me? People like my husband can't take care of animals. How do you expect them to care for an animal when they can barely care for themselves? Think about it. That's not a very wise solution to the problem."

I smiled and nodded, but disagreed silently. *Geez, Louise!* I thought. *What a wacko! She's totally focusing on what the residents* can't *do, instead of what they* can *do! She's so damn quick to box them in, to limit their potential.*

Jeanette finally returned with a pink plastic pitcher and set it on the table, close to him. "Sorry it took so long, Mr. Kay, but I had to go down to the cafeteria for the ice."

Mr. Kay turned his attention toward the window where drooping lilacs and a vacant, washed out birdhouse added to his gloom.

"How about we do some therapy, Mr. Kay?" Jeanette said. "Your ultimate goal is to become independent again. Since you're doing well with standing with a walker, one of the tasks we can work on is walking to the bathroom, so you can use it independently."

"My husband *can't* do that. We're paying for his care in here. Go get a nursing assistant—she can at least help him in that department. When he's home, I'll make him do it himself."

Jeanette could see that getting Mr. Kay to do his therapy with his wife in the room would be difficult, so she offered to come back later.

I shuddered upon exiting. "Geez, they're real charmers. I didn't realize how much pleasure you must get out of doing this job. The rewards must be overwhelming. Talk about the blame game!" In contrast, I received gifts of appreciation from clients in the beauty salon where I worked.

"It's normal for residents to be angry. They hate their situation and the unaccustomed feelings of dependence. They have no one to take it out on, except for us. At least his wife still comes to visit every so often. Most family members just drop them off and then visit an hour or so during the holidays. It's sad. During the holidays, this place should be empty. The residents should be home with their families. But they're here. The nursing assistants can have up to twenty patients per shift. They have to assist with dressing, toileting, and feeding needs. Most of the time, they're behind schedule because it takes time to fulfill tasks. The residents depend on the staff to make them happy, but we barely have time to care for their physical needs."

"The only people who can make them happy is themselves."

"Remember how Mom and Dad were?" Jeanette asked. "Can you believe it's been ten years already since Dad's injury? It's taken us so long to adjust and we still haven't really accepted the situation. I don't think Mom and Dad are happy even after a separation."

"I don't think it's possible."

Suddenly passion stirred. Trying hard to restrain her excitement, Jeanette whispered, "We've got to do something. You and me! We've got to open an adult family home where we can make people happy! You know we make a great team. We could really make a difference. Let's finish our business plan! It'll be perfect. Then, if Mom and Dad get sick and can't care for themselves, we'll have a place for them! We won't have to stick them in a nursing home."

I smiled at her idea. Maybe this was the missing link. After all, we understood and we had caregiving experience that had begun at the age of twelve. I thought about my job at the salon. No, I didn't want to work in the beauty industry forever. There had to be more to life. Even though I loved my job and my clients gave me gifts of appreciation and we shared great conversation, something inside told me I wasn't fulfilling my purpose. *Is this all there is in life? Grow up, get a job, get married, have children? Where is the sense of purpose?*

Where is the passion? Something was missing—I just didn't know what. An inner voice continued to whisper that I was meant to work with Jeanette. I wasn't supposed to be a nail technician forever.

My heart raced when Jeanette mentioned opening up an adult family home. We would make the perfect team! This *had* to be the missing link in our lives. This *had* to be the reason Dad suffered a head injury in the first place. This was what God wanted us to do! He was giving us direction and purpose in our lives!

Chapter 18

Leap of Faith

"Sean, I had such a realistic dream! I gave birth to a baby and we named her Allison!" I exclaimed, still trying to wake up and comprehend what I had seen. "I was breathing hard on a birthing table, you were sitting next to me for support, and there were several nurses gathered around. The doctor lifted up the baby and cheered, 'It's a girl!' Her name is to be Allison!"

Sean mumbled something in the darkness, "Allison... like that name... you get pregnant... call baby... Allison."

He rolled over the plush blanket and started snoring again, but I couldn't stop thinking about the prospect.

Many months later, Sean shocked me with his own prediction. "I think you're pregnant again," he said.

"Why do you say that?"

"I just know. I'm psychic."

"Don't say that. Psychics are evil."

"They are?"

"Yeah, in the Bible they're anti-God."

"They are? In my country they're considered normal."

"It's against the Bible," I stated.

"Where?"

"I don't know; it just is."

"I'm just telling you what I see. You're pregnant."

"You can tell me that I'm pregnant, but don't say you're psychic." After thinking over what he had told me, I complained, "What is everyone going to say when they find out I'm pregnant again? I'm only twenty-three!" Worse, I still looked and felt like a teenager.

"Who cares what people think? The timing is perfect. The kids will be three years apart and we can get the baby stage over with in a short amount of time."

"Yeah, I guess you're right, but after this, no more kids! I don't want people to think that I'm having too many babies too soon."

"You care too much about what people think of you."

Soon enough, I discovered, Sean was right. I was pregnant again. Positive that Mom would not approve of this pregnancy, I admitted to Jeanette that it would be embarrassing to have my coworkers meet her at the baby shower they were planning. Part of me wanted to keep her out of my life.

"You've got to invite her. Think of how upsetting it would be to her if you don't—you didn't even invite her to your wedding," Jeanette reminded me. "Didn't she want to be in the delivery room for Vanessa's birth?"

We chatted while cooking in the L-shaped kitchen of my newly purchased home. "Yeah, you're right. Anyway, things have been pretty good. It seems like she enjoys being around us now that we're adults. She went house hunting with Sean and me around Bonney Lake last month, and we actually enjoyed our time together." I hesitated, one last time, before agreeing to the idea.

Mom called me at work after I sent her the invitation. "Jeannine, you should really think about inviting Angie, Mike's girlfriend. It's the proper thing to do."

I stumbled over words and finally stammered, "Well—see—um—I—ah—don't know—" The thought of making this a family affair made my stomach jump. I was surprised at her request. I didn't know that she and Angie had made amends. The last time they were together was at Christmas, when Angie had made remarks hurtful to Mom, and then had sat in the car until Mom went out and fetched her. No one knew what was said, but whatever it was, Angie joined us during the rest of the ritual of opening gifts, sighing with annoyance every once in a while. I knew why she sighed so heavily; her blue eyes told me that she was agitated about our family's dysfunction. What if such eruptions happened at my baby shower, in front of my coworkers and clients? What would they think?

"It would be appropriate," Mom added. "She is Mike's girlfriend. They'll probably get married soon, so that would make her your sister-in-law. She's practically family already—."

I tried to stall for time, but Maria, a coworker, wanted to use the phone so I gave a quick answer. "I guess you're right. Okay."

Later, when I asked Mike about his marriage plans, he exclaimed, "Mom said that? Fuck, Angie and I have no plans of getting married. We never did! Just because we've got Kyle doesn't mean we're going to get married. Mom even went out and bought Angie a wedding dress! Can you believe that? A fucking wedding dress."

I was confused. At the baby shower Mom and Angie sat together but didn't say a word. They acted like total strangers to each other and to the rest of the crowd. They just watched everyone and everything that went on around me. Mom didn't warm up to Vanessa like she usually did. I was embarrassed too. What did the girls from work think? They were perched on the other side of the coffee table making delightful comments about each gift I opened, but there was an uneasy tension. Why was Mom so quiet? She didn't even attempt to make small talk, something so unlike her. Maybe she was ashamed of me. I felt even more alienated from her and regretted inviting her.

After the baby shower was over, I was more confused over our relationship than ever before. Perhaps her odd behavior was only a figment of my imagination; we really did have a normal mother/daughter relationship. It never occurred to me that she was probably uncomfortable with her role as my mother and that she felt like an insignificant part of my life. She might also have been feeling self-conscious and intimidated surrounded by a group of hairdressers, when she was forced to wear a wig because of her loss of hair from chemotherapy treatments. She had always been sensitive about her hair anyway. When Jeanette and I were growing up she made envious comments about our thick hair. As with several situations in her life, she felt she wasn't wanted or needed.

Mom's attitude changed the day Allison was born on August 8, 1995. Jeanette escorted her to my hospital room to visit Sean and me and the new baby. They entered the room laughing and smiling, followed by Vanessa giggling at the thought of a new baby sister, and Dustin curious about having a little cousin.

"Oh, look, there she is! She's such a little sweetheart." Mom squealed with delight when she saw the baby and caressed her fresh skin. Then she set a potted violet plant at my table as if she were proud of me. She proceeded to study the actions of the nurses and followed them with questions while they took the baby's temperature and changed the diaper. This made me feel nurtured and put new life into me. It gave me a wonderful energetic feeling. There was no shame with this baby, only joy.

Mom even came to our house with gifts and cheer. Then she was the queen of the party, around Sean's brothers and sisters. After she left, Sean's family talked about her charming personality. "You're lucky Jenne. Your mom's nice!"

The Sunday after Allison's birth, Sean convinced me to stay home and recuperate. I felt pangs of guilt. Usually Jeanette and I took Dad to church together. That way, neither one of us felt overwhelmed by the task. About one o'clock in the afternoon, the phone rang. I knew it was Jeanette with gossip about Sunday's outing.

"We were on the way to church," she told me, "when I saw a building that seemed to jump out at us. I'm tellin' you, Jeannine, this church is much more contemporary, and the music is way different. They even have a band instead of a organist, and they play upbeat inspirational music—it's huge!"

"Dad is always giving low scores to the pastor's sermons at the Presbyterian Church, anyway. What harm can it do?" I agreed. He thought that there was no Christian at the church who was as competent as he was. In fact, he confided to Jeanette and me on numerous occasions that he thought the pastor was dumb. "Can you believe that he doesn't even know who Ashpenaz was?" Dad complained, "As the leader of the church, he should be more knowledgeable of the Bible."

Another time, Dad got into an argument with a church member over when a person would receive the Holy Spirit. "God decides to give gifts whenever and to whomever He feels like it. You girls are the only two who will listen to me. Receiving the Holy Spirit has nothing to do with salvation and the people who are saved will go on to eternal life with or without the gift of the Holy Spirit. Anyway, it is not my problem, but his," he concluded.

157

Most people were afraid of Dad's behavior and interpreted his boisterous attitude as crazy. He would get into arguments with the parishioners over insignificant issues to prove that he was more biblically knowledgeable. "I do not know why I understand so much about life. I sometimes think I must be wrong or more people would understand."

Jeanette and I would nod in agreement to keep the peace.

"No one learns except through experience. I would like to pass on my wisdom to someone, but I guess it is not part of the plan. Each person has to make his own way. That is the system and I can't change it."

I had to admit, Dad was egotistical at times. He wasn't even afraid to raise his hand during the sermons when he thought the pastor was wrong. It left the entire congregation in a quandary over what to do with this strange man. Most times I held his arm down to keep him from disturbing everyone in the church. Once when I did this, a man assumed we were a couple and asked how long we had been married. To make the whole situation worse—even bizarre—I was eight months pregnant with Allison at the time. Disgusted, Jeanette and I decided to sit in the vacant fireside room and listen to the sermons on the loudspeaker without being a distraction or being bothered. We told Dad it was so he could drink coffee during the sermons. Though I wouldn't admit it, I came to the conclusion that Dad was right. Even Christians could be stupid.

Grappling with doubt about changing churches, I asked, "Is there anything better than Presbyterianism? How did people react to Dad?"

"Dad didn't raise his hand once. In fact, he rated the sermon and the pastor a perfect ten."

"Cool," I said, but wondered if the new church was as dedicated to showing the way to a personal relationship with Jesus, as our old church.

The following Sunday, I was ready to go. As we entered the bustling parking lot, men in red fluorescent vests directed us to a handicapped spot. More vehicles searched for open spaces along residential neighborhoods and side streets. *This is not a struggling church!*

"This doesn't even look like a church. Where's the stained glass windows? Where's the steeple?" I asked in awe and in doubt. How could they teach the beauty of God's word without the traditional trimmings?

"Told you it was different! Have you ever seen so many people? And the kids' classrooms are totally packed."

I wasn't prepared to hear electric guitar music performed over a loudspeaker, nor did I expect to watch the service on a huge screen in an overflow room that was specially prepared for anyone who couldn't fit into the contemporary sanctuary.

A man dressed in khaki slacks, a crème button down shirt and brown tie walked up to the podium and began giving the sermon.

I turned to Jeanette. "Is he the pastor?"

Jeanette nodded.

"Where is his black robe? Where is the pulpit?"

She only waved at me to quiet down. "Shh."

As the pastor spoke, a religious energy and fervor recharged the congregation. I eagerly leaned forward in my chair to hear what he had to say. In fact, he had the entire congregation in a trance. Dad listened intently and nodded to the beat of the pastor's words.

The pastor told the congregation to open their Bibles and turn to 1 John 2:18-19. "Dear children, this is the last hour; and as you have heard that the antichrist is coming. Even now many antichrists have come. 1 John 2:22-23 tells us a liar is the man who denies that Jesus is the Christ. Such a man is the antichrist—he denies both Father and the Son. Fix your gaze directly on the Lord Jesus. He will keep harm from you. He will save you from your destruction. Only with Jesus, can you do good."

He then proceeded to announce that the devil was doing its work again. Many false prophets would try to lead us away from the one true path. He concluded the service with reports that we must watch out for nonChristians. There were many "wolves in sheep's clothing".

I agreed with Jeanette. This was a church Dad could feel at home in. I just needed to think of a way to entice Sean to go. We could even buy tapes of the sermons we had missed from a convenient mini-store located outside the sanctuary. I did this often and listened to the pastor's talks while driving to and from work. I would leave the tapes out, hoping Sean would find one, get curious, and stick it into his tape player.

"Grab the person's hand who sits beside you, while I pray today. Turn to them and tell them you love them, and God is watching over them. If you see someone who is new to you, please introduce yourself and make a new friend."

Each person obediently found the hand of another, said 'It's nice to meet you,' and finally lowered his or her head.

"If you confess with your mouth that Jesus is Lord, and believe in your heart that God raised Him from the dead, you will be saved," the pastor prayed. "For it is with your heart that you believe and are justified, and it is with your mouth that you confess and are saved. As the Scripture says, 'Anyone who trusts in Him will never be put to shame.'" He spoke for the rest of the hour. Time flew by and soon he was closing the service. "O Lord, hear my voice; in the morning I lay my requests before you and wait in expectation.' Amen."

In unison, the congregation raised their heads, released their hands and then when the music started they reached for the heavens, perhaps longing that for one brief moment God would lower His own great hands and touch us all. There was something different about this pastor. Was it his young age? His passion for the "Word of God?" Or was it because it was the first time we had experienced enthusiasm, humor, and light during the sermons and hope that we will overcome our failures? We were drawn in. We just went along with the congregation, admitting to being humble and weak, gracious and meek.

"Girls," Dad said, "I'm concerned. I don't know how to speak in tongues yet and I wonder if I am the way God wants me. Since I can't speak in tongues, I wonder about the experience I've had. Shouldn't I be filled with the Holy Spirit? The book *Speaking Other Tongues* says that everyone who is holy and has the mind of God has been filled with the Holy Spirit and can speak Tongues. Since I can't, I wonder what is wrong with me."

I wondered also. Perhaps, we weren't Christian enough. Maybe we needed to try to be better Christians and speaking in tongues would be a worthy goal in God's eyes to try to achieve. The new church convinced me that what I had been taught for the majority of my life was true. I *was* born a sinner. I needed Jesus for salvation. For much of my young life, I had been fighting against living a truly righteous life and I hadn't immersed myself enough in the Word of God. Even Dad was concerned. Since he couldn't speak in tongues like some of the parishioners and he wasn't yet healed, maybe he needed to try harder. Even though he had read the Bible thirty-two times, what if he wasn't attentive enough in God's eyes? His mind told him he was far more Biblically advanced, but his heart left him in doubt. Was his faith not strong enough? Should he submerge his heart further in the Word?

My own insecurities flared up again. If we could convince Mom to go to this new church, she would see my dedication to the righteous path and she might learn to love me. Perhaps, she would see that I was maturing into a lovable woman. Now I was set on following the *right* path that only this church and a personal relationship with Jesus could fulfill. I was born again. My faith in Jesus was renewed. Today, He had saved me from my wicked ways. From now on, I was set on following the rules.

Jeanette and I decided to switch churches and took Dad to the newly discovered church from that Sunday on. We told Mom she had to at least try the church once. She smiled at our enthusiasm but refused to join us because of her own organ playing duties at her home church. Meanwhile, Dad repeatedly gave the new pastor's sermons a score of ten. Somehow the powers that gushed from this church felt magnified tenfold. We were immediately addicted to the music. In fact, everyone raised and swung their arms around; everyone spoke passionate prayers; powerful electric music filled the sanctuary. Our religious obedience intensified. This was a place of refuge for the discouraged. It was an answer from the Divine, and to make the situation even better, Dad stayed quiet during the entire service.

Dad continued to watch televangelists. "Jeannine. I've been watching Robert Schuller and I've come to the conclusion that man is programmed just like a computer. A sick man is programmed differently than a well man, a woman is programmed differently than a man, a Christian is programmed differently than a non-Christian and a child is programmed differently than an adult. We can not think differently than our programming but even with the programming, we have to make a choice about God, whether we are going to follow Him or ourselves. Whether we like it or not, we change. When I was a child, I was not a Christian. Now I am. I have found grace. As we mature, our programming changes."

My heart was set on a healing for Dad. Just like Dad, I began studying the televangelists on the Christian channel, and praying regularly for Jesus to heal him. A healing would solve Mom and Dad's problems, and all I needed was faith. There was power in numbers, we were taught, so if Dad, Jeanette, and I combined our faith, a definite healing was in our future. After the healing, Mom and Dad could be happy, and their problems would be forgotten. I was so relieved that I had found an answer. Because of this church, I had discovered the final road to God's grace. God would make sure that Dad didn't get hurt during the divorce, God was so good—He would make sure all was right and fair. After all, the Bible said we only needed faith the size of a mustard seed to move mountains. I had faith that God would resolve my parents' battle. Jeanette and I distanced ourselves from the divorce proceedings, knowing that by doing so, we would not only win God's approval righteously, but we'd gain Mom's acceptance. Life definitely couldn't get worse. The battle was over and we were out of the box. Finally, we were entering God's grace... or were we?

Chapter 19

Screwed

Far from being over, the real battle had just begun. *We should have helped Dad!* I raged when I read the papers from the final hearing that said Mom was awarded everything: the house, whatever was already in her possession, which included the automobiles, jewelry, bank accounts, the real estate properties, and her inheritance. Dad was awarded forty percent from the sale of the family home, which was to be held in a trust by his Guardian Ad Litem, Eliza Lott. He was given sixty percent of his retirement income, which would barely cover the expenses at the retirement facility.

The world, I began to understand, did not care. Jeanette and I had put our trust in Eliza's intelligence to determine that Dad was competent. Then, we put our trust in the law to grant what was fair. My trust was shaken. I didn't want money for myself and I didn't expect Mom to give me anything, but I'd hoped the courts would protect my father. I hated Mom for depriving Dad of everything he'd earned and saved, except for a pittance. I knew why. She assumed we were out to get her money and the only way we could get it was through him.

Too late, I wondered why I distanced myself from their two-year divorce battle in the first place. Why was it okay for Mom to have David's support but not okay for Dad to have our help? Staying out of their divorce proceedings didn't win Mom's affection. She still mistrusted us! How could we trust her, when she had never trusted us? Nor did we win God's approval. God wouldn't have ended it this way if we were in His favor.

I scanned Dad's humble room: Mike's old bed in a corner; a computer sitting on a child-sized desk; a recliner; a brass reading lamp; and a small poster of a shaggy dog that read, *I would never say I'm perfect, Lord, but I wish somebody would.*

"Girls, did you know I wrote the court appointed Guardian Ad Litem on numerous occasions and she's never written me back?" He showed us these letters.

4-5-95

To Eliza Lott, Guardian Ad Litem,

I am now, and may always be, slower than normal, but I have more time than normal to think and it's my opinion that my ability to think was not damaged in the injury and besides I am healing and changing. All of the psychology tests at the Puyallup hospital were based on time, and I am below normal in time response. My method is to train the part of the brain that was undamaged in the incident. I am convinced that you will be clever enough to determine that competency is not a function of speed. Like I contend, I am slower than a bullet but faster than a slug.

I have confidence in you and I'll do whatever you say. I appreciate your looking out for my rights.

Allen Louis Vance

5-9-95

Dear Eliza,

I can understand how/why the court appointed a temporary Guardian Ad Litem (GAL) for me during the divorce, but I don't think I need a permanent one. I even signed the paper for a temporary GAL. I am healing and a permanent guardian is unnecessary and undesirable. I am scared of Joy and David, and I will never, no never, sign the house over to Joy.

Joy refuses to recognize change. There was a time when I was totally dependent, but that time is past. Slow, yes. Incompetent, no. Like I say, slower than a bullet but faster than a slug.

Allen L. Vance

Jeanette and I skimmed over the letters and the Factual Overview with Dad in the room. We wondered what had prevented Eliza from seeing him as competent. Every slight mistake noted by Eliza was a blatant disrespect for Dad and a lack of concern for the truth. Jeanette pointed to a miserable string of words. "Look here, she wrote that he walks with a cane! He doesn't walk with a cane; he walks with a grocery basket! And she says Mom cared for Dad for seven years at home, then he was transferred to an adult family home, and now he lives at a retirement facility that Mom found. Doesn't say anything about me taking care of him. I was the one who found this place! Mom doesn't give us credit for anything."

"Look what Eliza says here," I added. "'In my dealings with Allen, he is able to communicate effectively. However, over the course of my representation, I have noticed an impairment of his judgment regarding money management issues and an apparent lack of empathy in his dealings with individuals. The doctor confirms that this is symptomatic of the type of brain injury Allen sustained.' Dad, who is this lady? I thought she was supposed to be your lawyer." I hated this woman for being blind and ignorant.

Dad grinned as though he didn't care that this was his life we were talking about. "She was a court-appointed attorney—I didn't have any money to hire a real attorney—and still don't. I guess the old saying 'you get what you pay for' is true." He chuckled. "Money doesn't grow on trees. I've checked!"

"Geez Louise." I rolled my eyes. "You *are* crazy!"

Dad stated slowly, "Normal people scare me," then did a strange, opened mouth snort, exposing a mouthful of gold-capped teeth.

"Come back to earth, Dad."

Jeanette pointed to another line of poisonous words written by his guardian. "'In April 1996, Allen took it upon himself to change the payee designations on his Social Security and Boeing pension income to have those payments mailed directly to him. This was contrary to the terms of the temporary order set by his wife and my warning that he was in violation of those orders. He applied these funds to his own use and did not pay his wife her share of the Boeing pension. A review of his expenditures during this period reveal that, among other things, Allen donated two hundred and seventy dollars to his church during May 1996, representing a 'ten-percent tithe of his gross income' from that month. He also paid his daughter, Jeanette, approximately two hundred dollars for a used television. This excessive expenditure is a direct result of his head injury."

"Hey, you didn't buy the television from Jeanette. I let you borrow the money. You mean just because you gave a ten percent tithe to the church and paid me back, she says you're not capable of handling money?" I asked. "Mom's new television didn't have rabbit ears. Did she expect you to use your old television forever?"

Jeanette agreed. "Yeah, everyone has a remote control at the nursing home. How can the court say buying a television with a remote is due to your head injury?" She continued to read from the papers, "'Joy Vance recommends that the parties' son, David, be guardian for his father.'"

"No!" Dad's face tightened.

"Whoa, Dad! Take it easy!" I said. His outburst satisfied us, but it also made us feel guilty for shoving the facts in his face.

"I'm only afraid of two people. Joy and David! I've written David several times. He's stopped visiting me and Joy has brainwashed him! I told them if I needed a guardian, I wanted it to be one of you girls! You're old enough and you listen to me."

"Jeannine, it gets worse," Jeanette said. "Under 'Recommendations' Eliza says because she doubts Allen's ability to handle large sums of money appropriately, she recommends that the promissory note and any other property be placed in a trust. She believes that because of his impaired judgment, he is only capable of managing fifty-five dollars for a monthly income, which would pay for his telephone and incidentals. She questions his ability to appropriately handle larger sums of money, based on his attempts to change the payee designations on his Social Security and Boeing pension."

"Oh my God!" I exploded. "After years of only getting twenty-five dollars a month as spending money, it's only fair that you reverted the payment back to yourself. It proves you *are* competent! Mom has had control for way too long!"

"I wanted to tell you something. Did you know that Eliza said I could have gone to jail for doing it? Can you imagine?" he said shrilly. "Me, in jail?" Then he erupted in laughter. His amusement at the irony continued to bother us.

"Did I tell you that all the letters I wrote to the court went ignored?" Dad stated, adding fuel to our fire. "I didn't want to sell the family home, but the judge says we have to."

"There's a court order to sell the home?" Jeanette asked. Then, without warning, her eyes lit up. She spit out a mangled fingernail tip and exclaimed, "Hey, maybe we can buy Mom's share of the house!"

"Yeah!" I agreed. I could read Jeanette's mind; we had just completed our business plan and were ready to shop for a home. "Man, the house is perfect! And the timing is perfect. If we stay on Mom's good side, I'm sure she will sell it to us! Can you imagine how awesome it will be for the residents to have such a great view and a huge yard?"

"The basement is large enough for a whole 'nother apartment and Mike can help remodel it!" Jeanette exclaimed.

"Girls, did you know it's over four thousand square feet, and I designed it to have many special features, like a built in vacuum system?" Dad asked, proud of his project and happy at the opportunity to remind us of his past capabilities, even though he had never finished the project.

"There's got to be a reason why Mom wants to sell the home! Remember when the pastor told us that we must follow God's plan? Well this must be it!" I exclaimed. Fresh hope excited me. I would do anything for the house; I would sacrifice my life for the house if it meant we could use it to for the adult family home.

Jeanette held the same idealistic hope that I did. "We're meant to help other people with disabilities! Dad, I bet when you built the home thirty years ago, you never thought it would one day be used to help others. It must be God's plan!"

Of course Mom would sell us her share of the family home! We would leave Dad's share alone. We should keep the house in the family, we reasoned. The fact that it wasn't finished made the purchase ideal and affordable. Once we cleared out the boxes, the home could be remodeled to be wheelchair accessible. Dad's past work would not only benefit himself, but others who had been dealt a similar fate. We sat back, comforted by our faith and fantasized about what the future might hold.

Chapter 20

City of Angels

A coworker announced that her psychic friend, Nancy, would visit soon and would be available to anyone who wanted a reading. All of us laughed at the idea of getting our future foretold and our past explained. We didn't want to get involved and even if we did, we wouldn't admit it. As Christians, we were taught that psychics were evil, and should be avoided. I didn't want to appear sinful by trying it out, but curiosity conquered my reservations.

The bells to the salon door jingled when the woman entered the salon. She talked loudly and laughed a lot. I couldn't see her, but I could hear her from behind the walls of my manicuring room where I worked on my client. She actually sounded like a lot of fun, not wicked and satanic as I had expected after listening to horror stories from church about the paranormal. *Why not? I might as well see what she has to say about my family.* I wasn't going to take anything she said seriously and I knew I could ask for forgiveness later.

A blond lady peered around the corner. "Hi, I'm Nancy!" She exhibited the upbeat temperament of a cheerleader.

"Hi, I'm Jeannine. Do you have time to do a reading for me right now?" I was eager to hear what she would say about me, but I was in the middle of working on my client and wouldn't get a break until much later in the day.

"Well, hon—I usually do them in private. Maybe after your client or something?"

"Come on in, it's okay." I considered my client, Wendy, a friend and assumed nothing Nancy would say could dig too deep into my soul. "Wendy, already knows everything about me anyway! Right, Wendy?"

"Just don't hurt me if Nancy says something you disagree with," Wendy joked as I filed her nails.

Nancy grabbed a director's chair and placed it close to us. She stroked the recent picture of Sean, Vanessa, Allison, and me on my desk, then smiled. "Wow, your husband would work five jobs to keep the family together! He has great love for all of you."

I agreed, "Yeah, that's for sure!" *Sean is particularly dedicated to us.*

She hesitated, then toyed with a bottle of pink nail polish before adding softly, "But I sense something wrong with the relationship with your mother."

"Oh, really? Well, she does have cancer." I quickly said. "Hey, try that pink over there... want me do a French manicure for you?"

She looked at her hands and chuckled at the thought. "On these stubs? No thanks. Hon, listen to me. I see your Mom is sick, maybe even fighting for her life, but I also sense something flawed between you two emotionally. Do you want to talk about it?"

My stomach tightened. I could feel my face get warm. Surprised that Nancy hit home so fast, I thought: *Maybe she was right—maybe we should do this in private.* I couldn't wait to tell Jeanette about this and asked if she was available to come by my house that evening. She was.

"She's coming over tonight to do a reading," I eagerly explained over the phone, forgetting everything I had been told in church about psychics. Apparently, Jeanette had forgotten also, because she agreed to meet us after work; she didn't seem to mind that we were embarking on potentially dangerous territory.

At the salon I had been attracted to Nancy's outgoing personality and her positive spirit. At my house, the feeling intensified. She felt like a long-lost sister or one of those cool aunts that everyone wants.

"Haaay! How are you gals doing!" She exclaimed as I opened the door to let her in.

"I don't know—you tell me!" I answered. We laughed and settled in the living room.

The large ebony lacquered painting from Vietnam, radiating shimmering goldfish served as the backdrop while she spoke. "First of all girls, I need to tell you a little bit about myself. I'm a Christian, just like you two. My ability is a gift from God, and I give all credit to Him. This is new to me—in fact I was just given this gift recently. As a child I yearned to go to church. I've always had a deep fascination with Jesus, but my family never went to church. Sometimes I would go with friends, and think, "Wow; they are so lucky to be able to go." My gift came to me after my mom passed away. I was asleep when all of a sudden a bright light filled my room. Oh, my God—let me tell you—at first I thought it was my mom, and I was about ready to freak out! But as soon as my eyes focused, I realized there were two illuminated forms standing next to my bed. I realized they were angels—took me long enough—must be the blonde in me!"

"Oh, my God, that would freak me out!" Jeanette grabbed one of my moss pillows.

"Yeah." Nancy laughed. "I was scared, but they told me to stop being afraid because they had a great message for me. They said that Jesus would come to me at a later time, and give me a special gift, and that I needn't be afraid to receive the gift. Soon, I would be working His will!"

"Man, that's amazing. Almost like in the Bible days!" I said, remembering Bible stories about angels visiting certain people.

"A month later, I was visited by a bright light, and soon an angel who resembled Jesus appeared at my side. I was still scared—even though I shouldn't have been. I mean, duh—the angels told me to remain calm!"

"Believe me, I would have freaked out too!" Jeanette mashed the pillow against her and fingered its fringe.

"The angel said, 'Be at peace my child; receive these gifts that I give you and go work my will.' At the same time he touched my left shoulder and I felt a warm glow go through my body. I'm a rational person, you know, and quite bold. I argued. I said, 'I don't deserve this gift! You've got the wrong person, mister!' But the angel just chuckled and told me to be at peace, for he would always be with me and I would have 'knowingness.' Then, just like that, the angel dissolved into the darkness. Man, I was so taken aback I didn't speak for three whole days! You can even ask my friends! Then, it was so weird, I could see people's angels, and I could sense things from people too. I can even communicate with them, and they are huge and magnificent!"

"Do we have one angel or many?" Jeanette asked.

"Oh, everyone has many, many angels. And yours are all around the living room laughing at our jokes!"

We scanned the living room, behind the crème leather couch, against the freshly painted, burnt orange fireplace, trying to envision beings with wings, but nothing out of the ordinary surfaced. I remembered watching a so-called angel expert talk about modern day angels on *Oprah*. She said that everyone had angels. I had smirked and thought she was imagining things and telling a big lie. Angels only existed back when Jesus was alive. But for some reason, what Nancy said resonated with me. I sensed a connection—even some truth, although I couldn't place my feeling.

"What can you tell us about Dad?" I asked.

"Well, he's depressed and lonely, but he's reluctant to admit it. And he somehow doesn't think his condition is as bad as others think it is."

"Yeah, that is true, it's something Mom complains about—in fact the Guardian Ad Litem even reported this 'flaw' in her ridiculous Factual Overview for the court." Jeanette rolled her eyes at me. Thoughts about Eliza Lott's lies surfaced temporarily in our minds.

"He's grateful for what he does have, though. And your Mom, she needs a man to care for her. She's lonely, too, and has replaced your Dad with someone else."

"Oh, my gosh, Dad complains that Mom has substituted David for him!" I exclaimed.

"Your mother needs to do more volunteer work; it makes her feel good." Nancy twirled a few strands of blond hair between her fingers.

My mind flashed to the last time I had visited the house. Mom had shown me her latest knitting project, a sweater for an orphan child. Her thoughtful gesture made me wonder if her blockade against Jeanette and me was only our imagination and that there was something definitely wrong with us.

"Girls, it looks like your mother is keeping a secret from a young man in her life."

Jeanette and I looked to each other. We couldn't figure out what that comment meant. *Who is the young man in her life? What is the secret?*

We asked for information about the adult family home business that we were planning. She said that more schooling was required: one twin to specialize in creative marketing and the other in business planning. Her comment impressed me because I had always wanted to go to school for business administration and Jeanette talked about going back to school for a marketing degree several times to me in private.

Nancy continued talking with the insight of a spiritual guide, impressing us as each hunch matched our life story. "You need a good management team. I see the numbers one, three, and five are significant. You'll be reluctant to get the state involved, but after the first year you'll work with the state. Beware! The state will cause many headaches during the first year. Yet your business will be successful thereafter. You'll need an accountant after six months. Your main focus will be three things: nutrition, physical exercise, and recreation. God will bring spirits to you and you'll be known for 'quality care.'" She concluded. "Looks like the business will be very successful!"

After Nancy left, we looked at each other, and then said, "We've got to call Dad!"

"Dad, we've just seen an angelic reader!" We exclaimed, reporting the encounter with Nancy almost word for word.

Her supernatural ability opened the windows of my mind. Before I had only believed what I was taught in church and by those who were considered authority. Here was someone who was not brought up in the church, but who imparted sound knowledge. My curiosity grew. I began to question the Christian teaching that psychics were evil. Our new friendship with Nancy and the new church inspired me to read and understand the Bible more. I immersed myself in it, just like the pastor advocated, deepening my faith by reading as much scripture as my time allowed. "How much better to get wisdom than gold, to choose understanding rather than silver!" Proverbs 16; 16 Anger toward Mom turned into compassion. I wished more than ever to win her heart. Someday she would see that I was on her side as well.

173

Maybe if I kept myself immersed in the Word of God, she would see my worth. The next time Jeanette and I visited with her, we told her of our encounter with Nancy, hoping we could give her peace of mind. I also gave her a gift certificate to see Nancy for Mother's Day; I didn't want her to be excluded from all the excitement we had experienced.

Mom thanked me for the gift and then asked if Nancy happened to mention how long she would live, since her cancer seemed to be taking over.

"Nancy said you're going to make it for a very long time," I lied.

Mom silently absorbed the hope in my answer. However, the following Sunday she returned the gift certificate, saying that it was against the Bible to see a psychic.

Chapter 21

Out for Justice

I dialed Mom's phone number, anxious and hopeful. The divorce was finally over and Dad, Jeanette, and I clung to the hope that somehow we could convince her to give us permission to buy her share of the family home. *Can't she see the larger plan? God's plan?* I had to stay focused, calm, and polite when I called her in order for our plan to work. I ignored the conversation with Sean about the family home. He pointed out that finishing the home would be a financial drain and time consuming. I only saw purchasing it as a real estate opportunity. My focus was to keep the home in the family.

"Hi Mom, it's Jeannine." I did my best to sound upbeat, but my insides were churning with worry.

"Oh," she said, as if she was disappointed it was only me. "Hi."

"Um, I heard the house is for sale. I was wondering if Sean and I could buy it." My mind itemized all the reasons she was still apprehensive around me: Jeanette and I weren't around while she fought against cancer and to make things worse, we gave continuous support to Dad. The apprehension in her voice told me she still thought of us as the enemy and our attempt to win her over made us look even more pathetic. But we were 24 years old. We were adults and we were going to prove our worth to her. We were going to open an adult family home and take care of other people who had gone through the same pain that our family had.

"Why would you want to buy the home, honey? You already have a nice house."

If she knew of our plan to open an adult family home, she would refuse our offer immediately. She didn't think we were capable of bettering the world. She didn't fill out college applications or help pay for our education, like she did for David.

"Why would you want to buy the family home?" Mom's question caused more confusion. I wasn't sure if her sugary voice was just a front. After all, as adults we had learned to be polite to each other—even when we were burning with anger inside. Her candy-coated voice made me feel guilty for hating her. Maybe I was being too hard on her.

"Well, it would be neat if Vanessa and Alli could grow up in a big house like I did." *How pathetic. She knows I'm lying; after all, Sean and I had just bought a house.* Even though Sean was actively remodeling it, it would never meet the potential the family home had.

"Honey, first of all you're going to have to get approved." Then she added, "You understand the reason behind why I can't sell the house to you, don't you?"

"Not really." My heart plunged at the thought that she had already made up her mind.

"It's in terrible condition, Jeannine. It just wouldn't be a good idea for you to buy it," she justified. "It's over thirty years old. Your father just didn't finish it the way it should have been finished."

My mouth wouldn't open to tell her all the reasons why she *should* sell us her share. Why couldn't I tell her that this should be a business transaction, and should not be personal? I hung up disappointed in myself. All I could think about was that Dad had built the home. Why would she refuse to sell it to us? The only explanation I could come up with was that she didn't love us. Hateful thoughts seared my soul; eventually, I was furious.

I couldn't help but brood about her refusal to listen to me—for days after the conversation. She didn't take my desires seriously. In fact, she totally disregarded anything that I had ever wanted. This was the first time I had asked for anything materialistic. It wasn't like I wanted her to hand it to me on a silver platter. We intended to pay her for whatever the house was worth.

When I talked with Jeanette and Dad about our business plan, I regained my confidence about the future. Together, we would be as strong as Zena, the warrior princess! We decided to reclaim our power and focus on the positive. If Mom wouldn't sell us the family home, we were going to help Dad win it back the right way—through the court system! Dad wasn't as passionate about buying back his home, but he went along with us.

I told Sean that we had to buy the house for the adult family home. I yearned for his support but his response was not what I had hoped for.

"I don't think you should do this. It might not work out the way you want it to, and face it, Jeannine, taking care of people is just not you."

"No, you don't understand! It's God's Plan!" I argued. Jeanette and I were divinely ordained to open a home for adults with disabilities to prove that Dad's injury didn't happen in vain. If we didn't try, we would feel incomplete. We continued with our plans seeing anyone who prevented us from moving forward as against God. I found a lawyer through the phone book and took time off work so Dad could see him immediately. I wasn't thinking. I was just doing, doing, doing; taking quick action before it was too late.

At last we found a lawyer located in the Southcenter area. I set up an appointment and made it to the office on time with Dad. A man with peppered hair called us into his office. My black heels clicked against the marble floors; Dad's tennis shoes squeaked and left a few black scuff marks.

In the office, I wanted to dwell on the injustices, yet hurting Mom or getting her in trouble was not in the plans. More than anything in the world, I still wanted to win her love. On the surface, she didn't appear mad at us. She still talked to us sweetly, as if nothing was wrong with our relationship, which caused more confusion. Maybe her mistrust toward us was just our imagination. My ambivalence over our relationship prevented me from opening my mouth and spilling out all that I felt. I blamed Dad's court-appointed Guardian Ad Litem, Eliza Lott, for his problems. I gave the lawyer an overview of the case and explained that Dad's unusual disposition was because of a hang gliding accident twelve years ago.

"Even though he doesn't appear competent, he's read a set of encyclopedias twice and the Bible thirty-four times! He's probably one of the smartest people I know."

"What's your Dad's name again?" The lawyer asked.

"It's Allen," I answered, feeling my confidence slip. Why couldn't the lawyer ask Dad for his name? He probably didn't believe anything I had just told him.

The lawyer turned to me and declared that we could call him Christopher. He finally directed his attention to Dad and asked, "Who was the President before Clinton, Allen?"

Searching for an adequate reply, Dad stared at the colorful awards and certificates against the glossy black wall. I stared at the floor, wishing I could, somehow, telepathically give Dad the information. Finally, after a moment, Dad answered with a familiar strained voice. "You know, that's a really good question." Then he laughed. "You got me. I don't know. And does it really matter? The whole system is shot anyway."

Dad thought this was some big joke. I tried to make excuses. "Um, I can barely remember what I did yesterday, much less who the president was." I wanted to tell the lawyer to ask Dad about the Bible. That would be proof—massive proof.

Christopher couldn't read my mind, and he obviously wasn't interested in the Bible. "Well, Allen, you'll need to get a competency test before I can do anything for you."

"A what? I've already—"

"You know, a psychiatric test." Christopher slowly and clearly enunciated each word. "The... doctor... will... give... you... questions. If... there... is... no... doubt... that... you... are... all... there—you... can... retain... me... as... your... lawyer."

His disposition changed as he looked to me. "So young lady, where are you from?"

"Federal Way."

"No, I mean, what is your background. Where are your ancestors from?"

"Well, both of my parents are from Portland, Oregon, but I've lived here all of my life. I was adopted when I was six months old."

"What I'm trying to ask is, where were you adopted from?"

"Oh. Korea."

"You look like an ex-girlfriend of mine. She was from Singapore. Was she a beauty!" He closed his eyes and a smile swept over his doughy face as he remembered good times possibly gone bad.

178

"Oh, that's nice." I stood up and moved away from the chair, giving Dad the hint that it was time to go.

Christopher snapped back to reality. "What do you do for work?" I pulled Dad up by his arm. "I work in a salon as a nail tech." Christopher's hands discreetly dropped under the polished walnut desk. "You know, I used to get manicures regularly. I need someone to come to the office. It's really hard to get out with my busy schedule. If you need work you could come to the office. I'm sure the girls would get their nails done too."

"Oh, well, thanks, but I keep pretty busy at the salon. If things get slow, I might consider your offer."

Immediately after arriving home, I looked up the phone number of Dad's psychiatrist. After reaching the office via a phone call, Jeanette and I made the necessary arrangements to take him to see Dr. Leslie Brain for the required psychiatric exam. We got straight to the point while cramming into her office, a cleared-out storage room, and told her that Dad needed to prove his competency so he could handle his own money.

Leslie, a tall lean woman, was awed at the sight of Jeanette and me, while we talked back and forth, completing each other's sentences. She shook her head from side to side, and rapped her nails against the commercial-sized filing cabinet. Her thin lips curled into a wrapping ribbon smile. We hoped it was a sign that she understood and would do her part in God's plan, by giving the test. We fell silent and waited for her to respond.

Leslie looked from Dad, to Jeanette, to me, then back to Dad again. "Twins are so interesting; they're just amazing—you are so lucky to have these two."

Dad liked the attention, and smiled. "I know. Did you know I have two biological sons who rarely talk to me? I had no idea that when we adopted the two girls that they would be the ones to take care of me." He looked to Jeanette and me for approval.

"Girls and boys are certainly different," the doctor agreed. "What made you and your wife decide to adopt these two?"

Dad gladly expounded on his happy past with Mom, while Jeanette and I waited patiently, knowing that he rarely had the opportunity to share his story.

Time passed quickly. Before we knew it, Leslie looked at her watch. "Oh, shoot. Sorry, folks, I'm late for another appointment. You know, girls, a competency test is remarkably expensive. I'm sure your father can't afford it and besides, it's just not something you can do without a court order. Allen, tell your lawyer that he needs to get you a court order before I or any doctor will give the test. The test is quite complicated anyway, I mean, we're talking thousands of dollars!" She fumbled with a key so she could lock up her office.

"Okay," Dad obediently replied.

"Good-bye Allen, it's been fun chatting with you!" she patted his shoulder as he strolled out the door between Jeanette and me.

Dad's loud laugh ricocheted off the wide corridor as we walked out of the hospital. "Boy, is she fun!"

Afraid that his unstable gait made him look slow in the head, Jeanette and I hissed, "Shh," together.

Embarrassed, I scolded, "Dad, everyone is going to think you're weird! Your loud laugh is what got you into trouble with the judge, lawyers and doctors in the first place."

"No normal person is so animated and blissful," Jeanette agreed. "No wonder everyone thinks you're crazy!"

"Girls," Dad shouted into our ears, "I don't suffer from insanity. I enjoy every minute of it!" Again, his voice boomed and echoed against the corridor and his boisterous laughter bounced off the thick glass doors on the way out of the building. Jeanette and I rolled our eyes. He was content for the day and the special attention from a female doctor was a bonus.

Jeanette and I managed to find a lawyer for Dad right away, before Mom sold the family home. Time was running out. Now any lawyer would do; anyone who was willing to give Dad a few moments to speak, believe that he was competent, and understand our desperation. Was there anyone in the world like this?

I discovered a lawyer in Federal Way, close to Dad's place, my work, and home. Jeanette and I took another day off work to get Dad there. I noticed the office was small and plain, without frills. There wasn't a receptionist, a leather couch, or fake smiles.

Mark, the lawyer, talked straight to Dad instead of through Jeanette and me. Dad got to talk about hang gliding and his injury, he talked about how he had been an engineer at Boeing for thirty-two years, and how he worked on the black box, so he couldn't tell Mark about his projects because everything was secret. He talked about how he was a Sunday School teacher, and an elder, among other things, and that currently he was on his thirty-fourth reading of the Bible.

After a lengthy discussion, Mark was convinced. Dad *was* competent. To our relief, he even saw the injustice in the case. Dad retained the man as his lawyer immediately. Maybe we weren't crazy after all.

7-12-96
Dear Joy,
I have hired a lawyer, Mark, and he has filed a petition to vacate the court's judgments.

You didn't keep the vow we made at our wedding and the Bible says God doesn't like that. I am still healing and will one day be near normal.

I now support eight children via three International organizations. That may seem illogical to you, but not to me. God is still my strength for money will pass away. I am grateful to you for the education about God, and I keep learning.

I will live as long as God wants me to and at the moment that may be a long time. I haven't fallen or been sick for over two years and I seem to be getting stronger and more capable every day. The other day I connected the TV cable and now I have more channels than I know what to do with.

Allen

12-28-96
Dear Joy,
You may discount this as the ravings of an injured man, but I think it's worth considering. I wrote you 24 times and you have *never* written me back, nor have you stopped the divorce that you started. I can only conclude that you consider me an undesirable liability. I should have expected it to end

this way. You have discounted me, thinking I am financially incompetent, but in the end that will be decided by a doctor. Since the injury, you have always done what served you best.

I miss being a part of your life but "c'est la vie" …I can learn to survive. I went shopping for birthday cards for you and David's and they were a big deal for me, and I assume they got delivered, but heard nothing.

I assume you had a good Thanksgiving and Christmas dinner, and I missed being a part of it. I will probably never get over you, but life must go on and I will always have God, even if humans leave, and they do. You lied to God. When you got married, you said "for better or worse," but as soon as "worse" came along you moved to the side.

I have been ignored. My ideas are not heard nor given consideration. It's like I am already dead.

Divorce is anti-God. You, as usual, will do as you please, but I want nothing to do with it. I am writing you again to express my pain at your rejection. The marriage vows were meaningless to you. Like the Bible says, you will stand before God alone and He will be the final judge. For me, nothing and nobody will separate me from God. One of the advantages of my injury is that I drew closer to God and became stronger in my faith. If God tests me with pain NOW, so be it. I may not like it, but what child likes a spanking?

Allen

A few days later, the lawyer called me while I was at work. "Hi Jeannine, Mark here. The reason I'm calling is that I need to go over some stuff with your Dad."

"Okay." I flipped through the wrinkled pages of the salon work schedule, attempting to find time to give Dad transportation. "I think I've got some time tomorrow."

"No."

"What?"

"See," he said slow and uneasy, "I need to see him alone."

"Oh, okay."

"You see, I talked to Eliza Lott and she's advised me that it would be best to see your Dad alone from now on. She said, from her past experience, that you girls are a bad influence on him and that you are only interested in his money. Don't get me wrong, I know you two are nice. It's just from now on, I need to proceed with caution."

"Okay, I don't mind. You can see him on your own."

"From now on, I'll go see him at the facility. Thanks for understanding."

"Sure. It's actually better for me. Now I don't have to take time off work to get him to his appointments." I tried to sound nonchalant, but inside my heart stung with anger. I just wanted the court to see Dad as a normal human being. Why can't they see beyond his physical body? I was sick of Mom's insistence that he was incompetent. What was she trying to do? Convince the rest of the world to see him as worthless too?

On the way home from church, after a motivational sermon about the need to go beyond "man's game," and to live as better Christians, Jeanette and I advised Dad that this time he needed to win "Man's Game". The pastor told us to use Jesus as a master coach—ever present with a watch, always urging us to better our time, jump a little higher, throw a little farther, and win the battle against Satan. Only problem was, Mom lived for Christ as well and she believed we were the evil ones. We were at war, both sides using Jesus to win. It was like a competitive football game. Whose side was God going to choose? I had forgotten that God is love. If we loved we wouldn't need strict rules and standards. If we loved we could live in peace. *PEACE. People Enjoying A Cohesive Environment.*

The phone call I received from Dad's newly retained lawyer was proof that there really was a war going on within the family. To win this war, we told Dad, "No more wearing sweats to court! You have to wear a navy blue suit, like you did at Boeing so people take you seriously. You have to play Man's Game!"

"But all my suits are at home with Joy," He complained. His once-black hair had turned nearly snow white; I blamed it on the stress from the divorce. At age sixty-seven, the wrinkles on his face seemed to steadily increase.

"Fine, then we'll take you shopping. I don't care if I get in trouble," I fumed, and turned the car around to head for Sears.

Jeanette agreed. "Mom already thinks we're evil anyway. What difference will it make? Dad, you deserve to get your case heard!"

Still, there was our fear of Mom, and it kept us from going to court with Dad and announcing what we believed to be the truth. We couldn't bear for her to be mad at us for supporting Dad. She already had the court system in the palm of her hand. We'd be looked at as money-hungry daughters. So Jeanette and I impatiently waited for Dad to call us over to his place after he returned from the hearing.

"How'd it go, Dad?" We asked, eager to discuss his victory.

"No one listened. I would like to pass on my wisdom to someone, but I guess it is not part of the plan. Each person has to make his own way. That is the system and I can't change it."

"What do you mean, Dad?" We asked again. "How did it go?"

"Not too well. They dismissed the case because I don't have a doctor's note that says I'm competent. Eliza argued that she was never my lawyer in the first place. And then she said, as further proof of my incompetence, I'm unable to understand this due to my brain injury. She said if I was as capable as I claim, I would have retained myself a lawyer sooner—" Dad stopped mid-sentence and laughed. "Isn't it ironic? The law is supposed to be about justice and getting to the truth, but all they know how to do is lie!"

Jeanette and I didn't laugh at his comment. We stood still and stared at him with frowns and crossed arms. "You know what their problem is, don't you?" Jeanette said, "They can't see past your body. Of course they're not going to talk to you. It would only prove that they were wrong the first time around."

Dad nodded in agreement. "Mark recommends I see a civil attorney as soon as possible so we can freeze the sale of the house. This could cost us some money. Is the house worth it?"

We didn't need to answer. Our minds were made up and Dad knew it. I had only one final question. "Dad, do you think Mom would let you buy the house since she won't sell it to me?"

Dad could read the intention behind the question. "I've asked Mark about the house. Mom has a buyer already, and she won't tell me what real estate agency she's going through. She's afraid I'll get involved and mess up the transaction. It might be too late to buy the house, girls," he concluded.

Chapter 22

Sixth Sense

On the way to work each day, I drove by a large billboard that read *"The Messengers: A true story they want told,"* with an image of a large graceful angel next to the words. If not stopped at the most convenient full service gas station near my house, I probably wouldn't have paid much attention to it. But because I drove by it so often, I assumed the sign was placed for me—literally and figuratively. My angels placed it there with purpose. In my heart, I knew that I was supposed to buy the book. I passed the huge billboard on the way to work several times that month before I told Sean that I thought my angels led me to it and I just *had* to get the book. "It must be a sign from God," I stated with faith and gratitude.

"Whatever you say!" Sean rolled his eyes in disbelief at my angel talk. In spite of this, as he always did, he supported me and found the book at the third bookstore he visited.

I read the book from cover to cover in two days, then gave it to Jeanette and Dad. The Messengers was about a businessman who remembered a life as Paul from the Bible, via a past life regression. His memories presented a vivid account of his life 2000 years ago, causing me to become interested in Paul's thoughts during his time with Jesus. It motivated me to study the Bible, especially the lives of Jesus, Paul, and the disciples.

Nick Bunick, the man who experienced the memory, didn't intend to publish the sessions at first for fear of risking his position as a prominent and respected businessman. Yet, after an encounter with an "angelic reader" and other angelic coincidences, his fear disappeared and the dialogue from his regression was published.

Dad was hesitant about reading the book at first. "The Bible says that man lives only once. Reincarnation isn't a Christian belief," he said.

I told him that, yes, our *body* may only live once, but our spirit within the body lives eternally. Maybe our spirit chooses to forget all it knows and take form in a new body after living in heaven for so long. Maybe we come down here to experience imperfection so that we can grow, evolve and eventually learn and appreciate what true perfection is. Maybe each life on earth offers an opportunity to better our spirit. It was a new concept that came to me after reading *The Messengers*. "I don't think it matters that there is no such thing as past lives. Didn't the book get you interested in Jesus, Dad? I know my faith in God has increased."

"You know, Jeannine," Dad said after his second reading. "You could be right and the book did get me thinking." We decided it would make a terrific gift for the pastor and bought him a copy for Christmas.

A curiosity about reincarnation emerged unexpectedly after we had finished the book. Dad, Jeanette and I had heard of the concept only a very few times, but had always discarded the thought. The Vietnamese lady who baby-sat for Jeanette and me had small Buddhist shrines in her apartment. I wondered if God would forgive me for exploring other religious beliefs. After thinking about it for many months, we concluded that if Christianity was truly the right way, God would lead us back. And if we were meant to look into different philosophies, God would present me with an opportunity.

A few clouds drifted over Mt. Rainier like giant swan feathers. Nancy, our new friend and clairvoyant, invited Jeanette and me to "do the Seattle scene" with her. We hung out by the pier, dropped in on the little shops, and ate lunch at *Ivars*. We munched on fried fish and chips. Between bites, we filled her in on all the details of Mom and Dad's divorce.

Out of the blue, she surprised us by saying, "I want to meet your Dad. Come on, let's go!"

We quickly picked up our belongings and headed for the retirement facility. Upon entering his room, Nancy announced over and over, "Ooh, wow! Your Dad has great spiritual presence!" She was so dramatic and exciting to be around. I was glad and amazed that she could see past his body, an ability we learned was hard for most.

The right side of his mouth was still lazy, as he spoke. "I want to tell you one thing, Nancy, I've learned more about God since my injury than I ever knew before. And if given the chance, I would go through all the adversity all over again. I asked for wisdom, and God gave me problems to solve! I have everything I need, right here and now." Dad sluggishly pointed to his chest and then his arm went wild as he pointed to his head. I liked that he didn't depend on others to make him happy. Depending on people only caused disappointments.

"Allen, can I do a quick healing prayer for you?" Nancy asked.

"Sure. I'd like that." Dad wiped his nose with the sleeve of his cobalt blue sweatshirt and grinned.

Jeanette and I assisted him to his bed and he lay down. Nancy knelt beside him. Her hands hovered just inches above his head. Then gently she moved them over his body, and finally above his toes. I wondered if she was feeling some sort of energy from God, as she prayed over parts of his body that needed healing. She mentioned problems with his digestive system and told us that he needed to eat better. It was true. Even though the facility offered three nutritious meals daily, Dad chose to skip most of them for store bought sweets. Mom blamed this habit on his head injury. Nancy even sensed that he had gall bladder surgery and the stones were removed.

During the process, I quietly wished for her to magically transform Dad back to his pre-injury days. Perhaps a miracle would occur that would shock Mom, Eliza Lott, and the judge. All our problems would suddenly be gone! A miracle would also prove that the Bible was right: God does move mountains and heal the sick when we have the faith the size of a mustard seed.

The air in the room was warm and pleasant. I felt at peace and sensed that Dad did too. After Nancy's prayer, Dad sat up calm and quiet. I fully expected his voice, balance and gait to be restored. He was silent—all of us were; then he spoke.

"That was soothing. Thank you. My muscles feel relaxed and more in control."

Jeanette and I noted that his voice wasn't as loud and strained as usual, but when he toddled back to his recliner, I felt disappointed. A miracle did not occur. When is God going to perform the miracle? I became even more envious of those who had recovered fully from an injury and claimed their healing was due to God's grace. We had prayed for almost thirteen years for God's grace, but with no results. Our family never received the miracle Christian leaders claimed we would earn for our faith. Do we not deserve God's grace? Is our faith not strong enough? Are we considered undeserving? God's lost souls? God's unchosen?

Although Dad wasn't healed, he thought it would be a good idea to have another healing prayer. We did too. Perhaps more prayer with Nancy was needed. Jeanette wasn't able to attend the succeeding meeting. This time, Dad sat comfortably in his light blue recliner. Nancy faced him in a metal fold-up chair and I perched myself on the edge of his bed, where the blue and red comforter revealed washed-out orange and yellow sheets. This time, Dad was going to be fully restored to his old self. I just knew it. The church had taught us all about God's grace from the beginning of time. Dad had even taught Jesus' miracle stories to his Sunday School students, and now he would be living proof.

Nancy closed her eyes in prayer in the middle of the large uninteresting room. Dad kept his eyes open as if he were participating in a strange staring contest. My nonverbal attempts to try to get him to relax went unnoticed.

After a moment of silence and prayer, Nancy began speaking in a slow and soothing voice. "You are of warriors. It is very hard being present in this human body. It is very loving of you to choose this life, but being in spirit form is much more pleasant."

What's going on? This doesn't sound like a normal prayer; it doesn't even sound like Nancy. I scrambled to find a pen and paper, worried that my noise would distract her. She continued. Her words were clear and monotone.

"It feels very slow here compared to the energy and light that I love. You taught many children, taught many families to farm and prosper. When we walked together, you were very loving, but impatient. You showed people how to prosper and they would not listen, and so you would not show them anymore. You loved many children when we walked together. You were a very wealthy farmer in a land of poverty. You herded many animals, and farmed food as well. Wealth was very comfortable to you, for you have knowingness of having nothing. You started with nothing and created great wealth and shared teachings with many who listened."

As fast as I could, I copied her words with a ballpoint pen and a scrap of paper.

Oblivious to my commotion, Nancy continued speaking. "This is the first time in this land. This journey that you are on now is very purposeful, for you have truly learned patience, which is why you chose to come back, to teach others of patience. To be a great warrior-teacher, you must be a great receiver. You wanted to experience patience. God is pleased. There are many days in front of you. It is greatly hoped that you truly learn receivership on every level. You are a great warrior once again."

I scribbled on the paper and then shoved the note in front of Dad's face. As slow as a tortoise, he searched for his reading glasses while Nancy continued. "This is the fourth time on this planet; many life-years ago you walked the holy Jewish lands. A great warrior with God, but you did not allow for patience."

After several attempts to get the frames on his face properly, Dad scrunched his nose to read my note through smudged glass. *Dad, ask her if you knew Jesus.*

"Did I know Jesus?" he obediently asked.

"Yes, you knew Jesus."

I scribbled, *Ask her if you were one of The Twelve*, and placed the note front of his face.

"Was I one of The Twelve?" Dad asked.

"No. A close relationship with him in your third lifetime, but remember God's time is a very short time. You have great knowingness now beyond all others, because you are remembering your walk with Jesus and His brothers, which were most important to you. Live in remembrance of receivership now and what this truly entails."

"Am I going to live again?" Dad asked on his own.

"Your spirit lives eternally, forever, and you can be transformed anytime at God's will."

"What am I supposed to do now?"

"We have great faith that you will walk your journey, and minister to help others, and you will be of allowance of receivership, as well as giving. God is most pleased with your patience. For it took great teaching for you to learn this. You have great knowingness of patience, warriorship, interpretation of thought, faith, and hope that love prevails over all. The Father is most pleased."

Dad searched for more questions, not yet ingesting what Nancy had said. "What is your definition of the Kingdom of God?"

"Seeking the fruits of the spirit: love, joy, peace, patience, kindness, goodness, faithfulness, gentleness, and self-control. You have great remembrance about the Kingdom; Heaven is a minor word for what the Kingdom is like. You know much more than you allow yourself to remember. The Father is very pleased."

When Nancy finally opened her eyes, Dad took off his glasses like an English gentleman and set them on a dusty TV tray. My hand hurt from writing so hard and fast but my mind raced with excitement. Late for another meeting, Nancy rummaged around in her purse for the car keys, ignorant of the profound effect her words had had on us, and unaware of our need for it. She gave Dad a hug, then me, and ran out the door.

I excitedly told my clients and the women at work about angels and Nancy's supernatural abilities. Later, when I thought about it, I felt embarrassed about getting so excited. *Who knows? Maybe they think I'm going crazy. Maybe I'm making a fool of myself.* The experience *did* feel outrageous, but at the same time it felt real.

My enthusiasm for the new church and Nancy's sixth sense did cause me to lose a few clients, but living for the Lord was worth it. I couldn't help but to share the experience. Angels? A past life with Jesus? Religious dedication? For some reason, the power and joy I felt made the challenges practically dissolve into a forgotten past. God had provided me with evidence that there was redemption in our struggle, motivating me to stay on the path and to help others.

I wished Mom was open to hear about our exciting experiences. No such luck. She continued to perceive Dad as weak and incapable.

Like the rest of the world, she believed he should do everything possible to get back to where he was as an engineer and elder. After the session with Nancy, I, however, saw Dad as a powerful teacher, capable of inspiring others—even in his disabled state. My mind changed. *Perhaps God doesn't see our disabilities or our faults. Maybe God focuses on our capabilities, our potential, our authentic power, our spirit. Why do we see less in ourselves? Why do we see less in others?*

Chapter 23

Civil Action

Jeanette and I felt an inner conviction that we were supposed to turn Dad's home into his legacy, even though we never asked him how he felt about the situation. If only Mom would trust us with the house, we would show her our worth. We would show her how much we could help others. Using our parents' house would be the ultimate way to prove to her that she was wrong about us. We made arrangements to take Dad to a civil lawyer. Did we have a case?

Nancy, with her usual good cheer, accompanied us on the trip to see the civil lawyer and gave Dad, Jeanette, and me a boost of confidence. The drive to Seattle was fun and positive. Insecure about driving on the busy downtown streets, I drove carefully, and everything fell into place. We located the building right away and found the perfect parking spot. We praised our angels and Jesus, of course, for our luck. Dad was just happy to get out for the day, and treated it all as one big adventure.

Even though the lawyer, Jeff Miller, was of small build, I trembled while Jeanette and I took turns describing our parent's situation, again emphasizing Dad's competency. Mr. Miller listened patiently to us rant about Eliza Lott, and how, in our opinion, Mom was guilty. Guilty of what? We didn't know. We didn't want to hurt her, but it was getting increasingly hard not to feel that she was the cause of Dad's impoverishment and our pain. Afterwards, I felt guilty.

"Dad, hand him the letter," I instructed. "Maybe this will do a better job of explaining the situation."

Dad attempted to put the letter on the conference table but the ataxia in his arm caused the two papers to fly out of control and float onto the floor. Jeanette and I quickly crawled under the table, retrieved them and handed them to the lawyer.

193

To Mr. Miller:

I would like to file a formal complaint concerning the law practices of Eliza Lott. She was appointed Guardian Ad Litem to me during my divorce trial. I was injured in a hang-gliding incident in 1984 that left me physically disabled. My speech, balance, and motor control skills were impaired. Yet I am competent and I have written statements from friends who can attest to this. I have a B.S. in Physics with minors in Math and Philosophy. I worked at Boeing for thirty-two years as an Engineer prior to my injury. I have read the Bible many times and a set of encyclopedias twice, along with numerous other books.

The following are ways Ms. Lott failed to perform her professional duty resulting in my loss of rights:

1) She mislead me to believing that she was my lawyer in my divorce proceedings.
2) She did not refer me to or recommend a divorce lawyer on my behalf. I defended myself during all hearings.
3) In two brief visits, amounting to no more than twenty minutes, she concluded I was incapable of handling my affairs.
4) She refused to acknowledge the competency test administered by my physician or admit that I should be given the chance to handle my money.
5) She failed to and was not interested in interviewing those persons who interact with me on a consistent basis; she only interviewed the Petitioner of the Divorce.
6) She failed to inform me of rescheduled divorce hearings. I spent wasted time and effort to go to hearings and depended on others for transportation. When I asked her why she didn't notify me, she said it was not her responsibility.

7) She ignored telephone calls, letters of inquiry, and comments made by me.
8) She never supplied me with my requested list of assets.
9) My "incompetence" was proven with two facts: 1) I donated ten percent of my income to the church 2) I purchased a two-hundred-dollar television, which I financed personally. She considered that excessive spending.
10) Against my wishes and ignoring my ownership rights, she gave away one of two Ocean Shores lots. The other was given to the Petitioner of the Divorce (Joy Vance).
11) Ms. Lott, for some reason unknown to me, has deliberately misrepresented my interest. Due to her biased opinion of me, I have now lost fifty percent of my community assets in my divorce hearing. As there was little or no communication on the part of Ms. Lott, I was forced to accept whatever was put forth in the hearings without my prior consent or knowledge.
12) Eliza Lott totally misrepresented me. She relayed her opinions of me to the court as fact.

Ms. Lott has done everything in her power to prevent me from being awarded fifty percent of my community assets in my divorce hearing. I hired a new lawyer to represent me, who petitioned to vacate the judgment and to renegotiate. Ms. Lott made sure she was there to ruin my credibility again during this hearing. Therefore I lost again. I will now have to spend my money for the cost of an appeal to try to win my rights back.

I am suing Eliza for malpractice, neglect, misrepresentation, relaying untruths to the court, and refusal to pursue my rights in the court of law for the following amounts: Five hundred thousand dollars to form the Allen Vance Foundation to aid in proper legal representation and fees for persons with disabilities. Four-hundred thousand dollars for pain and suffering, and one-hundred thousand dollars to go towards the opening of the Ad-Vance Living,

Inc. adult family home, elder care, and to rehabilitate persons who are recovering from head injuries.

Allen L. Vance

"Did you write this Allen or did you have some help?" Mr. Miller asked.

"I wrote it," Dad answered.

"What kind of engineer were you? An Electrical Engineer or a Mechanical Engineer?"

"Yes." Dad grinned, while explaining. "They didn't know what to do with me, so they made me both. Did you know I went to the University of Washington on company time and studied Electronics and Boeing paid for it? I was studying for a master's degree but never finished it."

"Why not?"

"Oh, I don't know. I wasn't a very obedient student and I asked too many embarrassing questions."

"Why were they embarrassing?"

"Oh, because the teacher couldn't answer them. It's a situation where the student knows more than the teacher. And the teacher wasn't going to admit that he wasn't prepared for the question. After all, the teacher had a degree. All that boils down to is that I thought for myself instead of taking information from books."

"Allen, were you ever in the military?"

"No. Because I worked at Boeing, I never had to go into the service. I got to stay home and make lots of money so Joy could buy lots of clothes." He laughed at the thought. "She hasn't stopped buying and look where it put me—stuck inside your office!"

Jeff caught on and laughed. "Allen, you're a quick wit. I believe you girls when you tell me that your father is 'all there.' What I need for you to do is go down to the courthouse archives and get copies of the entire case. Allen, have you thought about suing your wife? You know, you really should think about it."

Our eyes bulged at the thought. Mom was fighting cancer that had spread to her bones and to her liver. We didn't know how much longer she had to live and we didn't want her to get into trouble with the law.

Dad frowned and said, "No way!"

The following day I convinced Sean to help me retrieve Mom and Dad's divorce papers from the courthouse. We found Mom's original petition and declaration where she said Dad was both physically and mentally unable to take care of himself. She pointed out that Dad suffered injuries to the part of his brain that deals with judgments and attitudes, and because he complained while living at Jeanette's, she moved him back to an adult care facility.

Mom also insisted that the court-appointed guardian (or David) control Dad's share of the finances. She couldn't understand why Dad would demand control of his Social Security and pension money when he lacked the judgment to spend it wisely. Dad's counter argument was never heard. He wrote that there was nothing in writing that said his judgment was impaired. He wrote numerous letters to Mom to dissuade her from getting the divorce, and pointed out that she had accumulated almost thirty-five thousand dollars in excessive shopping debts, while he had incurred none.

We also found Dad's "Outpatient Follow-up Evaluation" test results from when Mom took him to the doctor back at the beginning of the divorce. The doctor said, based on what she had learned from Mom, that Dad had an impairment of judgment, lack of awareness of his limitations, and interpersonal rigidity. However, the doctor didn't feel she had sufficient information to make a clear recommendation about Dad's competence or lack of competence to manage his own money.

"No one but Mom has said that Dad was incompetent!" I exclaimed on the way home from the courthouse. "Maybe we do have a case!"

The final blow came from a letter I found hidden within the file that Mom had written:

Attn.: Ms. Eliza Lott
Subject: Vance Dissolution
Ms. Eliza Lott:

I have some concerns regarding the handling of information in the dissolution between my husband and myself. If my two hundred thousand-dollar inheritance is revealed to Allen, he would likely pass the information to our children. His severe brain damage was mostly in the cognitive area of the brain. As a couple, before Allen's accident, we did not share finances with the family, in order to prevent misinterpretations with regards to money issues. Our girls would pass the information on to the their friends and cousins, and that would be harmful to our family and my brother's family. I am there for my children and am ready to help them when it is appropriate. The knowledge of the inheritance would have a devastating effect on both my family and my brother's family. Our children are remembered in my will.

Allen cannot be counted on to use discretion in these areas because of the judgment-area injury. If there is a way you can process the inheritance information in your settlement recommendation to Allen without revealing the full amount, I will be eternally grateful.

I have always seen that Allen had the best care possible: the first eight years at home when I was sole caretaker, and top quality care in private care homes during the past two years. Even after he was no longer living at home, I provided transportation several times per week to doctors, therapy, lunches, etc. It is my desire to see this level of care continue as long as possible.

Thank you for your consideration.
Joy J. Vance

I shook as I read her letter; each word hit me like a bullet. My heart felt weak. The letter was evidence that my own mother hated me. She really did think that we were only out for her money. On the way home from Seattle, I didn't want Sean to know the damage done, so I silently stared at the letter in disbelief. I realized that even if we had complied with her, we wouldn't have been able to win her heart, or even any trust. After all, we weren't from her being, even after twenty-five years as her daughters, we were still considered adopted strong-willed children. Why did we try so hard to be accepted? If we had known all along that our attempts to win her love were futile, this letter wouldn't hurt so much.

Out of the blue, I became aware that I wasn't the one with the problem. Mom was the one who was boxed in! She was the one who blocked us out with her fears, and she did the same to Dad and Mike. The reason why she'd closed her heart to Mike remained a mystery.

I faxed the copied papers to Mr. Miller right away. The papers were confirmation that Mom had lied and the lawyer was negligent in her duty to Dad. There really wasn't any proof that Dad was incompetent. The lawyers and judge had relied on Mom's opinion without talking to Dad or his doctors!

Meanwhile, Dad searched the phone book for the real estate agent who was selling the family home so he could make an offer on Mom's share. After calling four agencies he located the selling agent. She said she needed to talk to Mom's lawyer before she could give him any information regarding the sale of the house.

Is Mr. Miller going to take Dad's case? Will all the papers I found help Dad win? Can Mr. Miller freeze the sale of the house? Soon after we had faxed him the papers from the courthouse archives, we began getting the same message again and again from his secretary. "I'm sorry, Mr. Miller is out of the office. May I take a message?"

What does that mean? Jeanette and I wondered. We were left hanging.

Chapter 24

Primal Fear

At least we could still hang on to our faith in the church, our trust in Jesus, and best of all, our hope in God. God wouldn't let us down and we wouldn't let God down. We made a big decision. We were going to continue with our attempt to open an adult family home, whether or not Mom gave us permission to buy her share. She couldn't stop us from fulfilling the purpose that God had given us. We were ready and willing to take on the world.

From my sister's diary:
3-12-97
I went to church and introduced myself to one of the pastors. I told him how the church has helped me. I can feel the difference and I appreciate that. It has helped my Dad too. Then I told him a little about our plan of opening up an adult family home and our mission to help others. He was very pleased and told me to contact the Mission directors so that they could pray for us. He offered full support!
I'm taking things one day at a time. Since Danny and I broke up, I am trying to enjoy being single and will hopefully find a man to keep me company. This has been a great learning experience.

Jeanette and I completed our business plan and requested a meeting with the great pastor at the thriving Christian Church. We had high hopes, high apple pie in the sky hopes! We were going to get support and prayers, finally. "The church will help us. After all," we joked, "Dad's the biggest Bible-thumpin' Christian there is!"

I worked hard to write a well-documented letter to the pastor regarding our plan to open a home for adults with disabilities and had it ready to give to him on Sunday. Maybe the pastor would let us put a notice in the bulletin so our need for used furniture donations from the congregation could be known. The letter requesting donations was in my purse ready to give to him after the service. I only half listened to the pastor give his sermon; my mind was preoccupied with questions: how should I approach him? Should I tell him that we were the ones who gave him the book *The Messengers*? If he had enjoyed it, he might be impressed with us and support our adult family home with prayers and used furniture donations. On the other hand, if he hadn't liked the book, he might not be willing to help us out. As I sat in the pew during the church service, and waited to hand the pastor the letter, I wasn't so sure. A buzz of doubt disturbed my head. Maybe it'll be better to keep my mouth shut about the book; he won't remember it was us anyway. There are too many people in the congregation giving him gifts and requesting his attention. I decided to give the letter without an accompanying speech.

It took only a few short spring days for Pastor Sterne to read over my letter and then call us for an appointment. When Jeanette and I nervously entered his contemporary office, I immediately noticed that his shelves were lined with books. Good, he likes to read! He must have enjoyed *The Messengers*. I couldn't wait to tell him how Dad and I had accidentally discovered the angel code.

It was only months after we had read the book. I sat on Dad's bed, rocking Allison to sleep, when I looked over at Dad's name framed with its meaning. Half of his first name was covered up, and only the letters ALL were exposed.

"Hey Dad, the first three letters of your name and the first three letters in Allison's name are the same!"

Dad laughed. "Isn't that ironic?"

Minutes later another realization hit me. "Dad, did you know that the first three letters in Vanessa's name and the first three letters in our last name are the same? Go look up the number three from your records."

Dad walked to the computer where he had meticulously collected and analyzed every number, person, and place mentioned in the Bible.

He typed his findings into an old Macintosh computer. After tapping on the keyboard for a few minutes, he said, "The number three means perfection, complete, solid, and divine."

"What does the number four-four-four mean? The number used by the angels to encourage Nick to publish his manuscript, *The Messengers?*"

Again, like a beginner at the piano, he clicked on a few keys with his forefinger. "The number four means created by God," he replied.

"So four, four, four means something like perfection created by God or Love." I stopped talking to soak in the information, then blurted, "Dad, look up the number twelve, because four plus four plus four equals twelve!"

I waited patiently for him to finish tapping on the keyboard. After a minute had passed, he swung around in his cheap office chair and stated, "Government Perfection."

"Hey Dad, maybe the code 444 means, a perfect government created by God or Love. Doesn't it say in the Bible that God is Love?" I exclaimed.

Jeanette and I sat in the pastor's office confident he would be sympathetic to our needs. When the pastor pulled *The Messengers* from his desk drawer, we became excited. He's read the book after all! I couldn't wait to tell him our good news.

He waited a moment before speaking. "Before the church can help you in any way, we need to straighten some things out." He pointed to highlighted areas in the book. "First of all, there is no such thing as reincarnation. Reincarnation is a pagan belief. You've gone outside basic Christian teachings when you read this book and I would say you are at the entrance of a New Age cult. You do know that the Heaven's Gate cult were New-Agers, don't you?"

I had heard about the group the day before from the news on the radio. Oh yeah, they're that weird group that killed themselves in California.

"You haven't been handing out this book to anyone else I hope— I've already warned the secretary and all of the leaders. See, Jesus wouldn't let his true flock run amuck."

I nodded like a cooperative child, as if every word he said was true, but inside my thoughts ran riot. But *The Messengers* is about

Jesus and confirms a lot of the teachings from the Bible! What the heck is New Age? I'll have to look that up later.

I knew what Jeanette was thinking as she slouched down further in the chair. But Dad believes *The Messengers* upholds the teachings of Christ and Dad should know. He's read the Bible thirty-four times!

"It's easy to get lost," Pastor Sterne told us. "You know, the Christian life should be one of great joy. We live knowing that God has forgiven us for every sin. We live knowing that God will provide for us and not burden us with more than we can bear. Yet even the most godly of us sometimes gets lost. Obviously, you girls got caught up in the trappings of the world and forgot to keep your eyes on Jesus. It's easy to do, but God knows you're just human and he makes allowances for that.

"God doesn't demand perfect obedience. He knows we're incapable of offering it. His main message to us today is to walk moment by moment in dependence upon His Spirit. If we fail to trust Him, we will sin. You must confess your sin specifically to Him and claim his forgiveness. Then turn from it and trust Him again. You might think that you aren't strong enough to do that. You might not have the power to change, but God will give you the power. You have to make the first move! That's what the Holy Spirit is all about. The power to live the Christian life comes from the Holy Spirit and from the knowledge that Jesus died for our sins, was resurrected, and sits in heaven at the right hand of the Father, where He prays for you continually. I hope that I've motivated you to live a life of righteousness."

He looked to the photo of Jesus on his desk and paused. "We need to fall in love with Jesus, he's got the answers—not us. We're not capable of joy or peace or love—no, not without Jesus!"

I continued to nod in agreement while Jeanette crossed her arms and sank down further, as if to disappear into the low overstuffed chair. We know all about this! I wanted to shout. We've lived and breathed this message for close to twenty-five years! We've immersed ourselves in the teachings of the church ever since I can remember— it's our roots! How dare you question our faith!

"All other religions have only evil messages to give," the pastor added, "and that is why we must never stray from the church."

Sensing our shock as defiance, he asked, "What does the law of the church demand?"

We looked toward each other searching for the answer he would want. "To love others?"

"Well, that too, but more importantly, perfect obedience. God doesn't grade on the curve when it comes to the law. In James 2:10, it says: 'Whoever keeps the whole law, yet stumbles in one point, he has become guilty of all.' Do you get that? You must live complete and righteous lives for if you fall, you are guilty. There are no ifs or buts in God's world. Stop living in man's world. The only way to salvation is through Jesus Christ. In order to get any support from the church, you'll need to study these five pages of scripture I've outlined. And then after you've done that, you can denounce the book by writing me a report."

I inhaled deeply incensed by his attitude, then exhaled slowly. Jeanette stared at him in disbelief. We were suddenly aware of his flaws. Religion had prevented him from being loving, from showing unconditional love, from loving without judgment. It boxed him in and blocked him from doing what he claimed Jesus would have done. Religion had limited him.

"You girls do know what happens to nonbelievers don't you? Hell is a place of outer darkness and deepest sorrow. A place prepared for the devil and his angels where there shall be weeping and wailing and gnashing of teeth, a place of grief and eternal regret on the part of those who have rejected the mercy, love and tenderness of the crucified Savior. Hell is for those who choose death rather than life, the unbelievers, the abominable, the murderers, sorcerers, idolaters, all liars, and those who have rejected and spurned the love and sacrifice of a bleeding Redeemer for doom, in spite of every entreaty and warning of the Holy Spirit. I'm just giving you truth and a warning. Look it up in the Bible. It's God's own goodness—not our own intelligence or sense of justice—that brings us a change of heart. Think of where you've come from. You have probably committed terrible sins. We all have fallen short of the mark. Yet God still loves you, and as you've been taught, he sent his only Son to die a horrible death so that you could be forgiven and be received as his children. Just immerse yourself in the Word of God and study the scriptures

I've suggested. They should help you understand Him. After that, the pastors and I will get together and discuss whether or not we feel you should be helped by our church." He closed his eyes and bowed.

While he prayed, I reflected on a passage from the Bible where Paul said in 2 Corinthians 10:7, *"You are looking only on the surface of things. If anyone is confident that he belongs to Christ, he should consider again that we belong to Christ just as much as he."*

After the pastor finished a private prayer to God, he spoke again to Jeanette and me. "You do understand now why we can't help you, don't you? How can a church support people who do not represent its beliefs?" Pastor Sterne didn't wait for us to answer and he wasn't open to discussion. Instead, he completed the meeting by praying long and hard for our salvation, and then pushed us out the door.

In the car Jeanette and I came alive. We freely voiced our disbelief over the lecture and the Pastor's rejection of our request for furniture donations from the congregation. "Did the past twenty-five years of dedication to the church mean nothing?" Jeanette wondered.

"What about Dad? He's the one who has read the Bible thirty-four times," I mentioned. "Christianity is who we are. All our lives we were taught that Jesus Christ would heal the sick and give us answers if we believed in his divine healing." But so far, even after numerous prayers from our entire family to heal Dad, Jesus had done nothing to solve our problems. Twelve years of praying to Jesus to perform a miracle on Dad had done nothing. Is the pastor right? Should we follow the rules?

Mom was like the pastor—on the surface she was considered a good Christian woman, in fact, one of the most dedicated—yet she failed to love. We had been taught to love Jesus, but we failed to love each other. Wasn't Jesus' message to derive power from the Father (who is the Source of All), but use it toward each other? Jesus wasn't a Christian, and he didn't advocate that we worship or fall in love with him. He also didn't want the people to use him as an idol. In fact, he was against idol worshipping. Jesus talked about claiming our authentic power, and loving our neighbor. Religion had taught us to love the messenger, but not the message. The Pastor had been so immersed in putting Jesus on a pedestal that he had forgotten to live the message. My family was guilty of this also. We focused on the love of power, instead of the power of love. During most of my life, I had wondered how anyone could stray from the church. After contemplating the situation, straying from my foundation seemed reasonable. Believing that there was only one way to truth was only boxing me in.

While Jeanette drove home, I stared out the window remembering our lives dedicated to the church. Both of us were silently absorbed in our own thoughts. I assumed, as a child, that Jesus would see Dad's dedication and then heal him. After all, he worked hard to improve the lives of many by teaching Sunday School, directing the choir and aiding the church in his role as an elder. Weren't we the perfect Christian family? How can we let go of all we've known? How can we let go of our history?

I exited the car more annoyed by the pastor's refusal to help than ever. Does our dedication to the Word mean nothing? I decided not to write the report against *The Messengers* like he expected. I didn't want to conform or be boxed in by his rules! I was tired of trying to prove myself to others. I was tired of trying to convince Mom and now the church that we were obedient Christians. I was tired of proving Dad's sanity and worth to the world. An urge from deep within told me I needed to fight this battle. I had to. After arriving home and resting, I sat down and wrote a letter to the Pastor. Dad and Jeanette did the same.

The letter written by Dad:
Dear Pastor I. M. Sterne,

You have proven that your church is not for the needy or those who don't think like you. You have also proven that the church believes a lie.

Jesus didn't limit himself to those who thought like him—in fact, none did. According to the Bible, He helped all who needed it, and all humans did. All the stories of Jesus in the Bible involved Jesus with someone who needed help, but who didn't think like Him. He even helped non-Jews. Should the church do less?

I can thrive without your help and I write this letter for the sake of my two daughters who are not yet disillusioned by your church. Have you ever considered that you might be wrong? For over thirty years, I was active in the Presbyterian Church, I was a ruling Elder, and I read the Bible cover-to-cover thirty-four times. I believed the Bible then, but no more. I have outgrown the Bible. Yes, it is possible, and, yes, I can see the faults in Christianity, for it does have them. We are taught a lie from childhood, but when we think for ourselves we find the truth. The Bible is man's words, not God's. No amount of analysis can degrade the truth and the truth can be known, but it takes thinking. Are you a thinker? You can be if you choose.

I think you have helped many and I always enjoy hearing you speak. You are the highest-rated speaker I have ever heard and I have listened to Billy Graham. Most of the church members don't realize what they have, but God does. Keep up the good work.

Sincerely, Allen

Jeanette's letter was very succinct:

Isn't God the ultimate expression of unconditional love?
Jeanette

My letter:
Dear Pastor I. M. Sterne,
Even though our religious foundation is not based on the book *The Messengers*, we enjoyed it and we will not denounce it. Our foundation is our faith in God. We had a strong faith in God long before the book came out, and we went through many tests and much analysis to prove it. When we were younger, we went through the motions and did all the right actions of being a "good Christian." But now we've learned that all that really doesn't matter. What matters is our strong faith in God. God looks at us from the inside, and He sees our hearts. In some places, people can't get to a Bible, but they have a strong belief in God. Not even Job had a Bible. God is

not going to punish those who are unable to get to a Bible and learn about Jesus. The Bible is not the only way to God, but it is a way. Dad has gone that route, and now he has outgrown the Bible and found God in other ways.

I will not be put in a box. Picture a warehouse full of boxes. In the boxes are groups of people; each box represent a organized religion. Everything on the outside is God, for God is Love and Huge! If the flaps are closed, we are blocked from seeing truth and attaining God's power. If the flaps are opened, we are exposed to the value of everyone. I'm not saying religion is wrong—some people need that—but after our conversation with you, we realize that we want to be open to all philosophies. I am not limited to one box. No, we're not New Age, for we don't even know the beliefs they hold. All I know is we have faith and love for God, and our decisions will be based on love, not fear.

I will not denounce the book *The Messengers.* I thought the book was enlightening, and it actually inspired me to read the Bible more closely. It did not get us an inch away from God. Nothing could do that, not the movies we see nor the clothes we wear, for God knows our hearts.
Jeannine Vance

April 10, 1997
Dear Allen, Jeannine & Jeanette

Allen, Jeannine, and Jeanette, I hold real concern for you and have kept you in prayer. If you personally deny God's plan of redemption as revealed in the Bible, I fear you are neither saint nor seeker. The cross is nonnegotiable for us. To miss the purpose and effectiveness of Jesus' sacrifice is to embrace grave deception (i.e. *The Messengers).*

I acknowledge that there may be some who attend this church who do not hold faith in these common areas. These people may be seekers who are in the process of being drawn to precious faith in Jesus. They are discovering their lost condition and their need for the Savior.

Allen, you characterized some scripture as "man's ideas." As you judge the relative truth of scripture for you, please carefully consider the whole testimony of Jesus. He was truly the Son of God and spoke His words in complete truth and authority, or He was a liar, mixing truth with falsehood. In the latter case, He would have embraced his own death as a fool, for the cross would have had no power to redeem men. And if men didn't need redeeming, He should not have died proclaiming Himself to be "God's Lamb" in fulfillment of all Old Testament sacrifice. Simply taking Him at His word will force you to decide one or the other. He can't be "one of many ways" to approach God for He claimed to be "the only way." If you reject His words, then all truth becomes relativistic and each man becomes his own final judge. You are entitled to that position, but should not mistake it as being a position that the church could *not* enjoy fellowship with.

The truth of the simple gospel message continues to contain the power to change lives and bring hope to people who are ready to receive it. Any hope that promises change without dealing with our sin is false hope. I'd like to suggest you to read some books by Christian authors.

Please know that the pastoral staff is aware of our dialogue and we are praying for you. I am certainly open to future discussion with you by letter or in person.

Sincerely,
Pastor I. M. Sterne

After we finished reading his letter, Dad had only a few comments to make to Jeanette and me. We decided not to continue our correspondence with the pastor. We agreed that Pastor Sterne had a right to believe whatever he wanted, and it wasn't our intention to change him. We could understand how difficult it would be to question what he had been taught. Letting go of all one knows was a difficult road to choose—we knew that much from experience.

Dad wanted us to remember that the Bible was written over sixty years after Jesus' death. Stories passed down from person to person could not have stayed one hundred percent accurate. He came to a conclusion that might be disturbing to some: the Bible is not the Word of God. It's man's *interpretation* of the Word of God. The writers of the Bible were not perfect; they were what Dad called, "filters". They filtered out what they wanted to and were as inadequate as we are today. Religion was formed by men for political reasons to gain control over the population. Religion was based on fear—fear against the government taking control.

We were stubborn. Dad had read the Bible straight through, thirty-four times. The three of us continued to call ourselves Christians, even though our beliefs collided with that of the pastor's. By the church's definition, in order to be considered a faithful Christian, we had to believe exactly what they told us to believe—we were not allowed to think on our own. Unfortunately, the pastor was bound by the limits of the church. I felt sorry for him.

At a snail's pace, our perception of organized religion changed. We concluded that organized religion had caused more deaths in the Name of God than anything else. The witch hunts of yesterday were instituted by the church. Many of the hate crimes today are caused by individuals refusing to focus on their own faults and instead focusing on someone else's actions and interpreting them as being opposed to God. In fact, according to *The Messengers* the same thing happened 2000 years ago: once Jesus started healing, the church thought he was a threat to their survival. They feared losing control over the people. They feared a loss of funds. Because of the healings conducted by Jesus, the synagogue followers were beginning to lose faith towards the church, which became the reason the religious leaders turned Jesus over to Roman officials.

I realized that it was my responsibility to discern truth from fabrication. I still loved many messages from the Bible, especially the books in the New Testament, but at the same time, I realized that I could not accept the Bible literally as the entire Word of God. I interpreted the positive messages as being from God, but the fear-based messages were unintentionally or intentionally added by men.

Dad told me that Christianity was a neat stepping stone, but he was not going to get stuck there. The men who wrote the Bible did the best they knew how, but they were just humans. He concluded his reflections with, "I got a lot out of the Bible, but don't stop there—at least I'm not".

After months of study and thought, the three of us decided it was time to move on. We could no longer call ourselves Christians because our opinions clashed with the pastor's. Little did we know that Dad's head injury could be considered a personal alarm to wake us up and move us over to a new ladder, called the spiritual ladder, where getting to the top and success had a totally different definition. Making sound decisions could be based on listening to our hearts, and success could be achieved by not needing or expecting. Happiness could be found by appreciating what we possessed inside, not by what we owned or achieved by the world's standards. The spiritual ladder had little to do with religion, salvation, and conventional beliefs and everything to do with forgiveness, awareness of The Source, and peace within. Dad's head injury marked the beginning of a long hard journey to self-discovery, first by letting go of past belief systems that had prevented us from living.

Our curiosity took us on a journey to explore religions from around the world. Gradually our traditional beliefs dissolved as each Sunday at church passed and we realized we no longer agreed with the pastor's sermons. Dependence on Christianity departed like a security blanket lost to a child. At first we were scared and sad, but as time went on and as our awareness expanded, we realized that we really had needed it only as a stepping stone. We didn't regret our Christian upbringing; we were happy with the lessons learned. Alternatively, by being open to different religions, we came to appreciate and respect the vast array of world philosophies and concluded that we were all worshipping the same God. The only variation is in the name used for God, perception and understanding. Practically any religion could have given us the tools we needed to live a spiritually productive life. At last, we were able to let go of the war within us. *WAR. We Are Right.*

Chapter 25

Pandora's Box

Within our own family, we were still continuously battling Mom. We were frustrated over Mr. Miller's decision not to take Dad's case. According to Mr. Miller, Dad was given 60 percent of his income and 40 percent of the sale from the home. Even though the money from the house was held in a trust by his court-appointed guardian ad litem and was not to be in his control, Dad was still given almost 50 percent of his total income. The properties, sold vehicles and household items that were placed in Mom's discretion were hardly worth fighting over. Ultimately, a civil suit would be much too costly. According to Dad, the division of property and monetary decisions were only surface concerns. Mom's control in ousting him from his house and indifference to his needs was what hurt the entire family. Mr. Miller would not take Dad's case because the legal system works to resolve monetary and physical losses—not emotional losses.

A few weeks after our session with the pastor, we learned that Mom had sold the home and just needed to wrap up the transaction by getting Dad to sign the paperwork. Dad complied. The new owners were thrilled at the great selling price Mom had offered them. They weren't aware that Dad had nothing to do with it. A few months later, he received an invitation from the new owners. "Dad," I said, "they want you to come over and look at what they did to the house. I guess they've already finished it."

"No. I don't want to go," he said, frowning.

"Are you sure? It might be interesting."

"No." When his eyes teared over, I stopped pushing the issue. Going back to the house would only torture Dad and reopen fresh wounds. I didn't want to be guilty of stirring up old ghosts. I wondered if suing Ms. Lott and keeping the anger alive with another court battle would only keep those wounds open. I didn't want to watch Dad suffer any longer.

Letting go of the house was like mourning the loss of a family member, especially since it was Dad's own handiwork and his only tie to a successful past. I felt powerless. Sadder than ever, I wondered why Mom had shut us out of the house and prevented us from buying it. Couldn't she see that we wanted to help others and that using the house for this would have been a legacy for Dad? I didn't want anything to do with her. I couldn't even drive by the old neighborhood. It was a war zone and my mother was the enemy.

Dad had learned several lessons from his divorce. "Justice is a 'Man' thing, and not God-given," he said. "There's no such thing as justice in the court room. If you want justice, don't go through the legal system and don't play Man's game. Winning a victory isn't worth the battle, for everyone loses in the end."

Dad decided to go against the divorce ruling arranged for him by the judge, lawyers, and even Mom regarding his living situation. He could not afford the increased rent of $400 per month at the retirement facility as he was only getting an additional $50 per month for his personal items. Without a word to more than a few friends, he moved in with Sean and me. Sean took a couple of days off to paint the spare bedroom, set up a U-shaped desk, and a new Compaq Presario computer for Dad. Jeanette and I alphabetized and pinned up the photos of 55 children Dad could now afford to sponsor via Children International. Being with his family made all the difference to Dad. He now enjoyed sitting in his blue recliner, even doing nothing but thinking. *Don't just do something, sit there* became his new motto and he chuckled whenever he said it. I teased that he was turning into Buddha.

When Mom found out about Dad's move, she called me, ostensibly to complain about our stealth. "Why didn't you at least tell David? He is your father's son. *He*, at least, should have been informed."

I couldn't stop thinking about the letter she had written that I had found at the courthouse, which had been copied and faxed to the lawyer. It confirmed to me in writing that she didn't trust us, and probably never had. From that point on, who cared if Mom got mad at me? I countered her objection over Dad's move with, "If Dad wanted David to know, he would have told David himself!" And then I hung up the telephone, without saying any more. I brooded yet again over the letter Mom had written. My heart still ached. I wanted Mom's love and acceptance most of all and that was the only thing in the world I just could not win.

Mom had moved Mike and his little son, Kyle, out to Bremerton, an old waterfront city located west of Tacoma, a vast port where WWII ships were repaired. She even replaced the fifth wheel Mike was living in for a small but more impressive two-thousand-dollar trailer. Mike was not content with his new living situation, and his son had little room to move around. "Better than nothing," he said, but he complained that there was no employment out there. Without a job, Mike didn't have the money for electricity; he solved the problem temporarily by using a propane burner to heat the place. Jeanette and I tried to convince him to go to the welfare office but he was totally against the idea, saying that he would never take handouts from the state. We didn't understand what the big deal was, but he believed that his pride was worth more than what the state would give him. I believed that Mom had pushed his self-worth so low, that he probably didn't think he deserved money, no matter where it came from. Unconsciously, he pushed abundance away.

At least Jeanette and I had each other to talk with regarding Mom's unfair treatment. Having someone to talk to was therapeutic. Eventually we found the humor, however dark, in Mom's actions. I would joke that one of us should write a book about our family. Jeanette and Dad would laugh and agree. As time progressed, I talked more often about writing a book. Jeanette and Dad didn't laugh; they nodded instead. Mom's boxed-up heart, and her inability to accept us turned into potential writing material. I told Dad and Jeanette to save their journal entries. Perhaps we would need them in the future.

Mike dealt with Mom's indifference alone. He and David were never close, even as young children. Mom nurtured David under her protective wings. Dad was guilty of playing favorites long before his injury. His attention too had always been on David. Dad looked down on those who didn't take education seriously and those who couldn't be bothered with climbing the corporate ladder. Success meant getting ahead at his job, and making money so his family would be happy. Money equated self-worth and was imperative for competing. Perhaps, because Dad placed value on professional vocations, he was not appreciative of Mike's unique talents. Mike was not one to play by the world's rules. He wanted no part of it. Money was needed to survive but he wasn't willing to sacrifice for it. A college education, business suits and conforming were not Mike's priorities.

Except for collect calls from Mike every so often, we hadn't heard from him since Dad was moved to an adult family home. We were surprised when we saw him at Jeanette's apartment for a visit. His hair was longer and fuller than I had ever seen it—it didn't glisten in the sun anymore.

"Hey Mike! When are you going to get your hair cut?" I asked.

"I decided just to fuck it. I like it this way!" He grinned. "But I do get it cut once a year whether it needs it or not.

I looked down and couldn't help but notice his hands. "Oh, my God, your nails."

"What, these? I use my pocket knife to cut these little guys." He proudly showed off callused, greased, stained and bloody nubs.

Eager to update him with the latest, Jeanette was the first to divulge the bad news. "Mom sold the house," she announced.

"Sold it?" Mike shrieked in disbelief, then immediately dropped to the low couch to roll a cigarette.

"We couldn't find a lawyer who would take Dad's case because he didn't have proof that he was competent, and then we couldn't find a doctor to do a competency test because he didn't have a court order. Now that the house is already sold, Dad doesn't want to go through another painful court disaster. He says he wants to let go of the whole ordeal," Jeanette explained.

"Yeah, well fuck it. By letting go, Dad can move on," he agreed.

"Hey Mike, did you know Mom got a two-hundred-thousand dollar inheritance from Grandpa King?"

"Fuck! Now I know where she got the money to build her dream home."

"Dream home?" Now it was Mike's turn to drop a bombshell.

"She already has a new house? I was wondering where she was going to live. I couldn't picture her in an apartment." I remembered how she had called me to ask if David could borrow Sean's truck to move her remaining belongings, but she had not divulged where they were moving. I hated her secrecy, so I had refused to help, making up a pathetic excuse that Sean's brother had borrowed the truck. After I hung up, my body trembled at the thought that I had refused her request. I was guilty of lying, which left me feeling horrible for days.

"You two don't know about the house? Actually, you could call it a castle. She and David moved into it just recently."

"They didn't tell us anything." Jeanette said.

"She actually let you see it?" I asked.

"Well, she only let me see it because she needed me to help move all her crap in, but she wouldn't let me stick around and visit. Man, you guys should see it! It's got a garage that could probably fit five or six cars and there's even a huge extra room above that! The front door probably costs more than my entire trailer." Mike finished rolling the cigarette, then stood up, unaware of how ripped and frayed his jeans looked. "Fuck. I need a smoke after this." He sauntered outside to the balcony.

My heart hurt for him. I remembered how disturbed he had been when Mom moved him out to Bremerton. Now he was having trouble finding work within walking distance, especially since he had no driver's license. He rode his bike miles just to get to the nearest store or food bank. Worst of all was his deep sense of insecurity founded on how little love and acceptance he had received from Mom. I held her responsible for every problem Mike had. We followed him out. The foliage from aged maple trees reflected off the sliding glass door of the apartment across from Jeanette's. "How many bedrooms?" I asked.

"From what I could count there are four—and the master bedroom has an adjoining bathroom with a purple toilet and tub!" He inhaled cheap cigarette tobacco. "Can you believe it? A fuckin' purple toilet. Shit, that just about blew my mind! I doubt Mom would ever invite you guys in, but shit, you guys should just drive over there and take a look. The entrance has a black marble floor, there's French doors to a den area and there's stairs that curve to the upper level."

"What does the outside of the house look like?" I asked.

"It's two stories high. There's big bay windows on both sides of the door, and the front is covered with a gray brick—."

"Well, where's all her stuff? Did she take everything with her?" Jeanette asked.

"Yeah, fuck—all her crap and Dad's—man, there's a lot of crap—the garage is full. There's a lot of stuff that's mine from when I was a kid too—and you guys' stuff, but she wouldn't let me take anything. She said we could talk about it later. She wouldn't even let me take my train set—the one I got for Christmas when I was a kid!" He paced from one side of the short, uneven balcony to the other like a trapped wild animal.

"That sucks!" Jeanette agreed. "So you moved all her crap and she didn't even let you take your old train set? Man, that's cruel."

Mike stopped pacing. "Wait a minute—I just remembered something. About a year ago, I was at the old house and I happened to walk into the dining room where Mom and David were. As soon as I rounded the corner, they started fiddling with a bunch of blueprints, rolled them up quickly and shit! I thought what the heck? So I just said, 'Hi guys, what's that?'"

"What did they say?" I asked.

"They both replied, 'Oh, it's nothing.' I believed them and didn't think anything big about it." He pressed the cigarette butt into an empty coffee can. "Damn, I should have known somethin' was up."

Shortly after Mike's visit, Jeanette visited Dad like she always did. We were in for another shock.

From Jeanette's Diary:

I was about to go to a friend's wedding and stopped to say hello to Dad. He said something to the effect of, "Mike is not my real child." I wasn't sure if I heard him right and said, "What? What do you mean? You mean Mom had an affair?" Dad shook his head and said that they had adopted Mike when he was just a baby. I was in shock and had to sit down. I felt so betrayed. I told Jeannine when we were at the wedding. We both sat through the reception, in a daze trying to come to grips with this new revelation while everyone else danced and celebrated. We agreed that it was not our place to tell Mike, but we were greatly hurt and it added to our disappointment in Mom and Dad. The next time I saw Dad, I said that he should tell Mike. He refused, but said I could do what I wanted with the information. Jeannine and I thought it was up to Mom and Dad to tell Mike the truth, and we felt like we were in a horrible dilemma. Finally, Dad wrote Mike a letter.

Dustin and I moved into our own apartment. After eight years together, Danny and I finally agreed to break up. I felt like he was holding me back from growing, like I was tied to a ball and chain and he felt the same way. We both went on with our lives, in separate directions.

Mike was free to come over. He needed a place to stay for a while and was using my living room to sleep. He decided since he was in the area that he would visit Dad. I knew that Dad had written a letter divulging the truth about Mike's adoption so I couldn't do much but stay home and wait. I fell asleep and when I awoke I heard Mike coming into the living room and saw him pacing back and forth. He told me that Dad had given him a letter that told him he was adopted. He showed me the letter:

Dear Michael,

The divorce is final and like I told Joy, I would tell you the truth about your origin. I raised four children, two boys and two girls, but Joy only bore David. You, like the girls, were adopted and few knew. I tell you now, not out of revenge but out of truth. I never knew your biological parents nor why you were made available for adoption and I hope the truth doesn't hurt you. You will always be my son and I will always be your father. Good luck.
Allen

Mike had stopped drinking prior to the news but this shock drove him to drink again. When he approached Mom with the letter she brushed him off, telling him they would talk about it later. He used alcohol to escape his pain temporarily, but this played havoc with his life. The alcohol was like a vicious cycle. Whenever he thought about his past, his mysterious disconnection with our parents and his current status as an adopted child, he drank. When he drank he was unable to work. Unable to work, he had all the time in the world to think, which led to more drinking.

He had always thought he was our parents' eldest son. Growing up as an oldest child, one usually feels a sense of pride. Mike didn't feel that. Parents usually talk about the eldest as being special because that child is the first to enter the couple's lives. Mike had never been able to figure out why he wasn't allowed into our parents' inner circle. Confused and hurt, he used alcohol to escape. Even after the truth was revealed, Mom refused to face Mike with the disclosure or discuss it.

I couldn't get Mike's adoption out of my mind. I shared it with a few coworkers. "Your brother's adopted? So what? Aren't you? What's the big deal?" They could not understand my dissonance. The concept of adoption seemed simple to most: match children who need parents with parents who want children. Everyone lives happily ever after.

I didn't know how to answer, although I wanted to say that we had been living a lie. Mike didn't know whom he belonged to or who he was any longer. It was like getting his roots pulled out from under him. At least Jeanette and I had twenty-five years to adjust to our adoption and we had each other to confide in. The realization that David was my parents' only biological child drove me to wonder if blood really was thicker than water. Mom had a special bond with David. A relationship she could not achieve with the rest of us. Mom and Dad's attachment to David was a natural instinct that was obvious for all to see, but it was not discussed. Love and a sense of responsibility came intuitively with David because he was Mom's biological son. On the other hand, she felt boxed in by the rest of us. Perhaps adapting to adopted children is easier when one has no children of one's own.

At least now many past events made sense and at least the nagging question of why David had always been the favorite child was finally answered. Unable to immediately accept the shocking news of adoption, Mike tried to forget by drinking the past away.

I remembered when we were younger, how Mom and Dad had tried their best to save Mike from temptation and danger. We had always thought that Mom was a perfectly good mother. She followed all the rules, like getting all of us involved with activities. For Mike it was music lessons and as many church activities as possible. Both Mom and Dad did the right things to encourage him to be well-rounded and successful. On one birthday for instance, they gave him an excursion with *Outward Bound*, an organization that works with troubled kids, hoping that that might save him. But the trouble wasn't him—it was my parents. They saw him as less than David and he became exactly what they believed him to be. They also expected David to succeed, and according to Mom, he was the most successful of us all.

As a child, Mike tried to make light of his hurt feelings. He gave us his theory when we were children. Mike would joke that either he was adopted or Mom had had an affair with the milkman. He just didn't feel like he belonged. We would grin in sympathy, but we never took such comments seriously.

Now, those old jokes came back to haunt us. Our childhood made total sense. We understood why Mom hadn't wanted us snooping around into her boxes. She had secrets. We finally understood why she could never find Mike's baby pictures, and why the three of us didn't have the power to make her happy, like David could. We became aware of what was wrong with us. The problem was not that we were strong-willed. Mom's lukewarm feelings toward Mike, Jeanette and me were because she had not birthed us. We didn't belong to her in the first place. The unconditional love was missing. We were only kids, but we sensed the difference.

My family's secrets were like a Pandora's Box. I had to find out why my parents had kept Mike's adoption a secret. Dad tried his best to explain why they'd adopted Mike. "Joy was ashamed and afraid because she couldn't conceive after twelve years of marriage. She thought people would look down on her if they knew. Since both our families lived in Portland and we resided in Federal Way, we thought we'd hire a local doctor to find a baby."

"But why were you ashamed?"

"It was different back then. You have to remember, I'm talking about the nineteen sixties when married women were expected to have children. Boeing transferred me to Huntsville, Alabama, so we packed our stuff and lived in an old trailer while there. You don't go around talking about problems, especially anything that had to do with sex. You did what you could to comply with the rules." Dad pondered his partial answer, then suddenly he started laughing. "Boy, was it hot in Huntsville, and Joy was afraid of the snakes. Heck, there was a big black snake under our trailer, and I climbed under there and shot it with a 25-caliber pistol. The people at church said, heck, they kept snakes like that in their chicken coups to kill the mice. They aren't poisonous. By gollie, that snake was six feet long when I pulled it out!"

"But when did you adopt Mike?" This was my pressing question, but I could not drag Dad back from memory lane.

"I want to tell you that once in Alabama I went out to explore the woods and when the people at church found out they said, 'You went out in the woods? Oh boy, there are lots of snakes out there!'"

"How old was Mike when you adopted him?"

"And I never went out in the woods again!" Dad crossed his arms apparently still in the past.

I snapped my fingers in front of his face and waved at him to get some attention.

"Oh… You want to know how old Michael was when we adopted him?"

"Yes, Dad. Please."

"While we were in Huntsville, the Federal Way doctor called us with news that there was a baby available. He told us it would be awhile—the young girl was still pregnant. By the way, did I ever tell you about the time we were almost kicked out by the church for inviting a colored family over? I invited Carson Brian and his family to my trailer for a picnic lunch and to swim in my above ground pool. After they left, the neighbors had a big Ta-do about it. They told the church and then the pastor called me into his office for a big talk. He said everyone in the park was about ready to kick us out. They thought—" Dad's voice deepened dramatically—" Oh no, Allen's inviting colored folk over. They were afraid that pretty soon the colored folks would move in."

"Yes, Dad, you've told us a million times."

"Oh."

"What did you do while you were waiting for the baby to be ready? What did Mom do?"

"Did I ever tell you about the time I got into a big argument with the Presbyterian pastor? He wanted to kick an unwed mother out of the congregation, but I refused and held a meeting with the other elders behind his back. Boy, was he upset when he found out about it!"

"Yes, Dad, you already told me that story."

"Oh." He laughed. "Okay... Your mother hid in the trailer for three months. She didn't show herself to anyone. Then when the doctor called, we drove to Federal Way to pick the baby up."

"Weird. How long did it take for the adoption process?"

"Only a couple of hours."

"But what about your families? What did you tell them?"

"On our drive back to Huntsville we thought, ah heck, we should tell our parents in Portland, so we back-tracked a little. Did you know that everyone commented about Mike's red hair?"

"No Dad, how could I possibly know that?"

"But I told them it was probably a throwback from a second or third cousin, and no one questioned me."

"What about Mom? Did she pretend to be tired from giving birth?"

"I think my sister-in-law thought it was strange that she recovered so quickly, but in those days, it wasn't proper to say anything."

"What did Mom say when you returned to Alabama with a baby?"

"Joy made sure that she didn't lie. She simply said that Michael was ours and that he was born in Tacoma. No one questioned her."

"Did you two ever talk about it afterwards?"

"No! Never."

"Why?"

"Because Joy decided it should be a secret."

"And you just went along with it?"

"Yes, you know me, I always go along with stupid things. Speaking of stupid things, would you mind gathering my Bible Study Fellowship folders and sticking them away in my closet?"

Dad's explanation only partially satisfied my curiosity. My family was not built on as solid a foundation as I had thought it was. Mike seemed to recover quickly. I, on the other hand, grieved over his plight. As children we have a certain amount of faith in our parents. We're taught to tell the truth, to be honest and to follow their example. We're given spankings for lying. We trust that our parents are right and want the best for us. We try not to question their motives. To find out that they had hidden the truth from us all this time caused me great bewilderment. I could only imagine how deceived Mike probably felt with the news. He was never the type to complain and he accepted the truth as if it didn't bother him too much. But he continued to drink the past away, causing an avalanche of future problems.

Chapter 26

The King and I

Mike's drinking caused us great and genuine anxiety. Mom's health—the cancer was spreading at an alarming rate—left us feeling more ambivalent. All I could think about was Mike's declining living conditions and how it was all Mom's fault. I began to really hate her. My heart burned with anger. Making amends with her was completely out of the question. When she called to invite Jeanette and me to her new house, the wounds were too raw. I wondered if I could ever talk to her again.

I tried to ignore her slurred words and obvious confusion, until Sean told me to go. "You need to go," he pushed. "It's time. Forget about the past."

"But, I don't want to forget about the past! And I'm not going to forgive her!" She had sold our family home to strangers and I didn't want to let it go. She was still the enemy. Anger lingered as I brooded over what could have been. Eventually though, I relented. My curiosity led Jeanette and me to visit her together. We took Dustin, Vanessa and Alli along as buffers. Whenever she was around her grandchildren, she smiled and talked sweetly.

As we approached the house we could see Mom's belongings through the bay windows. Her grand piano hidden under full boxes and crates. A house built to perfection, but flawed in many ways.

I detected some resentment in David's voice, even though "Hi," was all he said when he opened the door. He backed up so Jeanette, Dustin, Vanessa, and I could enter and then left to go watch television. The house was dark except for the flickers of light from the television, which led us to her room. We crept up the curved staircase and through the double doors on the right.

Mom rested in bed like royalty, among boxes heaving with belongings: clothes, jewelry, antique dolls and stuffed animals. Did these things satisfy her soul? Did they make her feel more elegant and refined? We knew better. Attachment to these things had blocked her from attaining true happiness with her adopted children.

"Girls, I just haven't had time to put these things away. It seems like we just got settled in. As soon as I feel up to it though…"

We had learned to ignore that phrase after hearing it many times while we lived at home. Rarely were things ever put away. When was she going to realize that we didn't care about all her possessions? Now we had to pretend we were happy for her. We praised the neat purple bathtub, exclaimed over all her dolls, and oohed and aahed over the view from the balcony where the neighbor's house was barely visible in the distance. Confronting her about Mike's adoption was completely out of the question. We could see that she was weak and frail, but was she at peace? She pretended to be alert and well, not wanting us to see her vulnerability. *Would she ever soften?* I wondered. *Would she ever open up to us?*

Mom strained to get a word out, only managing a whisper. "David!"

We waited for David to appear. Time stood still as Mom licked her once-rosy lips. She attempted to reach for the water glass, but was too weak. We pretended not to notice her struggle. Jeanette nudged me and pointed to the plastic bedside toilet. I knew that this was a further sign of deterioration.

"David!" She managed to groan out again. "David!" We could hear cheers from audience members of *Wheel of Fortune*, Mom's favorite game show, but David could not hear Mom.

Jeanette stepped out into the hall. "David! Mom wants you." Her voice sounded robust against Mom's frail one.

At last, he emerged. "Yes?"

"Go get the grandchildren their Christmas presents," she instructed.

"Okay." He disappeared.

Already March, I wondered if he would remember where the gifts were. We stayed by Mom's side and small-talked about *Wheel of*

Fortune. Mom said she currently liked *Jeopardy*. It didn't take much to guess why; it was one of David's favorite games.

Jeanette offered to come once a day and give her a meal since David worked up north and was away close to twelve hours a day. She knew from working in a nursing home that bedridden patients need to change position frequently to prevent bedsores. Jeanette shared more information about the benefits of home health care and the many services available to the housebound, as if Mom was only a patient of hers, not our mother.

"No, really, girls. I feel stronger than I look. I'm doing fine, thank you." Mom squeezed the words out through dry, peeling lips. Despite formalities, I could feel that she was still cautious of us. She didn't trust us. I could feel it in my bones, but I could never confront her. It was safer just to pretend everything was fine and dandy. Perhaps it was something we had learned from her. My sister and I smiled and pretended that we were not hurt or angry.

David returned with round Halloween tubs filled with Christmas gifts: an angel bear for Vanessa and coloring book and markers for Dustin. We made appreciative comments on the thoughtful gifts as we left the house.

"Is Mom going to die?" I asked Jeanette while getting into the car.

"No," she answered. "I've seen people look like that in nursing homes. They end up living for years."

The fear of her dying vanished because of Jeanette's reassurance. I resumed working at the salon and living life as if everything was normal. I told a few clients about Mom's condition but without emotion and compassion towards her situation.

Then my aunt called. "Jeannine, how's your mother doing?" she asked. My parents each had one brother whose families lived in Oregon State. Before Dad's injury, we used to travel to Portland to visit with them at least once a year. Afterwards the visits stopped. My aunt's phone call caught me off guard. Usually, she didn't corresponded with me. Rarely had I talked with my four cousins since Dad's injury.

"I don't know. Fine, I guess."

"Is she out of the nursing home yet?"

"Nursing home?"

"Yes. Didn't David tell you? She's been in a nursing home for a couple of weeks now."

"No, David didn't tell me anything."

"You mean David didn't tell you? Here, let me give you the name of the nursing facility."

Once again, I felt shocked. *Why doesn't Mom trust us? Why does she keep everything a secret?* Jeanette had been working in a nursing home for a couple years now; she would have made sure Mom had the best possible care. She could have checked on her every single day. Then I remembered what Jeanette had said; she had seen people live in nursing homes for years. *Mom will beat the cancer. Mom will regain her strength. She'll survive.*

From Jeanette's Diary:

3-28-97

I left a message on David's answering machine. I told him that Aunt Carole called Jeannine and informed her that Mom was in a nursing home. I told him not to be afraid to call me for help. He never called back.

Jeannine and I just got back from visiting Mom at the nursing home. She was oriented but confused throughout the conversation. For instance, Easter was on Sunday but she called it Christmas. She tries to appear strong, yet I know she's vulnerable. I asked a bunch of questions regarding her therapy and nursing care and gave her advice about how she can help herself. I distanced myself by asking questions I usually save for bedridden patients at work. Jeannine sat silently next to her with tears streaming down her face. Mom wasn't wearing her usual wig, either, which meant either she trusts us enough to let us see her without it, or she is too sick to keep up appearances. Probably too sick to put it on. I guess I have to let Mom be in control as long as she can and let her go. I have to stop interfering with her life.

Later Mike and I talked about our childhood. He said he remembers playing in the woods and wondering if he had been adopted, and whether he had another brother. He started smoking at thirteen and at seventeen he was living in an abandoned shack where newspapers were stored at one time. When his friend found out about Mike's situation, His friend's parents let him move in with their family. He also remembers Mom calling him a thief and liar.

3-31-97

This morning I picked up Mike and he's been staying at my place while I go to work. I called the nursing home and talked to the social worker. Mom is planning to be discharged, but when that happens no one will be home to care for her while David is at work. She is unable to care for herself. She'll need home health care and *Meals on Wheels*. Later the social worker called and told me that Mom reluctantly agreed to stay one more day at the nursing home until she can get those services. I told the social worker to tell Mom that we will visit her later after work. The social worker warned, "Your mom stated that it's none of your business," anticipating my attempt to help and refusing it. I was shocked. How could she say that?

I asked Jeannine why Mom would refuse help from us. We would have been there for her if she wanted us. Jeannine says it's because Mom doesn't want to give up control. I called the nursing home and the social worker told me Mom went home an hour and a half ago. I asked if she got any home health. She said she has hospice, a bath aide, and someone to assist with medication. I asked how she seemed, and she said she was actually in good spirits.

4-7-97

We went to the zoo with Nancy. She told us that Mom doesn't have much time left, and that her system is slowly shutting down. Her stomach is bloated and her legs are swollen.

4-20-97

David left me a message that Mom died. Called him back to find out when the funeral will be. Told him if he needs any help with anything to not hesitate to call. Also said if he needs help clearing out the house that Jeannine and I will help out. I also expressed my appreciation that he helped Mom and told him that it took a lot of strength for him and that we are all concerned for him. He was surprised! He opened up and spoke more, telling me how Mom was awake and coherent till Thursday. Then she started to sleep a lot. He said she wasn't in a lot of pain and that he had morphine drops for her. He also said he took a lot of time off work, especially the last week before she died and that he needs time to rest and catch up on work. So I'm pretty sure he got the message that I care about him. Maybe we all can be a family again!

"Your mother's white casket is just beautiful, girls. She always wanted the white casket. You did good." A long-time church member softly told Jeanette and me, attempting to fill the uncomfortable silence in the lobby of the sanctuary.

"Oh, really?" I said. *We did good?* I wondered while waiting for other family members to arrive. *But we didn't do anything—we weren't even included in her life. We were banished from her world. Did she even love us? No! She hated us! We were considered her enemies!* Church friends knew so much more about her than I ever did. I wondered what the point of going in and viewing the body in the casket was. Last good-byes should be said while the person is alive.

I peered into the dark sanctuary, anyway. There she was, in an expensive glossy casket. I could see her brown hair and her hands crossed over her chest. By the time I reached the casket, I saw that they had placed her wig too far over her forehead and her make-up was much brighter than she ever wore it. Her skin wasn't wrinkled with age, but unusually smooth and waxy. I wasn't sad that she was on the other side. I knew she was finally at peace. As I gazed down at her, I realized that my beliefs were unlike what she had tried to pass on. My church resided *in* me. I tried not to look for goodness outside of myself and I no longer believed that Jesus was the only one who could save me from evil. The answers to living a good, righteous life came from loving all things with an open heart. I had the power to create my own heaven, here on earth by radiating love, each moment. I didn't have to wait to be rewarded.

I realized that Mom had never seen our essence. She only saw our physical differences. She was the one who had boxed up her heart and shut us out, so that we had to constantly prove ourselves. We were outcasts and delinquents in her world. If only she could have understood that Dad's injury was not a tragic accident, but a wake-up call—an awakening! Instead, we waited many years for Jesus to perform His miracle on our family, only to be disappointed. Healing was our family's responsibility. We were so busy fighting amongst ourselves for a chance relationship with Jesus that we hurt each other in the process by not seeing each other's value.

Later in the day I talked Dad into going to the memorial service. Perhaps he would want to see the church where he directed the choir and Mom and David upheld his legacy. David had followed in Dad's footsteps by becoming an elder, Sunday School teacher, and youth group leader, and Mom had played the organ there until her death.

"No. I don't want to go," Dad said.

"Come on, Dad. Don't you want to see the members who knew you before your injury?"

"No."

"Come on, Dad. This is your wife we're talking about!"

"You mean ex-wife. Remember? She divorced me. She didn't see me as a person."

"Then why are you still wearing your wedding ring?"

He shrugged. After a long pause, he finally gave in. He agreed to go to the service. Then he added, "I think it is time to take off the ring." With that he attempted to remove the gold band, but it was stubborn and wouldn't move.

Jeanette and I helped him into the same navy blue suit he wore during the divorce trial. I slipped into a long black dress with printed spring flowers scattered about; each flower represented life; each white polka dot represented light from the heavens. The dress became my official "funeral wearing" outfit.

Members from the church greeted Dad with open arms and smiled in welcome. Most remembered Dad's former capabilities and his tragic fall, but Mom had failed to keep them up to date with his improvements. I wasn't surprised to see their raised eyebrows when I told them that I was taking care of Dad at my house.

Once at the church, Jeanette and I assisted Dad to the front row, just below the pastor's circular pulpit, where a cream tapestry with thick gold tassels adorned the crown of Jesus. I remembered how insignificant I had felt as a child, when I used stare up at the pastor while he spoke. I no longer felt so insignificant; I knew who I was. Mike followed, looking awkward and stiff, wearing—out of respect for Mom—an outdated three-piece suit, a size too big. His hair was still full and frizzy from being brushed back. David sat upright in another pew with George, Mom's soft-spoken male friend, who had remained a secret from Dad.

Sitting in the pew, I stared at the murals that decorated the sanctuary walls—Jesus washing the disciple's feet, and the burning bush had seemed larger when I was young. I tried hard to remember our family's good times and Mom's many caring attributes. When I hurt myself, she had bandaged my sores and murmured consoling words. When I drew a picture, no matter how ugly it was, she commented on my artistic ability and even gave me some suggestions. She accepted the bouquet of weeds I picked with delight and a warm smile. She gave Jeanette and me a hug after our violin concerts and told us we were doing great, and that she was pleased with our progress. She helped Jeanette and me send our Girl Scout crafts to the fair, so we could win ribbons, and perhaps increase our self-confidence. She shared in all of our accomplishments. She'd say things like, "Girls, unlike the boys, we *chose* you." I felt guilty for comparing her love for us with her love for David. After all, she *did* keep us involved with activities.

Mike shared the same feelings but kept to himself. Just like us, he had not wanted all the activities. He might have become a well rounded, successful adult if he had only been given love and acceptance as a child. Thinking about what Mom did to Mike made me the angriest. I was disgusted with her for giving him so little love that he felt he had no choice but to turn to alcohol to numb his hurt feelings. I hoped she suffered for destroying Mike's self-worth. She never told him how special and capable he was and he believed her lie. She didn't have the courage to question what she was taught. She couldn't see that we were so much more than our bodies! We were created in the image of God! God's Divine image, not the physical one. At our very core, we're perfect spiritual beings—it's our perception of who we are that is totally screwed up! If we remembered who we truly are, we would find value in ourselves and in our children and we wouldn't treat them like they were less important than our possessions.

Jeanette and I studied the bulletin. *Joy J. King Vance: December 4, 1929-April 20, 1997.* Jeanette pointed to the vanilla colored paper. "Look Jeannine. Even though Mike is the oldest, David is listed as the first honorary pallbearer."

"Yeah, you're right." I turned the paper over, searching for Sean's name. "Is Sean's name even on the list? Guess she forgot about all the gifts he gave her, or they're buried somewhere deep within her treasured things."

"The grandkids aren't mentioned in the list of survivors," Jeanette whispered.

"Well, I'm not surprised. None of them belong to David," I murmured.

The service rotated between the pastor talking, scriptures, and special music. I felt the stares of the congregation behind me. They probably wondered what had happened to our once happy family. Oddly, I didn't feel pain or sorrow about losing her. As if I was at a stranger's funeral, I felt nothing at all.

I reflected on the last telephone conversation with Mom only a week before her death.

"Jeannine," a strange voice had said, "Your mother wants to talk to you."

"Who is this?"

"Oh, this is Mrs. Hill from church. Your mother was too sick to dial your number. I figured out what the problem was. She didn't remember that it's long distance."

"Oh." *Why is another woman with Mom, instead of me?* A sudden flash of hope enveloped me. *Maybe Mom wants me to come over and take care of her!*

"Here's your mother."

I heard some rumbling and then Mom's weak voice. "Jeannine, did you find a house for your business?"

"Kind of. I mean there's one we're looking at."

"You do understand why I couldn't sell the home to you," she said weakly. "It needed too much work. It was just too old for it to be any good."

"Well, to tell you the truth," I countered, "the house we're looking at is just as bad. It's actually ten years older than your house and has rotting wood, but it's all we can afford."

"Jeannine, you have to be careful. Make sure you have it checked by an inspector."

"Yes, I already know that," I said, as if I was only a little miffed. I didn't want to talk about the house! My anger wanted to scream: *why the hell did you sell the house to total strangers when you knew that your own daughters wanted to buy it?* But of course, a rock in my throat prevented me from spitting out any words at all. Speaking to her had always been like speaking into an abyss. I struggled to put the words *love* and *mother* together. If she had loved us, she would have chosen me and Jeanette to be with her while she battled over her cancer, not a church member. I couldn't concentrate on the rest of the telephone conversation.

Her love was what we had needed most in our lives and it was the only gift we couldn't earn or didn't deserve. Her detachment prevented us from feeling good about ourselves and from gaining self-esteem. I wondered why I could never win her over. *Why does she consider us her enemy? Why doesn't she believe in us? Why are we considered outsiders and outcasts?*

I felt empty and hollow during the funeral. I refused to *feel* during the rest of the funeral. I didn't listen to the words of the pastor either. He only spoke of God's great promises for those who spent their life serving Him, and Mom had served the Lord, Jesus Christ for most of her life. She would be let in the doors to heaven with honors and grace. On the other hand, her strong-willed children and ex-husband would be left knocking. According to the church, we would burn in hell for all eternity because we didn't believe what they had preached for thousands of years. We had changed, instead of staying stagnant. *CHANGE. Circumstances Have Altered; New Great Experiences.*

When the funeral service ended Dad scratched his head and quietly confessed to Jeanette and me, "Everything I was taught was wrong. Everything I passed down to you kids was wrong. I should have told you to think for yourselves, instead of forcing you to believe what I was taught was right."

"It's okay Dad. Everything happens for a reason," we said, but swore that we wouldn't raise our kids the way Mom and Dad had raised us.

On the way home from the funeral service, the sun played hide and seek. It made itself known for a short time, then disappeared behind low clouds. Spring showers kissed the northwest, while Dad, Mike, Jeanette, and I talked about Mom.

"Whatever you do," Mike said between nibbling on a few nails. "Don't tell anyone, but I got a glimpse of the will!"

"What? What did it say?"

"Of course, David gets the house, cars, and everything else and he's named as her sole executor," he confided. "In fact, the will says if he doesn't want to give us anything, he doesn't have to!"

"So she actually left something for us?" I asked. The sun reappeared; its rays shimmered off the wet pavement and then shifted onto the moving traffic.

"The new house is David's. If there is any money left in the estate after covering medical and funeral expenses, then ten percent goes to the church and forty-five percent is to be divided between us kids, and the other forty-five percent is supposed be saved for college for the four grandkids. And if they don't use the money for college by the time they reach age thirty, then the money is supposed to go to Charles Wright Academy, David's high school."

"What about Dad?" Jeanette asked.

Mike withdrew gnawed fingers from his mouth. "Sorry Dad, no money for you. You're to stay out of the whole thing. If we contest or if Dad contests for us, we only get a dollar."

My insides churned. Mike and his three-year-old son were still living in a miniature trailer, sometimes without electricity. David, on the other hand, lived in the huge castle by himself, not required to share it with his brother.

"I'm surprised you two got anything!" Mike said.

"I'm surprised you didn't get more, Mike!" Jeanette said. "You're the one who helped her move all her crap and took the most abuse. Whatever I get, I should just give to you!"

"Fuck, no!" Mike exclaimed. "Jeanette, you need to keep whatever she gives you—don't give it to me."

We listened to the rain beat a rhythm on the earth during the rest of the trip home. When we pulled up to let Mike out, he stated, "Mom should have gotten rid of all her junk long ago. It was the move to her new house that killed her. Moving all those boxes was just too stressful."

We nodded in agreement.

Chapter 27

Proof of Life

Mom, at one time, had given Jeanette and me Dad's hospital records so we could see for ourselves the severity of his injury. Immediately after her death in 1997, I gathered them together, along with Dad's journal entries. I decided to write a book. Jeanette and Dad were enthusiastic and supported the idea. We felt free to speak and I would be the voice. For two years, I wrote little bits in the morning, after work and during nights when I couldn't sleep. I didn't know where I was headed, I just knew that it had to be done. Expressing myself through writing produced more pain than pleasure. It still took me an hour to write a paragraph, sometimes even a sentence. An inner drive told me a story was to be told so I continued to write without focus or direction. The only writing experience I had, after high school, was a Writing 101 course at a community college. I was slow at pushing out stories and I didn't have the confidence, but I persevered.

I was determined to record our family's story so that my children would know their roots. I added Dad's and Jeanette's journal entries and asked Mike to share his memories with me. This is what he wrote:

Memories from Mike:

So, you want some memories. I've worked a lifetime trying to forget this crap! I remember when you two first came here. Jeannine came first by two months. Jeanette was too sick to come to America. David was already telling on me. It was a crime to take a piece of bread without asking. I always got up very early so I could have some alone time. The very first time Jeannine laughed in our house I was up very early on a

Saturday morning, I think the last one before Christmas. She woke up and started crying. I was about seven years old. I went to her and started talking to her. She was six months old, probably freaked out, a lot of changes for a small baby. So I brought one of my toy cars in and started driving it over myself and pretended to be run over. She stopped crying. Then, when I started to run over her, she started to crack up. She thought it was the funniest thing in the world. I played with her for hours and by the time Mom and Dad got up, she was used to the place where she now lived. I remember going to pick Jeanette up. We drove to Eugene, Oregon, because for some reason Jeanette didn't come to Sea-Tac Airport. She was more secure than Jeannine, because, I think, she remembered Jeannine.

Now for the fights Mom and Dad had. Dad worked overtime every chance he got. I remember him coming home from work and being pissed because the house was a disaster area. He would clean the counters in the kitchen by sweeping his arm over them and spilling everything on the floor. This, of course, led to Mom being in tears, picking the crap off the floor whether it was broken or not. This went on for a very long time. I know one time, when I was nine or ten, I had seen enough of this; I went into the back yard and grabbed a piece of re-bar about three feet long and was going to use it on Dad, but Mom stopped me. I loved her so much, but Mom realized that that *would* have been a bad scene.

My attitude towards Mom changed as I got older. On school vacations when I was home, Mom would just sit there and watch TV. I would think, "Mom, the house is a mess; Dad will be home later and you haven't done anything." She brought on a lot of her misery. Dad finally quit being angry towards her by the time I was about twelve. He would come home and go to the bedroom and watch TV. Mom would still sleep in the same bed, but stay watching the TV in the family room until she got tired.

Meanwhile, David was doing great in school, I was doing average, I could never figure out what my problem was. I've pretty much blocked out my junior high memories and don't care to recall them. I remember being miserable from about the time I was twelve years old. By the time I was fifteen, I started smoking and drugging and it seemed to solve my problems. I had lots of friends in high school, and I started to buy my own clothes. I looked normal to my friends.

David was the center of Mom's life from the day he was born. He was the only child she actually bore, and I guess that's how it goes. Since I didn't go to college, I was just an idiot. I have nothing but bad memories of doing homework. I heard from Mom and Dad, "Why can't you just apply yourself like David?" I think David inherited Mom and Dad's natural intelligence for "book work." I knew when I was young that I would be very good with my hands. I think I've proved my point, finally at age thirty-two! It took me that long to buy the tools I needed to show anyone who cares how smart I am and that I am capable of construction. Unfortunately, Mom went and died so I can't even show her how wrong she was about me. She probably wouldn't have cared anyway! So here I am, I still drink too much, to try to forget, and I'm done writing 'cause I don't want to remember anymore.

Mike
P.S. Don't look back.

From Dad:

Joy eventually died of cancer, and David was named her executor. The worst part of the funeral was David's attitude. His refusing to speak to me really hurt. But, I'm not surprised; Joy brainwashed him for many years. I talked to a lot of people at my old church, but you can't know what it's like to have a "favored" son avoiding you. He wore a rhinestone cross pin to the funeral given to him by Joy, while the other kids got nothing. That wasn't fair. I find it very painful to write this. My final memories of Joy and David are largely bad and hurtful. I didn't know it would hurt so bad.

A few days later, I called David on a whim. I recalled the time when Mom had told me the Disney movies were for the grandchildren during one of my visits when I thought we were getting along. She put a tape in the VCR for Vanessa to watch and explained to me that she had started a collection for the grandchildren—maybe she told David to save the Disney movies out for them.

"No." David said over the phone. "She never told me anything about that."

Kneeling against the side of my bed, I suddenly felt like a beggar while I talked to him over the phone. Didn't he know that I wouldn't dare ask for anything that would be of value to him? "What about some old furniture? Is there any old furniture you would like to donate to the adult family home that Jeanette and I are about to open?"

"Not at the moment. I'm going through her things now," David said. I pictured him trying to sort through the boxes alone in the dark. *Hey, he doesn't have to be alone. We can make this a family project! Doesn't he remember when we were younger how we used to laugh and joke together about getting rid of Mom's stuff?* Then I realized that Mom wouldn't want me near her things and David was probably honoring her wishes.

"What about the family photos? Can I have those?" This time, I was clinging to hope that Mom might have left something for her grandchildren and me to remember her by.

"I can't find them at the moment, but I'll look."

Under the surface to my requests, I wanted my children to know the lineage of our family. I knew very little about my own grandparents. Both sets of grandparents lived in Oregon State. My father's parents, his only brother, and wife died from cancer after Dad's head injury. My mother's parents passed away shortly before Mom did. The last time we saw any of them were when we were very young. I had vague memories of my parent's families and of my cousins. Most of my life I had felt detached from who they were. After Mom's death, my curiosity got the best of me. I wondered what troubles and tribulations my grandparents experienced. How did they meet? What was life like to them? How did they overcome their problems? What were their accomplishments? What made them happiest? What legacy did they want to leave? These topics had never been discussed among us. We didn't investigate significant issues that cultivated in the past or under the surface. I didn't want my children to experience the emptiness that develops when the roots to family are so detached. I didn't want them to wind up unfulfilled. Roots gave a person a strong holding. They anchored a person. Strong roots could give confidence when self-doubt emerged. I wanted my children to know their roots so they could develop wings.

The silence grew unpleasant. I stood up suddenly, causing blood to flow wildly down my legs. My feet were being attacked with pins and needles. I had to say something. I asked another stupid question. "What about her collection of dolls? Can I have those?" Inwardly, I justified that the dolls would be great decorations for the residents at the adult family home.

"No. That collection goes to Enola, her friend from New York. She told me that specifically," David stated, and then he said in a sudden wave of frustration. "You know Jeannine, life is not always fair."

My face burned with shame. Of course, Mom hadn't wanted me to have anything and David only saw my phone call as a lame attempt to squeeze something out of him, just like Mom had probably warned him. "I know that. I just thought Mom might have left something for us." I noticed Sean in the bedroom doorway, listening to me.

"Well, it doesn't look like it to me," David said, followed by another, you're-wasting-my-time pause. "I've got things to do. Good-bye."

Embarrassed, I hung up the phone. Except for the bulletin from the memorial service, I had nothing to hold onto that said she was my mother, but I felt the worst for Mike; he had gone through the most neglect and received the least amount of love. Mom had deceived him. He had assumed all along that he was her natural son. I wished that I could solve Mike's problems by buying him his own "castle." He was worth so much more than Mom led him to believe. I blamed all of Mike's problems on her. I hated her for what she had done to him.

I remembered when Mom tried early on to teach Jeanette and me the right way. She would say, "Girls, think about your futures. Do you want to take Mike's wide path toward destruction, or David's righteous narrow path?" We didn't respond. I didn't want to be like either of them. I wanted to be me. Now she was punishing us for going against her version of the righteous path. She was punishing me for being me.

"Jeannine," Sean said after turning me around to face him. "You shouldn't have asked for anything. It made you look exactly what your Mom thought you were—a greedy beggar."

I knew Sean was right. I had done exactly like what Mom feared most about me. I felt like an idiot for acting on impulse, but I was just clinging to a last bit of hope. Now I had to come face to face with the truth: she didn't love me.

Sean put a strong arm around me. "You know that I don't think you're greedy. I've always loved you and you're an excellent mother." He was a man of few words but when he did speak, it was always something valuable and beneficial. "Hey, do you want anything to eat? I'll cook you whatever you want. I was thinking about making eggrolls this weekend."

I realized that not having Mom's love didn't mean I was less of a person. I wasn't going to stay unhappy over "what ifs". I had to move on, look to the future and let my past go. I had to break the chain of pain by learning from the imperfections in my life, then do better for my family. I wasn't going to raise Vanessa and Allison the way I had been raised. I believed in them, I knew who they really were and I could see their spirit. I knew they had potential to fulfill any dream they wanted. *I wasn't going to treat them as if they were a burden.* I had two beautiful, loving daughters and a supportive husband who wasn't afraid to tell me he loved me. Sean's love anchored me in the family we had consciously created together. Sean and I weren't *lucky,* like outsiders said when they saw us together; we worked very hard to maintain a close-knit family. We refused to let the world dictate how we would raise our children. *The key to our success is the appreciation we have for each other. The key to success is appreciating what we already have.*

I went back to work as if nothing happened. I knew Mom was in a better place and that she wasn't in pain. I had already prepared myself to be emotionally self-sufficient, anyway. I chose to give myself what

Mom could not. I not only taught myself how to survive, but the importance of living. At the same time, death didn't scare me. I knew that no matter what happened to me, I was always going to be okay.

It didn't take me long to recover from Mom's death. In fact, her life seemed like a dream. Little did I know that she would present herself via our dreams and other channels that were taught to us as evil by the church. I had no idea that a healing within the family would come after her death.

Chapter 28

Contact

"Today is July 28, 1997," Jeanette stated into a miniature handheld recorder. "A prayer meditation with Nancy—okay Nance, it's on."

I pointed to the lights overhead, ready to leave my chair at her request. "Nance, is it easier to meditate while the lights are out?" I asked inside my little manicuring room, taking advantage of the vacant salon while no one else was scheduled to work.

"Yeah, well it doesn't really matter to me, go ahead and leave it on if you want." She flipped blond hair behind her shoulders, clasped her hands and closed her eyes. Jeanette and I didn't want to appear rude and stare at her like Dad, but it was hard to keep our eyes off of her.

"So we're just going to get into the meditation, and while I'm doing this I want you guys to think about a lot of white light and Jesus, because it creates great energy." Nancy said.

I couldn't seem to get my mind on Jesus or white light, although Dad was engrossed with the thought. Instead, I stared into space and wondered if Nancy's extrasensory ability would give Dad an increased peace of mind. Dad obediently closed his eyes and bowed his head as if in church once again. I couldn't hold my concentration very well. Every once in a while I peeked and caught Jeanette doing the same. We waited in silence for about five minutes. Finally, Nancy raised her head and spoke with a new look in her eyes.

"Do not be afraid, be at peace, we have great messages to share with you. She, Nancy, is a great vehicle." Nancy looked straight at Dad; her words are confident, mild and pleasant. "You have fathered these girls through your heart. It is very wonderful, very loving; great rewards will come to you for this."

We opened our eyes and smiled at Dad. The glow from our smile caused him to grin sheepishly.

Nancy turned her attention to Jeanette and me with the conviction of an expert. "Great love for the two of you through this man." She continued in a deliberate meditative voice. "We wish to bring you great love and understanding of self, and purpose of each other. It is very important for you to stay on your path. Many people will drag you away from purpose. Do you understand what purpose is about? Truly, our understanding of purpose is simply to share your love with others. Many people misunderstand and seek outside of self. They're seeking outside of themselves for material things, thinking that this is purpose. Many are lost because of this thought. Thought and intentions are very powerful. Thought and intentions are not to be disregarded. What you think and what you intend are two different matters. Be aware of this and simply walk with the light of Christ. You are great with oneness, the three of you. Walk in love as one. This is very good. Very great teachers you are, very good."

Nancy directed her attention back to Dad. "We understand that you have traveled here many times. You walked many lands. Your purpose here on this plane is to be the great teacher that you have been. You are a great teacher. You must remember to honor your teachings. We understand that you are inhibited in the movement of your spirit. You are having some apprehension? No, you are having some thoughts of planning for your future and apprehensions of this. You are very loving, yet are not expressing to your fullest capability as the teacher you are called here to be. We understand that you are of great writing material. You, perhaps, could teach through writing a book or making a video, or some kind of communication in this life form. Perhaps a book, because of the circumstances you are in, would best suit the situation. For you to be a teacher through a book to be read and thought about. Great thoughts will come to this book to inspire others for many generations. It is a great and wonderful thing to do, not just for you to fulfill your teachings of love, but of future love for the people who love you now. Fulfilling your purpose will bring you the full circle of your plan.

"You need to perhaps push your physical body more than you have been. You've been relaxed too much and we are noticing that this day-by-day attitude is really not making you happy. You are not fulfilled with this. Perhaps pushing yourself to do things that others are not expecting you to do, will give you great passion such as you have not felt for some time." Nancy's cerulean eyes exhibited honesty during her meditation. Did she know the messages were as comforting as hot chocolate during a raging blizzard?

Words as rhythmic as poetry continued to flow from her soul. "Passion is very important. Passion means movement, movement is love. God is a God of movement. God is a God of Action. God is a God of creation. You cannot create without movement. You are all great creators—please remember to be the great creators that you are. You must have passion, for passion is love and love is movement. Do you see how these all connect with one another? It sounds simple, yet the importance of this connection is very powerful—especially for the future of the three of you and then the two of you working harmoniously together."

"You sir, you are a great warrior—you are a great presence amongst us." Nancy said with a loving gaze into Dad. "We are in great hope that you are in remembrance of the journeys many times before. You are not using your body or your mind in the capacity in which you came here. We understand that you have some limitations on your body, but that does not stop your mind. Use it wisely as you did before. You are one of God's chosen, do not forget this, please— most honorable for you to remember that passion. You are a very beautiful child. You are very beautiful, beautiful child of God. You have many with you, very many with you, they are great warriors of God, very loving, not all of them respond as you are aware. Great teacher. You are a great teacher!"

The miracle of a physical healing wasn't important to me anymore. I realized that I had limited Dad's worth by my negative perception of his disability. A true healing was one of emotional understanding, a broadening of mind, a deeper spiritual awareness. I had been conditioned to see his imperfections, when I should have focused on his everlasting spirit.

"It's very difficult to transition from spirit energy to body energy. It's very hard to do, but it's very worthy to do. We thank you for asking and today we're honored to be here with you—"

Nancy hesitated and looked to the blank wall as if she saw something between Dad and me; her brows rose and then furrowed. "Who is this woman who stands before us in this room?"

We looked toward the wall but there was only the mirror. I didn't see any woman. She continued to talk at the wall, then paused and listened for a moment. "Oh… oh, you are not of this planet."

Nancy attempted to explain the confusion for us. "She is not of this planet." She turned an ear toward the wall, attempting to make sense of it all.

"Oh, they cannot see—oh, I understand—Allen and the girls cannot see her."

Confident, Nancy finally turned back to us. "There is a woman here you cannot see. Apparently she is not of the physical form; however, she looks very physical to me."

Could it be Mom, I wondered? Through reading spiritual books, I understood that once our spirit transitions to the other side, we are able to view our life with unconditional love. There is no negativity or ego to block the soul from understanding the domino effect resulting from our life choices. We are able to see and feel the pain and pleasure we created from our choices while we inhabited this earth.

"She's come here today with understanding of—she says she knows of you from this lifetime."

Dad, Jeanette and I looked at each other with baffled eyes, not daring to interrupt, wondering if it could be Mom.

"She is very troubled… very sorrowful… as she should be. She misunderstood her time here with you. She is going through great teachings right now. She understands that she has much to learn of what you call yourself. The love you have in your hearts is nothing she could ever understand for she was always afraid of not having that love. So she is learning now of that love and she is grateful that you showed continuous unconditional love to her and you will be rewarded by the King many times beyond your comprehension. She is in a place of teachings where she is earning the way to the Kingdom day by day as we know on this planet, (for, as you know, there is no time in the universe) so she is in great teachings right now and learning. She is more sorrowful for the things she *did not* do rather than the things she *did* do and she said you would understand what

246

she is telling us. She misses you much and wants you to know that even though she wasn't supportive when she was on this physical level, she will be with you always in spirit. She must journey now, for her time here is over and she loves you and she is of great hope that when you meet again you will understand her weakness. She said you will know who this is. So be it."

Mom! My soul exploded with joy at her appearance and in pain at her quick exit. *Don't go! She's leaving us again. I don't want her to leave!* I left the room to find tissue in the bathroom, but Nancy continued as if the appearance of a departed one was a common occurrence.

"Well, what a wonderful visit that was from this woman. We also understand that we must always move forward. Forgiveness is everything—primarily forgiveness of self. For when you can forgive yourself, it is much easier to forgive others. Your life here on this planet is primarily your mirror. It is a mirror each and every day for you to learn from. The things you don't like about others are primarily things you do not like about yourself. Do you understand?"

I sat back down and studied the mirror behind Nancy as she spoke. It was natural to only see the body, the physical presence, but inside we are so much more. Deep within, we have an everlasting spirit.

Nancy continued to talk with her eyes closed. "This is very important to understand. It will help you grow greatly in your daily walk. It is very wonderful to understand what this means, for it will help you in the future. We understand you are great servants—great and powerful servants. You have been servants beyond most other human's understanding of this lifetime. You should be very honorable of self. When you are honoring self, you are living in God's light."

"You, sir," Nancy said to Dad. "You know that your time here is not long. You are aware of this. And you are very wise in your understanding—that it is important again for you to really comprehend the importance of your teachings. It is great hope of God the Father to have you continue with your teachings. Time is very different than time as we understand it to be here. You must understand that your time is not for long, yet it is very long."

Nancy's blue eyes then concentrated on Jeanette. "Oh, we are seeing a child in your life, a new child. You have a child already?"

"Yes, Dustin."

"A different child. You will be married and have a child."

"When?"

"Time is not of our time, it is very difficult for there is free choice and free will, depending on your ego. The mate in your life has prepared his heart for you. The Father has brought this—to you, so your ego will determine this mate and what is to be. It seems to me that you have some fears that have not yet been conquered about relationships. So perhaps you should look to the Father for understanding of these fears."

"Am I pregnant now?"

"We cannot tell this, we cannot tell this verbiage. You are frustrated in your work, in business that you are in. Do not worry, for God is Divine; He has a plan. Persevere, persevere through Him. We see that you are not in prayer of answers, you are in prayer of self only. Remember to pray for understanding of the business that you're in, because the work that you're doing is helping many—but if you do not do it Divinely, the doors will not open for you. This is your lesson this lifetime."

At last, she faced to me. "You, too, have great love in your life. I see a child. We are told that you too will be with a child, but you are not wanting. However, the Divine plan is that you are going to have another one."

Oh no! I faced Jeanette and shook my head no.

"This will be your last. You will have no others after this. Your body will be done producing and procreating at that time."

"Thank God." I murmured.

"You have great work to do. Your mate is with you for this eternity and next eternity. Do not forget to honor him as the man in your life. You, too, are doing very well in your prayer life. However, you need to pray more for self—self-needs and answers for self. That is the Divine plan for you at this time, for your ego is very balanced. However, it's very important, very important to forgive self of shortcomings. You are not forgiving of shortcomings. Time will tell you, time will give you wisdom. Look to your elders in your life for answers as well. Other elders, they know much. Do not pretend; do not hide your heart and your feelings. Forgiveness of your weaknesses is very important for you."

"You have very beautiful children," Nancy commended Dad. "You have great work to do, you're doing great work for the Father."

Too soon, her disposition changed. She scooted around in the pink director's chair, suddenly uncomfortable. "She is very anxious to come into her body. She is very stirred, very anxious to come into her vehicle, so we must go for now, we thank you for this time together here today. If you have any questions, look within for your answers. I repeat—be an example, be the teachers, go with your inner self. Peace in your heart, love to you, journey all together as you have been. I must go. Thank you, peace be with you, and to you and to you."

Nancy opened her eyes and smiled enthusiastically, meanwhile, she wiggled her upper body to an imagined tune of some oldies but goodies. "Did you have fun?"

"Yeah!" Dad, Jeanette and I cheered.

"No, really... Did you have fun?"

"Yeah! I liked it," Jeanette exclaimed. "Oh, my God, I'm speechless, Whoa—"

"Look, she can't even talk!" Nancy laughed.

"That doesn't happen very often." I joined in on the laughter. Jeanette quieted us by announcing it was Mom who came back.

"Really?" Nancy was stunned but Dad and I confirmed Jeanette's assumption.

"We couldn't see her, though," I said.

"I remember when I saw that spirit come up, I couldn't even see you guys anymore." Nancy looked toward the wall again, her voice softened. "I couldn't see you guys, all I saw was this woman—I'll try to describe her. This was a younger woman... brown hair, it was shorter—about to here." Nancy pointed to just above her shoulders. "And round face, and longer but pugged nose, beautiful smile. Yeah, beautiful smile. Not real big—but she wasn't a small woman, not small like you guys. They look different when they get spiritual. She had a robe on."

"That sounds like Joy when she was young," Dad said with a gaze so intense, he could probably look right through Nancy and see Mom, too, if he wanted.

"So what did she say?" Nancy asked.

"That she was sorry," I answered, "about not learning about unconditional love."

"She came to learn about love," Dad agreed.

Nancy snapped her fingers. "She didn't get it, and you guys were sent to her to teach her, but she didn't listen. She's sorry now. No, really. You guys knew about unconditional love just by being who you are."

"We were just two little kids!" Jeanette bellowed. "Why would she be jealous of two little kids?"

"She was jealous because you knew love and she didn't," Dad explained, gently.

"Look at the two of you," Nancy said. "The way you love each other, I mean, it's just... it's just all over the both of ya. It just glows—it shows!"

Jeanette and I looked to each other and then grinned.

"So what is Mom doing now?" Jeanette pondered. "I mean, what is this learning that she's doing? So does that means she's living another lifetime?"

"She's just learning about love, still trying to get it," Nancy answered. "She's living in the universe, learning about love on a whole different level because she didn't get it here. Don't stop, its like so-o important! Get it here, because if you don't get it here, you gotta go and still get it somewhere else. It's a drag!" She stopped short and looked at Dad. "Oh, I do remember something now, they said that you aren't pushing yourself hard enough! No sitting back for you! Forget that! Hey, I should do a reading for you guys right now. Want me to do a reading for you guys?"

"Yeah!"

"Maybe it'll match!" Nancy gave a nervous laugh and cleared her throat. "Okay, we'll, start with you, Allen. Ready, okay. Um, your health is really good but you're having some digestive problems. Drink a lot more fluids and perhaps *Metamucil* if you have to, but you gotta get yourself flushed out more regularly than what you're doing, okay? There are a lot of toxins in your body right now. So get that going. Are you having problems with your hearing?"

"No. I have trouble with understanding, but not hearing—"

"I think he's misinterpreting that," I interrupted. "It *is* his hearing and that's why he's not understanding!"

"What?" Dad shouted. An outburst of laughter bounced off the walls of my small manicuring room.

"I think it's your hearing, Dad." I rolled my eyes and turned toward Nancy. "You should hear how high the volume is on the TV in his room."

"Oh yeah, yeah well, we're seeing that you have some blockage in that one ear there," Nancy said. "As far as understanding goes, that could be it; it could also be a lack of oxygen going on in your bloodstream. So when was the last time you had your blood work done?"

"A long time ago."

"You might want to have the oxygen level checked out in his bloodstream, okay? But you got to start moving your body more, push yourself to do that, you know? You're a young man."

"Okay."

"I mean that."

"Do you have any questions for her, Dad?" I asked, eager to switch the attention over to me.

"Yes, I have two."

"Okay."

Dad unfolded his hands and scooted forward in the black director's chair. His green eyes gazed into Nancy. "How many more times do I have to do this?"

"Oh, you mean how many more times you have to come back here and do this?"

"Yes."

"This is your last gig!"

"WOW! Would you call me a master?"

"Yes."

"That's my two questions." A Cheshire cat smile decorated Dad's face with the charm of a birthday present.

"We wanted to get the name of who he was in his past life, but we'll get that later," I said.

"Yeah, I'm thinking that it's a cousin, I'm getting that you were a cousin of one of the disciples, a cousin, you're a cousin, or a really close friend of the family of one of the disciples. And you knew what was going on, but you weren't really in on the core group of what was going on, which is a great thing, it's a great thing."

"This is your last gig here, babe!"

All of us gazed at Dad.

"So, it's his last time—" Jeanette put two artificial nails in her mouth. A cracking sound alerted that one had broken, and then she popped the rest off with her hand. I watched her toil with it.

Dad's intense stare softened. Relieved, he sat back in the chair. "I don't want to go through this again."

"We're going to miss you, Dad," Jeanette and I said.

Nancy detected a hint of sorrow in our voices. "Just remember that you'll see him again in heaven, when you go home. Allen, tell your spirit guides and angels that you're done. Say, 'I'm done, I'm not going back to earth... you guys go!'"

We snickered at Nancy's suggestion.

Dad's eyes lit up again. "I like that!"

"You gotta tell me about the relationship!" Jeanette said, switching the attention to herself. We all knew she was talking about her new boyfriend, Simon. She had worked with Simon for a couple of years at a nursing home. They recently started dating and were considering a long-term commitment. Jeanette liked Simon's passion for education, Kenyan accent, poetic speech, awareness of spirituality and his ability to speak various languages and tribal dialects.

"Well, looks good to me! He's fine," Nancy answered. "What? Is it you?"

"I guess so."

"Are you afraid? What are you afraid of? You want Mr. Perfect?"

"Yeah."

"Oh, there's a little bit of an ego-gig going on there."

"He's good!"

"Are you perfect?"

"I'm not perfect. I never said I was!" She placed both hands on my manicuring desk. I could see that three acrylic nails were chewed off, five were chipped, and only two nails were still in perfect condition.

"Well then," Nancy asked. "Why do you expect him to be perfect?"

"Am I expecting him to be perfect?"

"Yeah—"

"I just feel like I'm going back in time."

"Yeah," I explained. "She met Danny when she was fifteen and he was twenty-one. And now she is twenty-five and she's going out with Simon, who is twenty-one. But Simon is very aware of spirituality and things like that."

"I think it just happened so fast and I wasn't expecting it," Jeanette said. "Maybe that's it. Then BAM! It happened, like whoa!"

"Good!" Nancy smiled. "That's the way it's supposed to happen. Perfect! That's called Divine Intervention. That's what happens when God puts two people together."

Jeanette pondered aloud, "So the spirit said that she sees a wedding and a baby..." She ripped off another artificial nail, causing me to wince.

"Sorry, Hon," Nancy raised her hands and shrugged. "My angels are never wrong, man! I'm tellin' you. Yeah, you're definitely getting married."

"I hope the marriage is before the baby," Jeanette confided.

Nancy nodded. "That would be good! You've already done the other route, girlfriend. Yeah, just concentrate on your friendship with him more than anything, that's my advice to you as your friend, concentrate on the friendship. Let him do what he wants, let him be the loving man that he wants to be! You're having a hard time with that aren't you?"

Jeanette nodded.

"Yeah, isn't that funny how first we complain that there's no love, now we complain that there's too much."

"A relationship is about learning," Dad stated.

"Learning about love." Nancy finished for him.

I rolled my eyes. "Can we please get off Jeanette and start talking about me?"

"There goes your ego, man!" Jeanette teased.

"Hey, I'm not the one with the ego problem... remember?"

Nancy interrupted before an argument ensued. "Jeanette, go walking with Dustin, take him to the park, play, walk, exercise a little bit! You're doing fine, you're doing a good job, honey; yeah, you're beautiful, okay?" Finally, she turned to me. "You're going on a vacation with Sean, looks like, four-day-weekend type thing."

"Yeah, Sean did ask me when he should take off work so we can go to Las Vegas. I picked the last week of September."

"Oh, okay. So you *are* going on a trip with Sean! Your health is good; um, you're not happy with your body are ya? What's going on?"

"My body feels weak and limp."

"Oh, okay. Could be because of the earth changes, too. People who are awake, they feel that way, their bodies are so heavy, then boom, they have a burst of energy, so it could be what that's all about. The more awake you are, the more the earth changes affect the physical body. The more asleep you are, you never notice! But drum up on your vitamins, you're a little low on protein."

"Nance, while you were meditating you talked about the book, too. I'm collecting notes right now, and I'm planning to write a book."

"Well, that'll be good, because then that'll be nice for your grandkids and stuff later on down the line. What a great, loving thing. Wow, you guys are going to be successful," Nancy concluded. "Well, you already are, you already are."

"I knew they would be!" Dad beamed with pride.

Chapter 29

Dreamcatchers

Life after Mom's death finally resumed some normalcy. Jeanette and I continued with our plans to open an adult family home. I worked in the salon, but my mind was not there. It was eager to start the business with Jeanette. At the same time, we continued our own internal spiritual search, this time without the help of the church. We began seeing signs from our surroundings that guided us into a new direction. The old adage, God works in mysterious ways, is true, I discovered. Fresh tools, spiritual books, and a Divine guidance would help us overcome future adversity. We could have prevented the pain from the very beginning if we had been willing to step out of the box and look at Dad's injury from a higher more evolved perspective. Peace eventually took over and finally set us free. *PEACE. People Enjoying A Cohesive Environment.*

"Jeannine," Dad called out sitting up in bed. I had replaced his faded orange and yellow sheet, with a blue one to match his comforter. "I've had an awful dream! I was talking with a group of church friends at a neighbor's house. Joy was by my side and being very nice. In a loving way, she asked if I want to go home now. I told her, no, I'd like to stay and talk a little longer. She agreed and stayed with me." He stopped to scratch his head. "Strangely, the people were slowly disappearing from the room."

As he talked about the dream, an interpretation presented itself in my mind: I could see the group of church friends and the neighbor's house as representing mainstream society—a group he could identify with. Mom's appearance "by his side" suggested that she supported him. She wanted to know if he was ready to go home; if he was ready to die and go to "heaven," and join her. But because Dad wanted to share his story, he still felt the need to stay here until "there was no one left in the room" to tell—and that is why the people were slowly disappearing. The neatest part of the dream was when Mom agreed to stay with him, proposing that she stood beside him during his talk. Even though we didn't make amends with Mom before her death, from the other side she was making him aware of her newly loving presence.

I opened the blinds to his bedroom thinking about how comforting the dream was. A hanging fuchsia planter jeweled with blooms, peaked through, the sun glittered from behind, contributing to the warmth I felt inside. Since I didn't know if I was right, I encouraged Dad to enter his dreams into his computer. Soon, it became a habit to ask about his dreams each morning and then give him my thoughts. I was surprised at how easy it was to read them, but I still wasn't sure if I was just imagining the answers. I decided to pay attention to my own dreams as well. Jeanette did the same. Dreams painted our black-and-white world with color. Each dream could provide an opportunity to find meaning behind our lives. Dreams, I learned, were treats from heaven.

"Jeannine, I had another bad dream." Dad's fingers wobbled through sparse, nearly white hair. "I wanted to go home, but Joy wouldn't let me." He attempted to rub sleepies from his eyes with one working hand.

"Dad," I announced with a smile, "Mom is giving you the message that even she doesn't want you to go home until you fulfill your purpose."

"But I want to go home now!"

"You're not supposed to. Not until your purpose is done."

"But I don't know what my purpose is."

"Whatever it may be—you are not done yet. And Mom understands this because she's able to see our life plans better from the other side. She doesn't want you to leave until your self-assigned purpose is complete."

I wondered if we only perceived some dreams as bad because, on this physical earth level, we disagreed with what our soul had chosen or, perhaps, bad dreams represented unresolved issues that need to be faced.

Dreams. I didn't understand the power in dreams. I didn't know that nighttime mystical images could be solved like puzzles. Dreams could be used to awaken us to face joys or fears, help discover who we really are, and tell us what to do with our feelings and our situations. Dreams had a mysterious language, which could be interpreted and used to give comfort and understanding. Now I believed all of us could tap into the "real world" restoring light, while dealing with the darkness in our daily lives.

I wondered what Sean had hidden in his own world at night. I caught him early in the morning trying to wake up so he could do his workout and then get ready for work. "Sean," I asked. "What did you dream about last night?"

"Forgot."

"Come on! You had six hours to dream. Plenty of time. You can at least tell me something. You can't deny that you do not dream any longer, because I caught you laughing in your sleep, once. Remember? When you woke you said that you, Vanessa, Alli, and I were floating down the strip in Las Vegas."

"Okay. I always dream about fishing boats."

"Are you on rough waters or smooth waters?"

"I don't know. I'm just in a boat."

"'Cuz, if you're on smooth waters it means your life is going smoothly, but if the water is rough it means you're having some rough emotions that you need to work through. And are you going against the current? Because if you're going against the current it means you are fighting against your emotions; you're going the wrong way and perhaps you need to try another route."

"I don't know. All I know is that I'm in a boat like the one I came to America in."

"If you're going with the flow, that's good. On the other hand, if there's a storm, then you're probably dealing with some disturbing emotions."

"I'm not on the water, I'm just in a boat." He stood up to leave the room.

"You mean you're on land? That's strange. Could that mean you don't have any emotions? I guess that's good. At least you're in the boat, because remember that dream you had a while ago when you missed the boat and you woke feeling really frustrated? That was a telling dream. Maybe you feel you've missed out on—"

"I did? I missed the boat?"

"Yes! Don't you remember?" I hollered as he left. "Geez, Sean, I remember your dreams better than you do!—Hey! What were you fishin' for anyway? You've got your catch right here at home!"

"I was looking for Little Mermaid," he teased from the hall.

In another one of Dad's telling dreams, he was assigned on a business trip for fourteen days, which interfered with his home plans. He agreed to go, but felt frustrated because he couldn't remember Mom's phone number. He wanted to call her and tell her that he was going to be late. I was surprised that he felt good as he woke, but everything made sense when I asked him why. He said he was putting his work ahead of his personal life—he considered the purpose and mission in this life as work. His home plans or spiritual life, including Mom, could wait. Dad agreed to carry out his work no matter how long it would take, even though it was taking longer than planned.

"Jeannine!" Dad howled, scaring me into thinking that he had just fallen out of bed. "I just had the same awful dream. I was late again."

I opened the blinds to his room and was surprised to see a hideous longhaired monster glaring in. *Oh, it's only the hanging fuchsia.* I made a mental note to clean up the dried leaves. "Well, where were you going?" I asked distracted.

"I was trying to get home, but everyone was walking so slow! I felt so frustrated"

"Again?" The dream reminded me of another dream he had where he had lost his watch. *He's losing time; he wants to go "home". Everyone is going too slow... oh my gosh, I'm going too slow!* I felt helpless and pressured to finish the manuscript of this book that I was struggling over. I needed to work quickly and get it published, so he could see his legacy on paper before he died. I wanted him to feel free to go home, but at the same time, I didn't want him to go. I also understood that God's delays are not God's denials and that if I rushed the process, there could be immediate failure. I tried to get the attention of his spirit guide or an angel, anyone in charge of this whole process, by shouting into the empty air of his bedroom, "I'm working as fast as I can!" Then I turned to Dad and demanded, "Tell your higher self that I get the picture!"

He nodded and agreed. Once I made it clear that I was aware of the messages in his dreams, the old dreams were replaced with dreams of Dad progressing slowly and "getting there," so he felt good in the mornings—a pleasant change from his usual frustration.

More dreams requested our attention and then later, as we figured them out, gave us peace of mind. Dad was baffled by a dream of houses, yet happy as he woke. He reminded me of a curious Shar pei puppy as he tried to explain the mystery he had seen the night before and then tilted his head while waiting for my response.

"There were three houses for sale," he said. "Three lots next to each other and two of them are only a story high, while the middle is three stories high."

I wasn't surprised to hear that all three houses needed work, but the group of faceless younger relatives who stood by, and were interested in the transaction intrigued me. I saw the three houses as Dad, Jeanette, and me; Dad was the tall one in the middle. The buyer represented whoever was going to publish the book. Because the homes were not in perfect condition, I understood that there was still work that needed to be done on the book and us. Could the group of faceless and younger relatives be interested readers?

Jeanette and I searched our own dreams, hoping to find messages that satisfied our own curiosity. I shared with Jeanette one of my own. "Oh my God! Boy, did I have a weird dream. I was walking around my front yard naked! Everyone was acknowledging me, passing my house and saying hi."

"The dream probably means that you feel like you're exposing yourself," she said. "That's why you were naked. The cool thing is that people were acknowledging you. They like you."

"Yeah, that was surprising, and weird at the same time. I felt so uncomfortable with the attention. And you'll never guess what Sean was doing."

"What? Were you guys, like, making out or something? Oh my God, was he naked too?"

"No, you dork! He was trying to keep me covered! He was trying to wrap a blanket around me. And get this, David was peeing in my yard. Then he turned around and said, 'Hi, Jeannine.'"

"Weird. But it's cool at the same time, because it means David is letting go of negativity and acknowledging you at the same time."

Jeanette shared one of her own dreams with Dad and me. She and I were driving through a forest on a cleared path late into the night. A huge truck tailgated us with unusually brilliant headlights.

"Geez, that's one of my biggest pet peeves! Were we annoyed?"

"No, actually we weren't. In fact, we felt totally at peace. At a certain point we stopped the car, got out and continued on the path through the forest. The tailgating truck stayed behind and lit the path with its headlights. I felt totally safe and happy during the journey. Isn't that a cool dream?"

"Yeah! That's awesome."

"Girls, don't leave me in the dark. What does the dream mean?"

"The forest path is our life path," I said.

"And you were the tailgating truck," Jeanette added.

"Me?" Dad hollered and pointed to himself as if we had just accused him of tailgating in real life. "But I would never tailgate anyone!"

"No, it's good that you were, because we knew that you were following us closely and supporting us. The second part of our life journey began when we left the car and walked the path without you. Your headlights helped us see our path in the dark." Jeanette said.

Each dream came undone as certain as the sun rose in the mornings. By afternoon, Dad and I were laughing over what we had just seen. I grinned at Dad and expounded on what the night had brought me. "A group of Jehovah's Witnesses were distributing literature among the houses in my neighborhood. When one came into our house, you walked out of the bedroom with your sweat suit on, but it was made of silver space suit material, and it had some brightly shining rings around the arms. You waddled into the living room, and then started laughing uncontrollably."

"Laughing uncontrollably?"

"Yeah, you know, the way you usually do, your high-pitched laugh where your face gets all happy and weird looking. You were bald, too, except for a few short white hairs, and you had the biggest smile. You almost looked like that Heaven's Gate cult leader. What was his name? His group committed suicide."

"Jim Jones?"

"No. I'm talking about the group from California. They all wore Nike shoes, they died with quarters in their hands so they could call home."

"Oh, I don't know who you're talking about." He swirled back and faced the computer ready to continue his one-finger typing.

"Anyway, I kind of figured out what the dream means. The rings symbolize a commitment or a bond, and they're around your arms, which means that you're reaching for something or you want to accomplish something. The spacesuit represents going 'out of the way,' or an untravelled way. You're coming out of a place where we usually sleep, but you're 'awake.' And you're laughing because you don't take yourself seriously. The people ran from you because they were scared of your 'out of this world' style and attitude."

Dad who was dressed in a thick forest-green sweat suit crossed his arms at my comment. "Are you telling me that I'm some sort of New Age nut?"

"Not really, I'm just telling you that everyone else thinks you are."

"But I'm a Christian," Dad argued. "I've always been a Christian! I may not be a Bible thumpin' Christian anymore, but I'm still a Christian."

"Dad, you're a Christian? What a joke. You're not a Christian anymore." I laughed.

"I'm not?"

"No. You've stopped reading the Bible. You don't go to church anymore, you don't even believe that the Christian belief is the right and only way."

"Oh. But you can't tell me that I'm not a Republican. My mother was a Republican, my father was a Republican and I've always voted as a Republican."

"Then, why did you vote for John Hagelin and the Natural Law party?"

He scratched his head at my comment.

"Dad, I'm sorry for being the devil's advocate about all this, but you cannot say that you're a Christian anymore—it would offend real Christians. You believe that we're all creators and that we have the power within to achieve whatever we want. You don't depend on Jesus anymore to do this for you."

"I've always thought of myself as a real Christian. What are people going to think when they find out I'm no longer one?"

"It's not going to change what people think about you. They're still going to think you're crazy, weird, and insane."

"I used to teach Sunday school, heck, I was a ruling Elder of the Presbyterian Church! I used to be against taking bits of philosophy from all over—it was called blasphemy." He sat like a bizarre, jovial king in his faded and blue, lazy boy chair and then pointed to Jeanette who just walked into the room. "I just found out that I'm not a Bible thumpin' Christian anymore. Do you know what Jeannine calls me now?" Dad exclaimed with a strained high pitch squeal, "a New Age nut!"

Jeanette rolled her eyes at Dad's banter.

"Dad, I did not call you a New Age nut," I countered. "I told you that *everyone else* thinks you're a New Age nut…"

"Did you know, girls," Dad said, "that everything great that has ever been accomplished in this world was done by people who were considered crazy? It's something worth thinking about, isn't it?"

Even though the metaphysical religion was not widely accepted, the philosophy made the most sense to Dad, Jeanette and me. After a few years of study, we completely released our old belief system and breathed in the New Age. Our new faith suggests that if we did not overcome our problems in a loving way, we would be faced with them continuously in this lifetime or another until we solved them using a positive spirit. We were finally taking responsibility for our happiness and life was treating us well because of it.

Chapter 30

The Peacemaker

I gave David a spiral-bound rough draft version of what I believed, at the time, to be my finished version of the family story. I delivered this to David, along with a letter from our father. Dad wrote:

1997
Dear David,
I write this letter to give you information. I do not expect you to answer or change. It is my opinion that you have been thoroughly "brainwashed" by Joy and are convinced you are right, but you're not. Let me give you some true facts. I am your biological father, I never physically injured you or Joy; we built many good memories together.

I, like God, will always love you no matter what you do. It pains me that you reject me, but it does nothing to diminish my love for you. I have fond memories of you as a baby, taking you to meet Dr. Neunherz, attending plays at the Academy, and delivering papers. You paid as you went along and I figure you owe me nothing.

I am doing okay and I understand that you don't understand me, but what you believe has no effect on my relationship with God. God and I are okay.

You are capable of thinking; don't let others think for you. I think some of my training was in error. Don't let that inhibit you.

Joy and I did a lot of good and bad things together and built many memories. I saw no fault in her during those years, but I changed and she didn't. In the end she divorced and

263

disliked me, then brainwashed you. It is time for you to think for yourself.

Everybody is egocentric. I believe that is part of our humanness, but acting with a basic motive of love or fear (or not-love) is a choice. Fear always ends up in pain, whereas love always ends up in joy. The problem is that "ends up in" is always long-term and people usually want a short-term (immediate) solution, and a short-term solution is frequently the opposite of a long-term solution.

One change is that I am no longer afraid of you. You can't hurt me more than your rejection. Now that your mother is gone, I get all my Boeing retirement and my Social Security which results in controlling more money than I ever did when she was alive. I am still a computer nerd and have both a Mac and an IBM-compatible. I have a man who is teaching me how to use the IBM compatible and I am slowly becoming an expert on it. I now send e-mail, fax, and surf the net. I have a scanner and printer connected to the compatible. The man calls my Mac a "door stop" because it is so old, but it works faultlessly and hasn't been shut off for over seven months. I am learning Latin and sign language and keeping busy.

Dad

A week later, I got an excited call from Jeanette. "Jeannine! Did you get your letter yet?"

"Letter? What are you talking about? It's eleven o' clock at night. Why are you calling me so late?"

"Just go look on your doorstep." She hung up.

Confused, I stumbled to the front door and looked around the cement step but didn't see anything. "What the hell is she talking about?"

Then, off to the side, I spotted three large manila envelopes: one marked for Dad, Mike, and me—from David. I slammed the door shut, raced into my room, jumped on the bed and ripped mine open.

Sean turned around from working on the computer and looked at me strangely for acting so frenzied.

"It's from David," I explained. David's letter was in response to after reading my version of the family story.

10/1998
Dear Jeannine:
   I am writing this letter in an attempt to mend the division between me and the rest of you. It has gone on much too long and it's time to do something about it. I am very sorry for all that I have done to cause any hatred or resentment towards me. Please accept my apology and try to forgive me.
   The cause of the resentment, as near as I can figure, (and Jeannine's book did a lot to clarify things) arises from two sources: Mom's favoritism and love for me coupled with a lack of love for the rest of you, and the disproportionate disbursement of her estate with me receiving more than the rest of you. I regret both of these outcomes. I wish I could change it all, but I guess that's impossible. I will attempt to change what I can.
   I guess I should also say that it was not always enjoyable being the "favorite." I hated it when I was used as a measuring stick for the performance of others. I know all of you had to put up with nonsense such as "Why can't you be more like David?" or "If you would only apply yourself, like David." I know those kinds of statements only made you resent and hate me. I remember one time in particular: Mike, Dad, Mom, and I were downstairs and Mike was in trouble for doing something (or not doing something), and Dad said "You're not doing your job, like David is." Then he paused, and I was thinking: what is he talking about—my job? I thought maybe he meant something about the paper route I had, but that didn't really make sense. Then he asked Mike, "Do you know what job I'm talking about?" Mike said, "Yes, being a good student." I would have gotten the answer wrong, but was angry that Dad was using me as a weapon, or a prod, to "motivate" Mike. I wanted to tell him, "Can't you see that's only going to make him hate me? It's not going to make him do more homework."

Being the favorite, or the "good" one who never does anything wrong, never screws up, and always does well in school was not always easy. Everyone expects you to never mess up. The pressure was overwhelming at times. I will say that Mom and Dad never pressured me to get good grades in school, and I am thankful for that. The pressure came from myself and the fact that since I had done well before, it was expected that I would continue doing well. It was the worst when I was in college. I had gone so far, and to fail at that point would have been a disgrace. There were many times when I had messed up on a test or something, or was behind in some classes and felt I just couldn't catch up, that I thought about committing suicide. I thought it would be so nice just to have it all end and not to have to worry anymore. I suppose everyone thinks that at some point in their life. But of course that would be the ultimate failure, and is a selfish solution, only hurting those that are left behind. So finally I prayed one time and said that I would just trust in God's strength to help me get through and accept His will for whatever would happen, and I promised to never consider suicide again. Although it has occurred to me from time to time since then, I have never seriously considered it again. I never wanted to be the favorite, I just wanted to be a brother and a son. At the time I thought the favoritism was based solely on what I did or didn't do, not on who I was (especially since I had no idea Mike was adopted). I guess I got that wrong, too.

The second issue, the one regarding money, needs much clarification and resolution. I was always taught that privacy, especially in regard to money matters, was beneficial, and that one should not go around sharing information about how much he makes, or how much he spends on things, or the details of agreements with other people. There is a quote from the movie *Driving Miss Daisy* that I have always liked. Miss Daisy asks Hoque how much her son is paying him to be her chauffeur, and he replies "Now, Miss Daisy, that 'tween him and me."' I thought that was a good philosophy and I still agree with it in some circumstances. However, in our family, keeping private and concealing information with regard to finances and money matters has caused nothing but assumptions, misunderstandings, and at last, resentment. In reading Jeannine's book, I realized that there have been several instances of this. After Dad's accident, I, as you well know, became Mom's confidant in many matters, whether I liked it or not. And I was sometimes very uncomfortable with that role. She needed the help and support, though, and although it may have been a mistake (one of many), I didn't see that I had any choice. I now believe it is very important that you have as much information as possible.

For a long time, I tried to figure out a way to help Mom clean out and finish the old house. I tried to encourage her to go through and get rid of most of the old junk in the house. We did a tiny bit, but didn't make much progress. She always wanted to put it off, or would just refuse to get rid of stuff I knew she'd never use. I couldn't understand why she wanted to keep the stuff (I'm sure you can relate) and it was a sore point between the two of us. Finally I gave up and just tried to rearrange and organize the junk so at least it was possible to move around. It seemed like it would be impossible to finish the house like that, though. Then, with the impending divorce and the sale of the house imminent, I suggested to her that we buy a house together. With the inheritance she had received from grandpa, she could afford the down payment. She wouldn't qualify for a very large mortgage, though, because of her limited monthly income. We decided that she would supply the down payment and put the house in my name so I could get a mortgage, which I would be able to do since I had a good monthly income, and at that time, little debt (most of my school loans were paid off by then). She did most of the looking, since I was at work during the days, and she would tell me about houses she had seen. We checked out a few of them together, but never found one that we both liked. Then I talked to a friend at church and he told me about the contractor who had built his house. Mom and I talked to him and he showed us books with all kinds of floor plans. Since he built directly for the buyer with no middleman, the cost of having a new house built was about the same as buying one a few years old. I didn't want too expensive a house because I knew that someday when Mom passed away I would be responsible for all the costs associated with the house (of course, that day came a lot sooner than I expected). Unfortunately, Mom had other ideas.

I let Mom look through the books for a plan she liked; I didn't really care that much, and I knew she'd pick something nice. I thought that what she finally chose was too much and objected, but Mom said she would pay the additional costs from her inheritance. It seemed like I was getting in over my head, but I didn't think I could tell her how to spend her money. Besides, as you all know, she was kind of like a force of nature; once she decided to do something, you couldn't stop her. I didn't have much more luck in that department than anyone else. We found a lot that seemed just right for the house. Unfortunately, there was a slight catch. The seller wanted to sell it and the lot next to it together (he got some kind of tax rollover benefit by doing that). So she bought them both. I was thinking she could turn around and sell the additional lot and come out fine, but Mom decided she wanted to keep it. Then, during the construction of the house, there were some upgrades Mom wanted beyond the standard ones offered in the estimate—for example, marble in the entry instead of wood, a fancier fireplace mantle, higher-grade carpet, and better appliances. The costs of these upgrades were split evenly between Mom and me and I paid my half by charging on credit cards.

When I originally suggested that Mom and I buy a house together, I never thought it would add up to all this. I just thought it would be a way for her to finally get into a house that was finished and not in need of so many repairs. I thought after all the years she spent in the unfinished house, that maybe she deserved to live at least a few years in a nice, finished one. At the time, she was in relatively good health—the cancer was there but her treatments had it in remission. I thought she would probably live at least a few more years. Also, I had originally thought that we would share expenses. I would earn back whatever she had put into the house by staying with her and helping to take care of her for the rest of her life.

Now, with so much invested in this new house, I was kind of uneasy to say the least. Of course, Mom had never intended for me to have to pay her back. She said that after the divorce was final, she would sign off the one hundred and sixty thousand-dollar promissory note that went toward the payment of the house so I would no longer be responsible to pay it back. Of course there was still one problem. It would still seem like she was just giving me that money as far as all of you were concerned. I hadn't foreseen this, and it was too late to do anything about it. With all the activity involved in moving, the promissory note was left alone and not addressed until Mom's health started failing. We knew that if she passed away and the note was still in effect, I would be responsible for paying that amount to her estate. Of course, I didn't have the money to do that and the only way I would be able to pay it would be to sell the house. Mom didn't want me to have to do that, so closely before her death, she wrote up a statement on a piece of paper that forgave the debt and had a Notary come to the house and notarize it for her.

I guess the best thing to have done would have been to just sell the house then, pay off the mortgage, and divide up what was left, even though the house was in my name and therefore not addressed in Mom's will. That would have avoided a lot of hard feelings between us. I wish that is what I had done. I don't even really want this big a house; it's kind of stupid for only one person, and I have thought about selling it many times since Mom died. We put so much into picking out the special things in it though, and I do have good memories of it with Mom (though her time here was short).

I wish things had turned out differently—I never would have suggested to her to go in on a house together if I had known it would lead to all this. I had never expected to rely on or even wanted money from my parents. I wanted everything I had to be earned by myself. It was a mistake and I am sorry for all the hurt it has caused. I know this letter doesn't change everything, but perhaps it helps a little.

Love, David

Also included is a letter from David to Dad.

Dear Dad,

I am very sorry for all the pain you have gone through since your accident, both physical and emotional, and I am especially sorry for the hurt that I have caused you. I love you and I was glad to get your calls a couple of weeks ago saying that you love me. I have to say I was shocked to hear you say that because it seemed to come out of the blue, and I don't recall you ever telling me that you loved me, even before your accident. It was coincidental too, because I got a call from the real estate agent who sold the family home a couple of days before you called me. I hadn't talked to him in almost two years but he asked me how I was doing and if things were any better between you and me. He knew that there were strained relations between us and had encouraged me to keep in touch with you. He is a very nice, Christian man and was very supportive through the difficult time of selling the house. Then, a couple of days after I talked to him, I got the letter from you. I wonder if there is any connection.

I hope you accept my apology and can forgive me. Things may never be the same, but perhaps this is a step in the right direction.

Love, David

Chapter 31

Frequency

*Do not conform any longer to the pattern of this world, but
be transformed by the renewing of your mind. Romans 12:2*

Two years went by and I was still struggling over the manuscript.
I decided to visit a psychic to see if I was on the right track. I paid
five dollars for five minutes of a psychic's time at an informal
clairvoyant gathering held in a bookstore. I didn't care who I saw or
who saw me. I trusted that my angels and spirit guides would lead me
to the right person. A young psychic nearest the entrance immediately
caught my attention. I sat at her table and learned her name was Lisa.
Lisa asked me for a personal item so she could read the energy
surrounding it. I handed her the gold ring that Sean had given me
when I was sixteen. Perhaps my history would be found within the
energy of the band. She turned on the timer and studied the ring for a
few seconds. "Jeannine, even though things are a little off-balance,
they're coming to a point, and it looks like the book is close to being
centered. You have an immense spiritual guide behind you who wants
to give you a message. He's ecstatic that you've come here today
because he's wanted to tell you that you'll be able to write with flow."
"Write with flow? What does that mean?"
She handed my ring back. "God will bring messages to you
through your pen."
*Big deal—I've been trying to write for the past two years now. I
want to know how I get what I've written published!* "Does that mean
I'll be able to write better?"

"He doesn't want to communicate through the computer. You need to write the old-fashioned way. And if it flows easily and fluently, it's from Him; if you have trouble, it's not Him."

"Okay." I fiddled with my ring, confused about what she was telling me. "Does that mean when I make revisions to the book, the words will flow better?" I examined the bookshelves around me, depressed by this thought: *"Shoot! Does that mean I have to revise my book for the hundredth time?"* Staring at the multitude of published books around me, I became jealous of each author. The lively best sellers bothered me the most; each one represented a success story.

"You need to set up a time that is just yours and His. And write next to the fountain at your house."

"Do you mean that little fountain that Sean gave me for Christmas?"

Lisa shrugged. "I don't know. I see water from outside."

"You mean the hot tub outside?" I became flustered at her lack of information, especially since she wasn't telling me which route I needed to take to get my book published. "There's no water in our hot tub; there's only a bunch of slugs and bugs."

She shrugged again. "I don't know... you just need to be next to the water. It'll help things flow better."

My heart sank when the timer went off with an annoying beep. She still hadn't told me what route to use to get my manuscript published, which was the only reason I went to see her, and now my time was up.

The next day, January 27th 1999, I did what she suggested. Outside, the northwest air was cold and unfeeling. Two rhododendron bushes drooped outside my front window, impatiently waiting for spring's melody. I set up my little fountain, ran some water into it, placed a figurine of a Chinese man holding a fishing rod with his miniature fish hanging off the end next to the couch, and plugged the unit into the wall. I found a legal pad, arranged my fringed orange and moss pillows behind me and wrote the words, "Authentic Power" at the top of the page. Under those two words, I wrote, "What is authentic power?"

Suddenly, the pen moved and without giving a thought to what I was writing, I composed an answer effortlessly.

Authentic power is reaching within yourself for positive feelings instead of gaining it from outside sources. If someone can take your power away, it is not real. Real power cannot be taken away from you. Authentic power can only be given away.

My soul jumped. For two years I had struggled to write. Each sentence I wrote in my drafts was arranged and rearranged in my head, again after I had typed it onto the computer, and then again after I examined it on paper. Still, my sentences were stilted, choppy and flat. This time, my brain felt like it was on autopilot. There was no thinking required. I wrote another question. I had never felt calm and joyful when writing, but I did now.

"How do I claim my authentic power?"

Find out who you are and you will discover that after all, you are a spirit using a human body. Realize you are capable of anything you want. You can change the world by changing yourself first.

I was amazed. "How do I change myself?"

The pen continued to give an answer at a quick speed. *Accept who you are, realize there is nothing wrong with you. Forgive yourself for any shortcomings you think you have. Realize that where you are on your path is exactly where you should be, but allow change. Change means growth, growth is love, and love is power.*

What should I do with my authentic power? I didn't wait for the answer, I just wrote.

Use it to change yourself, then your world. Use it to accept yourself, then your world. Use it to please yourself, then your world. Use it to forgive yourself, then your world. Use it to educate yourself, then your world. Use it to feel joyful, then make the world joyful.

How do I make myself happy?

Accept the situation and realize it's all part of a higher plan that was designed and prepared by you for you. On the other side your higher self is actually happy with where you are, so why can't you be?

As I became one with nature, my crimson rhododendrons woke, danced and celebrated in my imagination. The wise old juniper smothered with snow joined the party. Wow! I was impressed and excited. My words had never flowed with so much grace and love; never before had they come with this confidence and certainty. I could turn the switch on in my head, and an answer would be whispered in my ear. I was astonished. Never before had I been able to tap into knowledge as easily as turning on a light bulb. I asked, "What should I do now?"

Set your goal and it will be granted. You are very powerful—yet you do not realize it. Your doubt, which is the same as fear, is preventing you from moving forward spiritually, changing, evolving.

"Are there any questions that will not be answered?"

The pen moved quickly. The universe, and all of its wonders, had opened up to me. *Only the answers that will help you or someone else will be answered. Questions that have little significance in their chosen journey will not be answered. What the higher self wants you to know will be given to you.*

I wondered how I could determine whether the answers came from me, a spirit, or even God.

It is you all the time. We're just here to give you support, to see the whole picture and present it to you. The channel to us is now open. We will guide and support you through everything. Everything. Use this gift to your benefit. We love you.

Suddenly, a strange thought entered my mind. I wondered if Mom was around me and wrote the question down.

Yes, when you want her to be.

Mom, are you here?

Yes.

Tell me something; give me a message.

You are loved by me. I'm so proud of you.

Were you proud of me when I was a child? Tell me something I have forgotten.

You were just a baby, but when we first adopted you girls, I thought you were sooo cute. I dressed you up like little dolls and cuddled with you. I thought, these girls are going to make it. They're going to make something of themselves. And I'm going to help them be the best.

I was amazed at the thought. Can you tell me something about your life Mom?

Yes, I was a happy child even though we were poor. My mother was a strict Nazarene, but we were happy with the situation. My brother, Clyde, got on my nerves often. He was curious too and constantly at my door. When I met your father, I liked him a lot, but I played hard to get. He took me to all sorts of places and my parents were pleased. They could see his potential. At first I didn't tell them he wasn't religious, but eventually I did.

You're on the other side. You know everything. Why did you fill the house with so much stuff?

You know, it was out of ignorance, Jeannine. I thought those things would give me value, but what I found was they de-valued me. I would have earned more esteem if I had given, instead buying all the things I thought I wanted. But I believed I needed them in this world you still live in, and that, let me tell you, is only an illusion. You will enter reality and find only joy, and through me now I hope you will find some joy.

How do I know it is you?

Of course, I cannot give you proof but what I can give you is a part of myself that is already in you. And that is my joy, my peace and my love.

What was one of the funniest things Jeanette and I did?

You girls were always getting into things and I didn't know what to do because there was so much stuff! So I spied on you a lot. I watched you girls.

That's a scary thought.

And you, Jeannine, were always the leader, the one to get into stuff or at least con Jeanette into helping. And I thought, this girl is going to get herself in trouble one day with the law.

What was so funny about that?

Well, now that I look at it from a higher perspective, I see you were just curious. I thought you were manipulative and sneaky, but you were only curious. You wanted to know what everything was and there was nothing wrong with that. I think it's funny now, because I sure gave you a lot to be curious about. And I wish I hadn't caused so much trouble for you girls.

Are you mad that I wrote this book?

No, of course not! You can do anything you want and I will still love you. Look at where your curiosity has gotten you! It's gotten the best of you!! You keep asking questions and you will never stop. The attribute I thought was the worst about you, was really what has helped you become so successful. We are so slow and ignorant when we are on earth!

How powerful are you on the other side?

There are many who are more powerful than me, but if my intention is for good, my power is increased. If I wish negativity, I'm nearly powerless.

So your intention is clearly seen?

Yes, on the other side, you can choose goodness or negativity, but it is to your benefit to choose goodness.

Why?

It makes you feel good. It fills you with a sense of joy and accomplishment, and fulfillment.

What happens if you choose negativity?

Your power becomes depleted or weak. You're not as happy.

Sounds like me now!

No, it's different.

Then why do I feel so bad?

Because you are not aware of the results, but there are many. You are changing the world, just by changing yourself first.

When will I realize my goals?

Remember, there is goodness in patience. Be patient, learn what your Dad has learned.

What was it like when you crossed over?

Very painful at first, but my pain came from my ignorance. I did not know the pain I had caused you girls along with your father and Mike. I thought I was a good mother who did the best she could in raising her children. In fact, I thought I was an excellent mother because I followed all the rules; I did what my mother did. Yet, I did not break the cycle of pain. Did you know my mother and I had a strained relationship? I should have been honest with you girls regarding my relationship with my mother because it would have helped our relationship. But no, I put a shell around me and it hurt me in the end as much as it hurt you girls and Mike. You girls, along with Mike, are very honest and loving toward your children and I commend you. I wish I knew as much as you do about children, this world you live in and truth. So I felt all the pain I had caused and I didn't realize how tremendous it was. It makes me sad to think about how weak I was. I didn't realize how weak I was until I felt the pain. It makes me amazed when I watch you girls and your father and Mike. You all are so full of determination and perseverance. Even Mike, I know he has a difficult living situation, but he is full of determination to make everything work and he will.

What do you do every day?

I do what I want to do. If I feel like playing the organ, I play the organ. If I feel like taking a warm bath, I take a warm bath. If I feel like entering one of your dreams, I enter one of your dreams.

That's too weird; it almost seems too much like earth. I don't like that. I was hoping it would be totally different.

Oh, it is totally different. There is a sense of total freedom and we don't suppress ourselves from our wisdom. We are very much aware of who we really are and we love ourselves, if you can believe it. On earth we spend a lot of time hating ourselves and our situations. We are actually creating our own hell by doing so. But here there is only unconditional love. You feel it immediately when you transition and you breathe a sigh of relief that it's all over.

So once you immediately took your last breath, what happened?

Of course, just like you hear, there was a tunnel and then a bright light that fills your soul with renewed energy and you think why the "hell" did I go to earth and miss out on all this energy and love? And then your friends and family greet you, such as Grandpa and Nana were waiting for me. They were so happy to see me again and vice versa. They told me that they were proud of the effort I made and that it is a hard journey to take. They love me unconditionally and taught me how to forgive myself. Then I get to see my life review and feel all the emotions that I had inflicted on others. That was painful even though I was filled with unconditional love. Of course my guides were with me. They told me I ignored their presence most of the time while I was on earth, but that I could do better next time and encouraged me to make another trip down, but I am not ready yet. I don't want to go.

Then there is such a thing as fear on the other side?

No, it has nothing to do with fear, but with reservation. I want to succeed this time and I have all the time in the universe to make another trip down, so I will wait until I've had my share of heaven.

When will that be?

Who knows? I have all the time in the world, and I'm in no hurry. A part of me wants to be here when your father transitions.

Yes, but can't your higher self be there, while your lower self is somewhere on earth?

Of course, but I want my entire self to greet your father. He deserves that much. He deserves all of me.

How can there be total peace and love and joy when you said it was very painful to transition to the other side?

While I transitioned, a part of myself wanted to feel the pain. In fact, everyone wants to feel the pain because there is such unconditional love you know nothing can really hurt you. So even though there was pain in my heart, there was love in my soul.

What is the worst thing about death?

The people you leave behind, the unsaid good-byes and unsaid appreciation. The unfinished business. It is sad for the people left on earth, but for those who transition, there is only joy and peace and love. We try to communicate to our loved ones on earth and lucky for me you three are receptive. You listen for me, you watch for me so it makes my job a lot easier. I like that. There are so many here with me who try to communicate with their loved ones, but they are so full of depression and pain they do not listen. Just keep the channels open for us!

What is the best thing about death?

Not living in pain and ignorance and suppression and depression any longer. Being so close to The Source that you cannot imagine why you would choose to go down there. But it was definitely worth the trip. What you learn in a lifetime you take with you for all eternity. It's wonderful the opportunity to learn, grow and evolve. But for now, for me, I will wait here for your father.

With that, Mom was gone. I still had unanswered questions. Was her lack of feelings toward us just a figment of my imagination? She didn't gossip and she wasn't a complainer—what did she do that was so wrong?

She played by the rules.

How could that be so wrong?

She didn't live from her heart.

How is living by the rules so dangerous?

Living by the rules is dangerous because you are actually going against the flow of life, according to a higher grander plan. You are living according to society's standards and society's perception of what is right and wrong, not by your own spiritual concept of right and wrong. Society does not know what is right for you. Living by the rules is living in fear. Only your heart knows what is right for you.

How does one live by the heart?

Ask yourself, what would love do? What is the most loving thing you could do at the moment? Are you helping or hindering the situation? Are you moving forward or staying stagnant? Let go of control. Only by letting go of control can you be truly free.

How does one discern whether they are living by the rules or living from one's heart?

When you live by your heart, the majority of the world will believe that what you are doing is wrong. They will say what you are doing does not conform to their standards or doesn't make sense. If you are living by your heart you are listening to your intuition—you are making decisions based on love, passion, purpose, creativity, and desire instead of fear of rejection, self-doubt, negativity, jealousy, and judgment.

Why did I feel sadness from my relationship with Mom?

She let society dictate her actions. She adopted you so the world would respect her, she was a stay-at-home mother because she thought it was the right thing to do (even though it didn't give her joy), and she presented a pretty family picture so society would approve (even though she felt empty inside). Living by society's standards did nothing to warm her soul. Living by the rules made her miserable. If she wanted to create a successful family, she should have lived from the inside out, instead of the outside in. Thoughts are extremely powerful. With thoughts you can build up and tear down; you can uplift and you can destroy.

What would people think if they knew I was having this conversation? They would think I was crazy!

What does it matter what others think of you? What they think does not change who you really are. What you think of yourself, is what matters. Are you going to let your self-doubt control you or are you going to control your self-doubt? Are you going to claim your authentic power? Giving love is worth much more than playing by the rules and looking presentable for society.

"Zowee," I wrote. "I feel great! My confidence has risen!"

You've waited long enough. There is much work to be done.

Gifts from God

After the discovery that I could tap into my inner spirit, I wrote in a journal on daily basis. As my metaphysical beliefs progressed, I became aware that we are all spiritual beings temporarily using a body while on earth to experience love, peace and joy in a tangible sense. The doorway to unconditional love is by way of compassion. The definition of compassion is sorrow for the sufferings or trouble of another, accompanied by an urge to help. All the great masters were compassionate. For me, compassion is opening my heart to my mother. Today, I see her not only as "my mother," but as a human being with vulnerable feelings, insecurities and imperfections. I accept her for who she was instead of trying to change her by placing unrealistic expectations. Holding on to a boxed-up grudge hurts me in the long run much more than anyone else.

Dad, Jeanette and I continue to enjoy spiritually uplifting books and have furthered our studies of Metaphysics. Just recently, Dad and I earned a Bachelor of Metaphysical Science Degree. Our spiritual studies continue to draw us closer. Switching faiths did not come easy. The world will put a person through a magnitude of shame for not conforming to its beliefs and traditions. Changing religions took time—for me it took five years of personal study to dilute the old. Ironically, as a Christian, I used to be the one who judged others for their lack of belief. I couldn't comprehend how anyone could *not* believe. I was led to believe that Christianity was the best way and the only way. I was taught to fear anything that wasn't like me.

The easy part came with embracing the new. My spiritual study group friends accept my sister, Dad and me with unconditional love. We meet together each week to discuss books on spirituality. We believe in living the Christ Consciousness and manifesting His love, but without forcing our own belief on someone else; we believe in peace. All religions and all philosophies deserve respect and receive respect. Everyone interprets spirituality in a unique way. What a new concept for us! "Picking and choosing" is not considered blasphemous—picking and choosing actually leads us to truths from all over the world. My reading group friends understand that fear, self-doubt, guilt, or anything associated with negativity is the enemy. They know that Satan is only a figment of the imagination.

Today, I believe in getting answers directly from the Source. I refuse to live as if there is a religious war going on. I choose Christ but I choose the spiritual concept of the Christ Consciousness: use the same Divine power He used to create my own miracles instead of waiting for him to do the work for me.

Thirty years back Mom and Dad, with the best intentions, opened their home and hearts to two babies who were found in a box. They called us "Gifts from God." Now it is our privilege to return the favor. Sean, Jeanette and I share the joy and responsibility of caring for Dad. He continues to live in our home. He shares his love by sponsoring 60 children from around the world. My mom speaks to me with an all-knowing loving voice whenever I need her. Her spiritual presence fills my heart with peace. My parents are my own "Gifts from God."

For more information, and family photos check out:
www.ad-vanceliving.com
Would you like a website designed for your business?
Contact the author at: **Jeanninevance@yahoo.com**

ABOUT THE AUTHOR

Jeannine Vance, a Generation-X voice and author of *Twins Found in a Box: Adapting to Adoption* writes her story for anyone who has ever felt out of place. As a Korean adoptee, she has first hand experience dealing with loss of roots and feelings of self-doubt. At a young age, Jeannine has had to adapt to adoption, challenging relationships, her father's injury, and her mother's death.

Today, Jeannine is married with two daughters. She meditates, interprets dreams and writes automatically and hesitantly. She views life with a sarcastic sense of humor, yet at the same time she is passionate about her purpose. "It's okay to pursue truth by questioning our beliefs. In fact, asking questions is our responsibility."